Mutated Symbols in Law and Pop Culture

This book is part of the Peter Lang Media and Communication list.
Every volume is peer reviewed and meets
the highest quality standards for content and production.

PETER LANG
New York • Bern • Berlin
Brussels • Vienna • Oxford • Warsaw

Carmen M. Cusack

Mutated Symbols in Law and Pop Culture

PETER LANG
New York • Bern • Berlin
Brussels • Vienna • Oxford • Warsaw

Library of Congress Cataloging-in-Publication Data

Names: Cusack, Carmen M., author.
Title: Mutated symbols in law and pop culture / Carmen M. Cusack.
Description: New York: Peter Lang, 2018.
Includes bibliographical references.
Identifiers: LCCN 2018015412 | ISBN 978-1-4331-5193-4 (hardback: alk. paper)
ISBN 978-1-4331-5197-2 (paperback: alk. paper)
ISBN 978-1-4331-5194-1 (ebook pdf)
ISBN 978-1-4331-5195-8 (epub) | ISBN 978-1-4331-5196-5 (mobi)
Subjects: LCSH: Symbolism in law. | Symbolism. | Sociological jurisprudence. |
Law and art. | Culture and law.
Classification: LCC K195.S95.C87 2018 | DDC 340/148—dc23
LC record available at https://lccn.loc.gov/2018015412
DOI 10.3726/b14176

Bibliographic information published by **Die Deutsche Nationalbibliothek**.
Die Deutsche Nationalbibliothek lists this publication in the "Deutsche Nationalbibliografie"; detailed bibliographic data are available on the Internet at http://dnb.d-nb.de/.

The paper in this book meets the guidelines for permanence and durability of the Committee on Production Guidelines for Book Longevity of the Council of Library Resources.

Printed in the United States of America

Thank you to King Zulu, King Rex, and Charaka.

CONTENTS

FIGURES

INTRODUCTION

Mutated Symbols in Law and Pop Culture plays with iconic representations of fusion, liminality, dispossession, and development. Mutations embody life because they illustrate phases and progression. Mutations and mutants fascinate the public. They are depicted by artists, including James Franco, Cary Elwes, Sara Bareilles, The Smashing Pumpkins, Quvenzhané Wallis, Pablo Picasso, Alicia Keys, Katie Perry, Debbie Reynolds, Maddie Ziegler, the Olsen twins, Mark McGrath, and Paul Simon. This book discusses physiological manifestations of mutations, such as beauty and specialness (e.g., white tigers); aesthetic (e.g., redheads); innovation (e.g., Mormonism); and prowess (e.g., tuxedos). *Mutated Symbols in Law and Pop Culture* focuses on strata that are popularly contemplated in culture and by the law; for example, primordial states (e.g., sleep); supranatural physicality (e.g., bionic); irresistible impulse (e.g., psychopath); queer semantic shift (e.g., "gay"); and class (e.g., Leo).

Mutated Symbols in Law and Pop Culture interweaves interdisciplinary analyses because mutations exceed defined ranges. For example, symbology and culture evocatively synergize in constitutional law. A symbol becomes legally protected if it is intended to communicate a particularized message that is likely to be understood by observers. This book demonstrates that mutations may not be sufficiently protected as speech. Even though symbolism of mutations is the subject of study, the meaning of specific symbols may not be understood by the public. Symbols of mutation may identify cultural desires, embrace zeniths, and transform mundane or worn events into fantasies. Perhaps as a means of preserving, defending, and protecting mutations, culture has exhibited and spotlighted them.

Mutated Symbols in Law and Pop Culture focuses on nine discrete topics that serve as bridges between justice, cultural, social, and behavioral studies and other related disciplines. These topics are proximate to contemporary analyses and traditional perspectives. Each chapter identifies hot trends that seem to bend society as they endure. The subjects change and progress; and in their wake, new considerations develop about foundational and ephemeral experiences, including love, sex, marriage, art, language, and human-animal relationships.

Chapter One divulges shrouded sentiments and motives manipulating weddings. Focus on the proprietary significance of nuptials is at an all-time high. What was once taken to be the *status quo* is now controversial. Weddings were considered to be beautiful zeniths of brides' lives and fresh beginnings for grooms, who transcended boyhood and assumed rightful manhood. Now, many weddings are *ad hoc*, performative, and platforms for self-expression. They portray vanity, rebellion, politics, feminism, divorce, bestiality, blended-families, liberality, "wegotism," finality, irreverence, and other non-traditional tangents and influences. Chapter Ones spurs discussion on a taboo topic, desacralizaiton of marriage. This topic is woven throughout the book, and is particularly important in Chapters Seven and Nine. When brides and grooms nuncupate, they affirm society's premise—union and establishment. Eroding, revamping, or altering marriage redesigns religion, law, and family, seemingly inextricable pillars of human civilization.

Chapter Two delves into frightening and pacifying splinters of humans' psyches. At night, self-critiques, pleasure, agendas, and warnings seep through a disabled layer of consciousness to guide, protect, and encourage. People, who do not sleep (e.g., pernoctation), may experience morbid fear of their mothers, sex, and abuse. Sleep symbolically has mutated because traditionally it symbolizes "heavenly peace" (IlonAtzMusic, 2015). Biblical narratives (e.g., Book of Daniel) portray sleep as a state in which revelations from God may reveal His will and where angels may communicate with God's followers (I Samuel 28:5–7; Matthew 1:18:25). Post-Freudian analyses of dreams and nightmares symbologize objects and spaces, whereas Biblical dreams literalized fantastic imagery when dreamers woke and endured tremendous miracles, battles, and tribulations (Cusack, 2015a). The unconscious state has been treated as pure and sacrosanct. It is unavoidable, and appears to be a human right (Jayal, 2012). Inmates deprived of sleep may be entitled to protection under the Eighth Amendment (Clarke, 2015; Lochridge, 2017). To enforce this traditional and humanist view, the law has consistently classified burglary as a felony. Burglary is the intent to enter and commit a crime inside a dwelling at night. Now, the law considers sexual contact with a sleeping person to be violative. Although some jurisdictions create a rebuttable presumption, a few have failed to specify that consent, requiring knowing voluntariness, has not been granted when parties are sleeping. Sleepers are protected by some laws; but, the First Amendment protects parents' rights to raise their children, including imbuing them with fear before bedtime. Parents may communicate horrid tales disrupting sleep; and yet, possibly inciting permanently mutated perceptions. Nightmares continue to be the subject of teen movies, songs, and stories because of teens' unique position between childhood and adulthood (Perry, 2010; Swift, 2014, 2017).

Bionism is "iconic" (Madonna, 2015). For millennia, humans have fantasized that bionism correlated with overcoming fate and death. Bionism has been symbolized by medical devices (e.g., prostheses), conservation (e.g., DNA banks), and technology (e.g., pornography). Differently abled individuals are the subject of Chapter Three, which analyzes Walt Disney's descant of bias, specialness, impairments, similitude, and synthesis. Special people and animals are heroes. Although civilization has continuously rejected special creatures, symbolically society has evolved to recognize their power and effects. World Heavyweight Boxing Champion Mike Tyson orates an emboldening verse on Madonna's song "Iconic" on *Rebel Heart* (Madonna, 2015; Menash, 2010).

> I'm the best the world has ever seen
> I'm the best ever
> I'm somebody you'll never forget
> 'Cause I work hard and sweated my tears
> Can't be stopped
> I'm never falling again, and if I did I'll come back. (Madonna, 2015)

Tyson's tenacity is evident in special individuals and society's present response to alternate and rare forms. Madonna's lyrics reveal dualistic intentions in honoring "superstars" (Madonna, 2015). Her attitude is somewhat bitter toward normative types.

> If you tried and fail, get up again
> Destiny will choose you in the end
> If you don't make the choice
> And you don't use your voice
> Someone else will speak for you instead
> What you want is just within your reach …
> You pay with sweat and tears
> And overcome your fears …
> 'I can't,' 'icon'
> Two letters apart
> One step away from being lost in the dark
> Just shine your light like a beautiful star
> Show the world, who you are. …
> Baby, don't you know you were meant to be
> Born to be, meant to be
> Iconic … Ironic …
> Tell me I'm no good, and I'll be great
> Say I have to fight, and I can't wait
> Standing in the wings
> A butterfly that stings
> I will rise above 'cause it's my fate. (Madonna, 2015)

In a performative irony, she chose Chance The Rapper to rap the following verse:

> Firefly change when they catch ya'
> Wanna put ya' in their net for their light glow
> Yellow brick highway. …
> An idol. …
> Just to find how it feel to fall back. …
> Put it on your wall
> Put me in the school book
> Put me in your laws
> Put me in the desk
> And in the synagogues
> Firefly glow when they catch ya'
> Catch ya' when ya' lights go dim
> Wanna turn you to a letter in their logo
> Wanna stick you in a jar with a pen
> You an icon. (Madonna, 2015)

Although her perspective sympathizes with the mediocracy, a social system rewarding mediocrity, her willingness to share her "icon" status with individuals experiencing failure and struggling for self-redemption demonstrates "super" elitism (Madonna, 2015; Nelson, 2017). Chapter Three explores how machines have replaced humans. For example, Christina Aguilera's song "*Desnudate*" describes interchangeability between computer screens and human bodies (Aguilera, 2010). The title is a singular reflexive command, "Get Naked" (Aguilera, 2010). "Naked" is a term of art used in internet jargon. It means to be unapparent.

> Whisper all your fetishes inside my ear
> *Asi me gusta, papi* [i.e., 'That's the way I like it, daddy']
> My domain is shame-free so lose your fear
> *Amarrame* [i.e., 'Tie me']
> Nothing's too much or too little, too soft or severe
> *No pares* [i.e., 'Do not stop' or 'Do not give birth']
> Madame seduction has only one rule while you're here
> You got to …
> *Desnudate*, get naked. (Aguilera, 2010)

Aguilera's software inhibits her sexuality. Rather than fumble with the outside world, she finds pleasure through her hard drive. She is successful in her music career because she promises women sexual equality with men, who have internet pornography to supplant their sexual subservience. Her freemium is a slacktivist homage to internet pornography.

Chapter Four discusses why psychopathy is ubiquitous, not anomalous. Psychopathy may be mental, physical, and sexual. This chapter honestly considers the possibility that the American Psychological Association (APA) misunderstands human behavior. APA classifies psychopathy as an abnormality rather than a momentary lapse in judgment. Psychopathy may be bad decision-making, not illness. For example, nonconsensual insemination between intimate partners may exhibit narcissism, callousness, selfishness, manipulation, egocentricity, grandiosity, and lack of empathy (Chivers, 2017). Yet, according to typical figures, only two or three percent of nonconsensual inseminators are psychopaths. The APA's "psychopathy" is an envisionment of sin by mental health professionals. As morality decays, widely accepted fantasies about psychopathy have drifted from reality; and are now symbolically related to mental healthcare. Standard APA analyses no longer describe a psychotically deviant portion of the population. Psychopathy is a system of thought, not a genetic or mental characteristic. Chapter Four discusses the example of prostitution. Prostitution is conceived as psychopathy rather than victimization, exploitation, and immorality. It is a willful and self-directed activity for dominance and establishment. The song "Babylon" by David Gray insinuates that sin is complicated (Gray, 2013).

> Friday night I'm going nowhere
> All the lights are changing green to red
> Turning over TV stations
> Situations running through my head
> Looking back through time
> You know it's clear that I've been blind
> I've been a fool
> To open up my heart to all that jealousy, that bitterness, that ridicule
> Saturday I'm running wild …
> Moving through the crowds, I'm pushing
> Chemicals are rushing in my bloodstream …
> You know I'm seeing it so clear
> I've been afraid …
> Admit to some of those bad mistakes I've made
> And if you want it
> Come and get it
> Crying out loud
> The love that I was
> Giving you was
> Never in doubt
> Let go of your heart
> Let go of your head
> And feel it now
> Babylon. …
> Turning back for home
> You know I'm feeling so alone, I can't believe
> Climbing. (Gray, 2013)

Babylon is a symbol for individuals choosing to think and behave psychopathically in specific instances.

Chapter Five exposits definitions of the word "gay." This sensitive chapter defends free speech and homosexuality while pointing to American happiness as a dwindling vestige. Americans' levity and tolerance seems to have senesced. Yet, use of the word "gay" to mean "contrary" or "uninteresting" offers new hope. If the word "gay" can be treated as a homophone of the word-use meaning "homosexual," rather than as a slur, then it may demonstrate that Americans are willing to expand culture rather than attack mutations. Gays have been likened to transsexuals, pedophiles, zoophiles, rapists, and other non-sequiturs. However, the homosexual community has leveled the playing field by breaking foundations. They changed attitudes toward masculinity and femininity; then, they made underground lifestyles into a form of popular culture; next, they legitimized sexual revolutions by campaigning for reproductive freedom; and finally, they joined tradition and exercised a right to marry (Cusack, 2015). Now, their best strategy is to return to a happy state and overcome bigotry by surrendering to the times, which call for use of new and old meanings of the word "gay."

Redheads are iconic. Marilyn Monroe has been portrayed as a redhead in early photographs. Audrey Hepburn, Jaqueline Kennedy Onassis, Princess Grace of Monaco, Chris Farley, Prince Harry of Wales, Donald Trump, and other media darlings have captured the lime light by donning rouged coiffures. Their hair color declares "mutiny!" It rebels against the norm and allegedly recessive hair colors. It simultaneously places brown and blonde hair into the same class while remaining separate. Redheads have been ostracized and labeled. Some have been victims of discrimination and hate crimes; and banished as homewreckers and bad neighbors. Their rarity has spurred some radicals to decry their rights to eliminate unwanted pregnancies. Their hair is a bastion of dissimilitude. Therefore, it is a standard of human appearance "quite rightly" (Donovan, 1966). Redheads may appear to self-deprecate to appease people, who are attracted to their hair, but cannot possess or permeate it. Depictions of redheads offer audiences new attitudes toward assimilation, normativity, humanity, and automation; and their unusualness claims a stake in future conversations about mutations. Therefore, those redheads with highly unusual appearances, in their physical persons and entertainment roles, are discussed in Chapter Six.

Sara Silverman described a musical about Church of Latter-day Saints, *Book of Mormon*, as "mind blowing [and] special" (Silverman, 2012). She joked that she "wish[ed] not-rich people could see it" because "they'd love it" (Silverman, 2012). Her joke demonstrates why Americans' view of Mormons may be twisted and unrelated to their freedom of worship. An irrelevant understanding by the public of a vulnerable group may result in religious suppression and bigotry. Mormonism is rarely discussed by mainstream pundits except when they synthesize scandal. Scandals voyeuristically may be inflamed by the justice system using unconstitutional and unacceptably fictionalized accounts. Elites may excuse high-tech pogroms by reciting historical information and controversial insight in order to queerify and intellectualize Church foundations. Sympathetic Americans may be reluctant to voice concerns about mistreatment and unconstitutional deprivation experienced by Mormons. They may be unaware of distinctions between groups (i.e., fundamentalists); and hesitate to controvert the majority due to their fear of possibly supporting illegal activities. Their beliefs are likely informed by the press, which harvests malicious perspectives towards Mormons to conjure enemies. These people may also comprise the justice system, which may behave as a crusade for religiously intolerant, Americanized, and mainstream Christianity. Crusades are not limited to anti-Mormon legislation and legal interpretations. Muslims and other groups are persecuted by xenophobic laws and programized agendas. Outcomes denying religious equality and freedom are pre-organized and routinized by supremacist culture, oligarchical mentalities, and pervertization and defilement of sacredness. One goal is hysterization; another is isolation; and a third goal is distraction. Rulers persecute seemingly helpless and docile religious leaders and members to distract from economic tyranny. For example, people in plural marriages differently distribute and invest wealth than traditional Americans. Persecutors implicitly tout a homogenous banner demanding that Americans identify with the government's projected *status quo* in opposition against foreigners. Mormons are treated, not as an organic religious group and important link between New World inhabitants, but as a dirty blight or a shrouded radical fringe. Chapter Seven untethers various threads of the American narrative against Mormons and Muslims. It also opens doors for mainstream America to reconsider their values; for example, in light of a recent Utah Supreme Court case holding that abuse likely results when parents hit children and recent alterations to the minimum age for consent in Utah's marriage statute (Cusack, in-press; In re K.B., 2017).

Chapter Eight is about Leonardo DiCaprio. Leo is the voice of Hollywood, California. He is film and movies. His work is represented by actors in cinema and television; and he has influenced music videos, viral videos, and theater. His work is unparalleled, and therefore, he becomes his characters. Other actors simulate his work and nod to him in their performances. His characters may be described interchangeably with his actual identity. For example, Jack Dawson from *Titanic* is Leo, and vice versa (DiCaprio, 1997). His work is timeless and contemporary. For example, *Titanic* played in theaters in America to celebrate the film's 20th birthday (Audubon Nature Institute, 2016; DiCaprio, 1997). Through his films, Leo directs American culture and ethos. His responsibility to his audience is, not to be truthful or fulfill their expectations, but to envision the future and interpret it. He communicates using archetypes so that his wishes and insights may be understood and obeyed. Leo's stereotypes always glorify, but occasionally reprimand certain elements of human societies. It is this facet of his work that renders him personally vulnerable. Yet, his commitment to portraying depraved souls shows his goodwill, and often leaves him unscathed. His humanitarian and environmental work has politicized saving animals, the ocean, and other Earthly touchstones. To shuck glamour in favor of political prowess may indicate madness experienced by actors, such as John Cusack, Dan Ackroyd, Susan Sarandon, and Kevin Costner (Bermúdez Acosta, 2012). His tenderhearted nature mutates female affection to transform young girls into shrewd women capable of taking-on men. He provides insight, opportunity, and backdrop to their emotions, which contextualizes many females in spite of a world that would reduce them to the status of deviants. He builds emotional cities for psyches banished beyond society. His work is summarized by *Titanic*, but as the incumbent Academy Award winner for best actor, his future roles promise to restore the offspring of current generations to their once esteemed innocence and purity (DiCaprio, 1997). His work is not blameless; and, he may be accused of corrupting fragile plans. However, he is empowered by his ability to do so, and would likely not take that for granted, which appears to be accounted in his performance and devotion to his craft. In the end, the hero lives on; but, one day he will physically die. Only then will Hollywood, and the world, understand the gravitas of his devotion to them.

Mutations are most evident in white tigers. Figuratively and literally, this special species embodies change. They stand for their friends, meaning they are visible at zoos and promote conservation of all wildlife and captive species. Their exhibition denounces spoiling natural resources; and it helps to bring valuable tourist dollars to cities in need, such as New Orleans, Louisiana, home of white tiger brothers. Artists are inspired by white tigers because they have mutated audiences. One artistic collaborative, *Our Last Night*, penned "White Tiger," a love song to a white tiger (OurLastNightBand, 2016; Woodrow, 2015, 2017). The brothers in the band sing, "captivated by a perfect view;" "my faith in love was born again," an homage to salvation; "I can tell you were a different breed from the way you looked;" and "I saw you standing there. Butterflies. All I could do is stare," potentially citing the brothers, whose zoo logo depicted a butterfly, a shark, and a white tiger (Woodrow, 2015). "It's like an angel walked into me;" "nothing can keep us from never leaving this place;" and "they fit together so perfectly" (Woodrow, 2015). Woody Woodrow, the bassist mutates performance art when he crowd surfs on his back while playing the bass guitar (JaneeZanda, 2017). The vegan surfs to the bar where a bartender drips shock-art Goldschläger down his throat, undoubtedly discomforting his body, but promoting his band's power to bring in revenue to the house bar at Meet Factory in Prague, Czech Republic (Saiko, 2017; Woodrow, 2017). Holding signs with the lyrics "there's no place that I'd rather be," dozens of crowd members helped Woodrow "to decide what kind of king [he is] going to be" (Furious Trailer, 2017; Goskascience, 2012; JaneeZanda, 2017; The GypsyNesters, 2011). When Woody surfs them, they refrain from betrayal, such as gratuitously touching his genitals or instrument, a Tin Man (i.e., Tin Woodman) bass (Haley, 1939). He surfs their palms with dignity (Our Last Night, 2015). He mutates the relationship between a band, which normally reigns on stage, and the crowd positioned at their feet. He glorifies them by submitting his whole body to their touch, not merely his fingertips to a few privileged front row guests. In a glorious wave, he rises to the stage where he takes the center symbolically. The two brothers sing around him and he marches ceremoniously into unguarded artistic fields. His skill as a professional yogi is identifiable, and his patience towards the crowds' affection is humbling. The meaty performance leaves their audience with something to "sink" their "teeth" into (Woodrow, 2015). The cinnamon schnapps' gold flakes float inside the yoga instructor's stomach while he stoically stands like a rock "star[]" (Woodrow, 2015, 2017). Interpretations vary (Biggie Smalls, 2009). For example, perhaps this is a mating ball (Cusack, 2015). Serpentine images grace this homage to the white tiger. The audience's fingers rustle leaves only Woody can see. Chords are played by their abdomens when he passes over them with his weight. This blue blood of indie rock is not shadow boxed by the attention, but he gives himself over to his bandmates, who unify in one bodily movement driven by drums. Another interpretation is that the ocean, formed by his fans, likes the surfer's tickle on its rippling surface. Cutting the glassy surface charms the waters, who could otherwise destroy intruders, including an artist or a yogi. Sharks are in view when he enters the water, but the ocean tells them to hold-off. They push him forward and he exists the water unharmed, for now. Art is performed by the crowd when they "ignoran[tly]" appear to accept his alcohol consumption in spite of his deified image (Woodrow, 2012). They appease his whim by settling their tabs and drinking more. The crowd is invited to feel that "this time we're going to be on top" (Furious Trailer, 2017). Chapter Nine uncovers trending topics relating to white tigers, such as the Second Amendment and superhero comic books (LizaQuin, 2016). Aesthetic reeve and fashion designer Roberto Cavalli synopsized white tigers, who realistically and impressionistically were depicted on clothing in his 2018 Spring collection, when he said "to look [and] to appear" "special [and] wild" "is my brand" (Cavalli, 2011, 2017a, 2017b; Cunningham-Reid, 2002). Saint Laurent (2017), like Roberto Cavalli and other designers this season, honored the spirit of white tigers on an Eiffel Tower catwalk in Paris, France (Bayoucool2, n.d.).

Mutated Symbols in Law and Pop Culture is a conversation. The text may be cohesive or seemingly contradictory because literal, figurative, and intended boundaries are shifting in society and within this work. Geico's gecko lizard sagely has described scenario-based perspectives that encompass modern analysis and civility. In various modern *satsangs*, the gecko has said, "It's good for me, what'd you think," and "I'm not sure exactly what happened here" (Funny Commercials, 2015). He relies on scenarios that have "stood the test of time" because he "is hot" (Funny Commercials, 2015). Therefore, they seem to be "very compelling," like the government's authority in civil rights cases (Funny Commercials, 2015). Analysis of sociolegal and pop cultural mutations in light of law, science, and politics "is some really strong stuff" (Funny Commercials, 2015; Holt, 2014).

References

Aguilera, C. (2010). *Desnudate*. On *Bionic*. New York, NY: RCA Records.

Audubon Nature Institute. (2016, November 7). White tiger celebrates 20th birthday! Retrieved from https://www.youtube.com/watch?v=tkYEJQjoBz4

Bayoucool2. (n.d.). *Youtube.com*. Retrieved from https://www.youtube.com/user/Bayoucool2/videos

Bermúdez Acosta, J. (2012, April 4). Rehabilitación de zonas contaminadas con hidrocarburos: Biorremediación de residuos petrolizados. Estudio de caso en la comunidad costera de "reina," Cienfuegos, Cuba. España: Editorial Académica Española.

Biggie Smalls. (2009, May 7). Biggie smalls – Ten crack commandments. Retrieved from https://www.youtube.com/watch?v=ZYb_8MM1tGQ

Cavalli, R. (2011, November 20). Runway TV – Roberto Cavalli interview 2011. Retrieved from https://www.youtube.com/watch?v=YZNP96wWgJI

Cavalli, R. (2017a). Cavalli class 2018. Look book. Retrieved from http://www.robertocavalli.com/us_en/brands/cavalli-class/man/lookbook.html

Cavalli, R. (2017b). Roberto Cavalli spring/summer 2018. Retrieved from https://www.youtube.com/watch?v=CoaOjOzRG1w

Chivers, T. (2017, August 29). How to spot a psychopath. *The Telegraph*. Retrieved from http://www.telegraph.co.uk/books/non-fiction/spot-psychopath/

Clarke, M. (2015, January 10). Fifth circuit: Sleep deprivation may violate eighth amendment loaded. *Prison Legal News*, 46. Retrieved from https://www.prisonlegalnews.org/news/2015/jan/10/fifth-circuit-sleep-deprivation-may-violate-eighth-amendment/

Cunningham-Reid, F. (2002). *The real country house*. Retrieved from http://www.fionacunninghamreid.com/films/film-the-real-country-house/

Cusack, C. M. (2015a). *Animals, deviance, and sex*. Cambridge: Cambridge Scholars Publishing.

Cusack, C. M. (2015b). *Criminal justice handbook on masculinity, male aggression, and sexuality*. Springfield, IL: Charles C Thomas.

Cusack, C. M. (in-press). White tigers and corporal discipline of minors. *International Journal of Research Studies in Medical and Health Sciences (IJRSMHS)*.

DiCaprio, L. (1997). *Titanic*. Hollywood, CA: Paramount Pictures.

Donovan. (1966). "Mellow yellow." *Song Facts*. Retrieved from http://www.songfacts.com/detail.php?id=2554

Funny Commercials. (2015, June 14). Top 10 the best and funny Geico lizard insurance TV commercials of all time. Retrieved from https://www.youtube.com/watch?v=1GthI90L1Dg

Furious Trailer. (2017, November 20). Black panther white panther trailer (2018) Marvel superhero movie HD. Retrieved from https://www.youtube.com/watch?v=OAN_uQ4u2JQ

Goskascience. (2012, November 22). Peeing statues in Prague. Retrieved from https://www.youtube.com/watch?v=nb7BAkUS2v8

Gray, D. (2013, July 30). David Gray – "Babylon" official video. Retrieved from https://www.youtube.com/watch?v=zI_SBAkdKzc

Haley, J. J. (1939). *The wizard of oz*. Beverly Hills, CA: Metro-Goldwyn-Mayer Studios.

Holt, K. (2014, July 9). My slideshow Madonna, Michael Jackson, Freddie Mercury, Lady Gaga. Retrieved from https://www.youtube.com/watch?v=EZiGXNqZEz4

IlonAtzMusic. (2015, December 23). Silent night (Spanish, English, Finnish & Swedish version) – cover by Ilon. Retrieved from https://www.youtube.com/watch?v=lVSwpWL8pBE

In re K.B., 2017 UT App 210 (4th D. Juv. Ct., November 16, 2017).

JaneeZanda. (2017, November 5). Our last night – white tiger – Prague 2017. Retrieved from https://www.youtube.com/watch?v=eX5hvuXWkJk

Jayal, N. G. (2012, March 13). Supreme Court's stance on sleep is a step forward. *Daily Mail*. Retrieved from http://www.dailymail.co.uk/indiahome/indianews/article-2114671/Supreme-Courts-stance-sleep-step-forward.html

LizaQuin. (2016, December 13). Holywar x Alicia Keys (LizaQuin 1 min cover). Retrieved from https://www.youtube.com/watch?v=pfsOYwVTreU&list=PLNDJyxHvf5JWUl-HFuUF52xHrMG-8Pxsv&index=6

Lochridge, M. (2017). *Lochridge's prison adventures*. Prisons Foundations. Retrieved from www.PrisonsFoundation.org

Madonna. (2015). *Rebel heart*. Santa Monica, CA: Interscope.

Menash, P. (2010). *Spartacus: War of the damned*. Hollywood, CA: Raimi Productions.

Nelson, J. (2017, September 6). How Madonna is raising Malawi: Inside her tireless work helping children and fighting poverty in Africa. *People*. Retrieved from http://people.com/music/madonna-raising-malawi-charity-helping-orphans-fight-poverty-africa/

Our Last Night. (2015, July 26). Our last night – dark horse (warped tour 2015 @ Tinley Park, Chicago IL). Retrieved from https://www.youtube.com/watch?v=1J9DmkXki6g

OurLastNightBand. (2016, May 24). Our last night – "white tiger" (official). Retrieved from https://www.youtube.com/watch?v=c1Q81M2yT7I

Perry, K. (2010, August 10). Katy Perry – teenage dream (official). KatyPerryVEVO. Retrieved from https://www.youtube.com/watch?v=98WtmW-lfeE

Saiko, B. (2017, November 4). Woody Woodrow crowdsurfing in Prague. Retrieved from https://www.youtube.com/watch?v=iB1vCQiPZQs

Saint Laurent. (2017). Saint Laurent spring/summer 2018. Retrieved from https://www.youtube.com/watch?v=zCI7uh3aDYQ

Silverman, S. (2012, February 6). @SarahKSilverman. *Twitter*. Retrieved from https://twitter.com/sarahksilverman/status/166747378634858497?lang=en

Swift, T. (2014, November 10). Taylor Swift – blank space. TaylorSwiftVEVO. Retrieved from https://www.youtube.com/watch?v=e-ORhEE9VVg

Swift, T. (2017, August 27). Taylor Swift – look what you made me do. TaylorSwiftVEVO. Retrieved from https://www.youtube.com/watch?v=3tmd-ClpJxA

The GypsyNesters. (2011, August 4). The amazing astronomical clock of Prague. Retrieved from https://www.youtube.com/watch?v=NebyX6-GUTM

Woodrow, W. (2012). *Age of ignorance*. Hollywood, CA: Epitaph.

Woodrow, W. (2015). White tiger. On *Younger dreams*. Hollywood, CA: Epitaph.

Woodrow, W. (2017, October 25). Conversation with Woody Woodrow of *Our Last Night* during a tour of Europe.

· 1 ·

WEDDING

Tuxedo

Tuxedos are emblematic of union, monogamy, and blending. They represent a groom's commitment to blending his heritage with the bride's. The bride wears white because traditionally, she is unaware of the sexual commitments. Her fertility is inevident and her sexuality is unrepresented. However, the groom's attire speaks for both parties. Traditionally dressed in black and white, he symbolizes their union. He is her father and all other males present in the wedding party or at the wedding wearing tuxedos. He is nondistinct, and this symbolizes blending. Monogamy is distinctly uttered by her gown, as well as his cummerbund. His cummerbund suggests that his loins are guarded. He is chased as well. The crowd observing this amalgamation defiles the groom, who seeks to be wed in secrecy. A tuxedo, which modestly covers his body with several layers, represents everyone. It is a symbol of blending.

A tuxedo is a shadow (O'Connell, 2013). It slips onto the groom long before the procession. He wears the role, which drags him to the church. He wears the tuxedo in his bedroom, in his car, at his job, and around his finger months or weeks before he marries. In gay weddings, both grooms wear tuxedos (Carmen M. Cusack, 2013). Informally dressed grooms will wear a semblance of their own interpretation of a tuxedo years, months, or weeks before the celebration. Tuxedos shadow grooms, drawing their souls to the alter, and affirmatively, to the bedroom. The shadow lifts from their skin to reveal a man, who is no longer living in society's caldron of thoughts and dreams; but instead, is a ruler of his castle and the maker of his spouse's dream world.

Formal wear mimics weddings. No occasion is more formal than the union between a virginal female and her prince. Occasions calling for black tie and formal attire mimic the very core and spirit of severity—a wedding. Wedding parties are designed to appear reverential, serious, given-over, and submissive to hierarchy. Wedding tuxedos are distinguishable from other kinds. For example, tuxedo varieties include the white dinner jacket, colored jackets, coat tails, and framed or notched lapels. Also, a "Canadian tuxedo," for example, describes an all-denim get-up, such as the outfits worn by Britney Spears and Justin Timberlake to the American Music Awards (Walano, 2016). Tuxedos call to possibility, which is pantomimed when formal attire is donned.

Formal wear was epitomized by "business partner[s]" and "gay lover[s]," Siegfried Fischbacher and Uwe Ludwig Horn, known as Siegfried and Roy, who transformed tuxedos from eveningwear to elaborate, sequined performances (*Globe*, 2017, p. 6). Tuxedos "mushroomed" from mere vestiges of marriage to "emotional" expressions of white tigers and their withheld potential for "devastation" (*Globe*, 2017, p. 7). "Vegas crowds were shocked by the famed duo's appearance" (*Globe*, 2017, p. 6). Their hair, movements, makeup, and radiance indicated to crowds that tuxedos had mutated and become integrated into gay subculture (Chivu Chivu, 2017; Hutchings, 1993). Protégé Darren Romeo wears their sequined, white tiger pattern tuxedo jacket on stage when he reveals Hollywood, a gargantuan white tiger (Carmen M. Cusack, 2016a). Romeo is married to a female magician's assistant (VMS, n.d.).

Tuxedos invite analytical frames of reference. For example, participants in weddings, partygoers, and even television viewers, who watch formal occasions (e.g., Academy Awards), analyze the meaning, appropriateness, aesthetic, craftsmanship, message, and command that tuxedos portray (CBS News, 2015). This analysis is shared, and therefore, unitive between observers. The tuxedo transforms into a form of currency, which is fungible when an opinion, either positive, neutral, or negative, is expressed and relayed.

Through their work, The Smashing Pumpkins, including D'arcy Wretzky, James Iha, and Billy Corgan, develop an analysis of formal ties. In "Today," front man Corgan's bowtie represents professional attire (i.e., uniform) and discipline (The Smashing Pumpkins, 1993). He is an ice cream truck driver (Christina Cusack, 2006, 2012; Love, 1995). His band frolics, but his uniform denotes the difference between rock and roll and hard work. His tuxedo, including an ascot, in "Tonight, Tonight" is steampunk (The Smashing Pumpkins, 1995b). The video created in 1996 preceded *Titanic*, and may have inspired director James Cameron (DiCaprio, 1997; The Smashing Pumpkins, 1995b). It is reminiscent of Led Zeppelin and the Hindenburg (i.e., "Oh, the humanity!") (Morrison, 1937). The album title, *Mellon Collie and the Infinite Sadness*, suggests a phoneticized mutation of "melancholy," and seems to describe a dog rather than an emotion (The Smashing Pumpkins, 1995b). The dog may be orangish (e.g., Lassie) or sculpted from cantaloupe (Lassie, 1954; Sade, 2018). A melon-colored collie is differentiable from a black and white (i.e., tuxedo) collie. Yet, the quasi-mysterious spelling of "mellon" leaves the source of its inspiration to the imagination. While "Today" depicts gender-bending within the band (e.g., Iha wearing a dress), it also depicts Corgan and his bandmates abstaining from young love, lust, group sex, and homosexual, amorous affection (The Smashing Pumpkins, 1993). Corgan is deprived of young, heterosexual, and passionate kisses; and therefore, is downtrodden. He is sublimated with ample rabblerousing and exuberance emanating from his bandmates to help him overcome his malaise and devotion to duty. "Tonight, Tonight" presents a constricted love affair that, although exciting due to dangerousness and unexpectedness, lacks genuine affection and privacy (The Smashing Pumpkins, 1995b). In "Today," The Smashing Pumpkins (1993) defy "the man" by painting the ice cream truck in rainbow colors and riding off-road (The Smashing Pumpkins, 1995a). In "Tonight, Tonight," the couple's adventure is precipitated by a voyage and a spectacular send-off, like a wedding (The Smashing Pumpkins, 1995b). It is static, two dimensional, and phony, albeit threatening. The tuxedo maintains its integrity throughout the adventure, demonstrating its rigidity and symbolic impenetrability (The Smashing Pumpkins, 2012).

Throughout the ages, tuxedos have represented different forms of power, wealth, and height. For example, a description of semiformal attire from the 1920s points out that tuxedos have not always been considered the pinnacle of formal attire as they have become due to their prominence in wedding ceremonies and visibility on television.

> A gentleman's semiformal suit, called a tuxedo, was made of black or dark blue worsted material. Unlike a full-dress suit, the tuxedo jacket had no tails and the

> tuxedo pants were trimmed, if at all, in very narrow braid or ribbon. The tuxedo vest could be black or white, but, unlike the obligatory full-dress white tie, tuxedos ties were always black. Men usually completed their tuxedo outfit with all the same accessories as the full-dress suit, except that instead of top hats they would wear dark, dome-shaped hats called bowlers. Tuxedos were appropriate attire at the theater, small dinner parties, entertaining in the home, and dining in a restaurant. (Batchelor, 2017)

The tuxedo loomed between truly dapper and stunning ensembles and the average suit. Zoot suits came into fashion in the 1940s thereby further morphing the tuxedo and all other suits (Daniels, 2017). Some styles have developed since then, while other trends, such as winged collars, have remained constant throughout past centuries (Batchelor, 2017).

Tuxedo fur is a description of animals with black fur and white chests. The Clinton family cat, Socks, was a tuxedo cat (Rodham Clinton, 1998, 2016). He was very famous for receiving letters. Socks, and his companion, Buddy, received hundreds of thousands of letters. Socks' mailbox was the second most active in the White House. He received more mail monthly than President Thomas Jefferson. The significance of his tuxedo is evident in the respect that children ascribed to his position as First Pet. They asked him by post whether he was an elected representative of animals; a Goodwill Ambassador; or a powerful member of the animal kingdom. His tuxedo suggested that he may be well-off; and children inquired about his salary. Hillary Rodham Clinton propitiously collected letters to Socks and published a book entitled *Dear Socks, Dear Buddy*; and shared some proceeds with the National Park Foundation (NPF), which oversees protection of "83 million acres" of "spectacular" "God's creation" (Rodham Clinton, 2016). NPF President Jim Maddy commented that the book was about "safeguarding" "future" "fondness" for "American knowledge" (Rodham Clinton, 2016). The relationship was about "engaging" and "dedicating" "compelling" "public" interest in animals and nature. Socks' tuxedo helped to sew interest in his cause (Rodham Clinton, 2016).

Bo, President Barrack Obama's dog, is an example of a tuxedo animal, whose ambassador status brought attention to the significance and historical place of the tuxedo (Schneiderman, 2009). Bo was described as a "good" dog, who had paid "keen" attention to authority, style, and charm (Schneiderman, 2009). Like the formal wear, Bo wore his position in a manner that nodded at all others. Tuxedos are specific, and yet ubiquitous, throughout weddings. Bo was not breedist, but an every-dog. His interpretation of the tuxedo is what defined the Obama era. Obama's nod to typical Americans (e.g., working-class mothers) was Bo's style strategy. His curls wafted without pretense, but the formality of his tuxedo presided in a nonchalant air. Bo's goodness radiated through his attire, like the President's respect for America. His attire signified a change in American weddings. He blended black and white effortlessness, rather than symbolize purposefulness. Obama did also by toppling hundreds of years of tradition in favor of new beginnings for homosexual partners granted the right to wed by his administration and the U.S. Supreme Court. President Obama, a heterosexual male committed to a woman through partnering and marriage, understood the solemnity of Bo's fur without admonishing differences. His companion, Sunny, was all-black. First Dog Sunny was also an ambassador, who represented peaceful cohabitation with Bo and the Obamas. She was added to their family and invited new flavors and attitudes; for example, all black tuxes. Her *laissez fair* attitude and sheepish demeanor were a compliment to the White House, which was run superiorly, often times by persons sporting tuxes and other formal wear, who resembled her.

Song

Songs are symbolic because they witness to the spirit, entrance the mind, and move the body (Blind Fox, 2017; White Tiger, 2016; Yague & Gare, 2016). The wedding processional is a traditional element (U.S. Army, n.d.). Like the purpose of marriage, it is exclusively relegated to ceremonious union. Because the wedding processional traditionally announced the bride, and often her father, nontraditional wedding parties have rebelled. Dances, lip-syncing, costumes, props, and other bold departures symbolize hybridized families, homes, and sex lives finding their place in mainstream culture and federal law (Our Last Night, 2015).

The wedding dance is atypically placed in the wedding procession to symbolize hybridization of family-life and entertainment. With guests fixated on their appearance in wedding videos that undoubtedly will appear on Facebook and other medias, they seem disconnected from the wedding party, but for their entertainment value (Ben, 2008; Newstreetmelody Beats, 2015). The groom is often the butt of a joke, but stands in contrast to the bride, who is reduced to a mere attendant at her future husband's *fête*. Marches are somber occasions at which the bride admits to having no future beyond her big day. She shines most brightly on this occasion because afterwards she will attend to her home life. She will synergize with her abode and become one with its energy (Die Heart Crew, 2011). She is a living embodiment of her husband's property. The dance, new to this century, suggests that women have more to look forward to—party guests. They now may arouse the public eye with their attendance to nightclubs and saloons without accompaniment by males, such as fathers, male escorts, or pimps. At some weddings, acrobats have been hired to pose as wedding attendants to arouse the crowd with vastly complex athletic stunts (Hattel, 2013). These feats, while disingenuous, are genuinely entertaining, unlike other weddings entrances in which the bride's party meekly fumbles down the aisle to dance tunes; and the groom's buddies pretend to be intoxicated before the main event, the reception. This is the new tradition, shocking people; it symbolizes hate rather than love. It tells on the wedding couple upfront—"We party, and do not intend to stay married our entire lives. We rather enjoy each other's company now than make a somber commitment." By the end of the march, the wedding proceeds in a typical fashion, with a member of the clergy or government presiding over their love. However, this too has been eradicated in favor of unconventional unions. For example, at some weddings, ministers have dressed in costume, and at others, members of the government may supply comedy in the form of raps, etc. Children have been recruited to participate in this mockery as well. What were once tokens of spring and eternal love have been transformed into talent shows where children demonstrate that their parents' investments in dancing and singing lessons were worth the while. In the end, the union may last, however through a traditional lens, it is doomed from the start (Carmen M. Cusack, 2012b).

Wedding songs are a general invitation to the public to experience new varieties of musical styles, such as rap. Many members of older generations have little experience listening to the lyrics of raps music, which can be crafty and full of double *entendres*. Rap-cents (i.e., a specific accent used by rap artists to emulate urban idiosyncrasies) may be lampooned by grooms and brides, who crave rejection from older leaders or relatives. Lyrics may be pleasant odes to love and marriage; and yet, rap-cents denote lack of respect for family inception and historical ties between community members at the wedding (Schlamme, 1993). Rap-cents are phony tributes to culture unrealistically aspired to by those, whose are distant from urban life. A similar comment could be made of phony country western accents. Some brides, grooms, wedding party members, or attendants deliver toasts and speeches using rap songs. Lyrics have been dubbed to harmless and family-friendly songs, such as the television show theme song for *Fresh Prince of Bel Aire*, as well as sex and drug laden tunes, such as Eminem's song, "Please Stand Up" (ABC News, 2017; D. J. Jazzy Jeff, 1996; Eminem, 2000; Flaming Lips & Badu, 2012; Heine, 2007; Killer Mike & Big Boi, 2003; OutKast, Scar, & Sleepy Brown, 2006). Eminem's lyrics include the following verse:

> I probably got a couple of screws up in my head loose
> But no worse than what's going on in your parents' bedrooms
> Sometimes, I wanna get on TV and just let loose, but can't
> But it's cool for Tom Green to hump a dead moose
> 'My bum is on your lips, my bum is on your lips'
> And if I'm lucky, you might just give it a little kiss
> And that's the message that we deliver to little kids
> And expect them not to know what a woman's clitoris is
> Of course they gonna know what intercourse is
> By the time they hit fourth grade
> They got the Discovery Channel, don't they?
> 'We ain't nothing but mammals.' Well, some of us cannibals
> Who cut other people open like cantaloupes
> But if we can hump dead animals and antelopes
> Then there's no reason that a man and another man can't elope
> But if you feel like I feel, I got the antidote
> Women wave your pantyhose, sing the chorus and it goes. (Eminem, 2000)

A maid of honor toasted a rap using his tune (ABC News, 2017; Bloodhound Gang, 1999). She reminisced about how the bride and groom met. The groom was less than impressive. "Taylor said, 'Who cares? You freaks! He's six feet, Italian, and very sweet'. … Through thick and thin you got your family by your side, now it's time to toast to the groom and the bride" (ABC News, 2017).

"Wedding March," a traditional tune, decries virginity; but, the song takes a dark turn at its inception (Peterson, 2015). "Wedding March" was composed by Felix Mendelssohn to add a musical dimension to William Shakespeare's *A Midsummer Night's Dream* (Peterson, 2015). Brides and grooms may be unaware of the song's connection to Shakespeare, but symbolism of that magnitude is not easily shrouded. "Symbols transform the atomized and alienated individual of modernity into a psychic holism of time and space" (Rowland, 2011). Symbols in Shakespeare, as viewed by Carl Jung, are "strategies for regeneration" that "shied" "any radical change in the power relations between men and women in their societies" (Rowland, 2011). Shakespeare's work, brought to the forefront of culture at weddings, is a "transitional experience, with its healing realm of play between dreams and objective reality, between enchantment and demystification" (Frosch, 2007; Rowland, 2011).

Many of Shakespeare's works demystify sex for young people, who read his perverted epiphanies in school. Pairing the "Wedding March" with *A Midsummer Night's Dream* results in "a positive future and … amity with the often disturbing regressive elements still alive within adult psyches" (Frosch, 2007, p. 485). Innocuous absorption of the art "overrid[es] the ironic and dark notes that" are prevalent in any relationship (Frosch, 2007, p. 485). Shakespeare's vision of undemoralized sexuality "recreates for" the marital couple "a new beginning, including the new beginning of love," perhaps "in the promise of a wished-for child" (Frosch, 2007, p. 485). "*A Midsummer Night's Dream* addresses the evolution of psychosexual stability, the resolution of oedipal conflict, and the consequent ability for proper gender identity and adult heterosexual intimacy" (Hartman, 1983). The play is popularly performed by inmates, whose sentences resembles the bride and groom's commitment to sharing a single life and home (Wilcox, 2011). The "presence of imagination" in the processional evokes Shakespearean delights and ethos, with its whimsy, color, snuffed passion, and "social unpleasantness" (Fisher, 2004; Hunter, 2003). The wedding party "comes at the moment of awakening from a dream in which" the bride and groom pretended to be wealthy and independent from their parents' success for many months or years while planning their wedding (Fisher, 2004; Frosch, 2007; Hunter, 2003; Palombo, 1983; Wilcox, 2011). The stark reality of starting a life together is "matched" by their "current feelings" undoubtedly harboring "a repressed libidinal fantasy of childhood," which evaporates before the attendants' eyes (Palombo, 1983, p. 301). For the maids and bachelors listening to the music and fantasizing about a wedding of their own, the song "illustrates the ability of the matching process to go beyond the narrow logical categories of waking thought to reach deeper levels of experience otherwise inaccessible to the dreamer" (Palombo, 1983, p. 301). Single individuals must rely on "censorship mechanisms" to protect their ears lest they marry too soon under the delusion that they can ever truly escape life under their parents' wings (Palombo, 1983, p. 301). They may "sense a snicket" and hope for "the universal experience of losing control" (Tuft, Gjelsvik, & Nakken, 2015).

"Bridal Chorus" is a common bridal processional. Richard Wagner composed the tune for *Lohengrin* (Peterson, 2015; Spenser, 1590). Using an opera to guide the bride fictionalizes the groom's need to kill his father. He does not walk in the processional with his father, like the bride—the first clue that his father is different from the bride's. The second clue is patriarchy. To inherit the wealth needed to sustain the bride, the groom must socially kill—that is outdo—his father and all his ancestors. Use of fiction is a formulaic answer to unresolved and unquenched desire to murder (Paul, 2014).

> This formula is concerned with resolving the inevitable dilemma that arises in the succession of one generation by another, and more specifically the passage of a junior man to full senior status. This transition is fraught with ambivalence in both directions, so that the junior man must accomplish his ascendency without becoming guilty of the crime of displacing—usually represented in the narrative as killing—a man who already occupies the senior position. (Paul, 2014, p. 289)

"[O]ne of the outcomes of the succession scenario is that the succeeding junior male must be represented as an 'innocent heir'" (Paul, 2014, p. 289). In this regard, he is like the bride. This is why her processional music suits him and his unspoken agenda. "[H]e must remain untainted by the violence inherent in succession while nonetheless replacing the previous occupant of senior status. Because this required result is impossible to accomplish in reality, symbolic means must be found to allow it to occur at least in fiction" (Paul, 2014, p. 289). The crowd pretends that the focus is on the bride; however, "inner processes of individuation are clearly visible in the development of the" wedding, "which [takes] place in the context of the social, political, and psychological values of European patriarchal culture" (Clarkson, 1989). "Bridal Chorus'" "creative process … work[s] through early developmental conflicts" and supposed conclusions, which "may expect the constellation of early … relationships to be reflected in their" maturation (Graham, 1978). Resolutions are "hypothesized" because "confusion about the identity of" a murderable "father" is "reflected" on the son (Graham, 1978). During the processional, "the nature of his paternal introject, and … this confusion, [are] demonstrated in his … handling of the occasion" (Graham, 1978). "[T]he myth of the birth of a hero is used" by the father to praise himself and the bride in case he may access her after the groom has spoiled her virginity (Graham, 1978). "[T]o demonstrate this" he relies on the power of his "background" (e.g., career and relatives) to "indicat[e] his own" innocence (Graham, 1978). Disavowal during the processional by the groom's father of any rivalry with the groom is a self-generated form of "confusion about his father's identity, and certain aspects of his hypothesized early oedipal conflict" (Graham, 1978). Psychosocial "modifications" of attendants' concept of the groom and bride are made in response to the groom's father's behavior during the procession, which all but ignores him and his once-bride, the groom's mother. "[I]nferences are made as to how the" groom's father prevented the groom's mother from being used as a "familial object" to satisfy needs for "relations and oedipal conflicts" (Graham, 1978).

Bride

A bride represents purity, but also lust (Demanarig, 2012; Falb et al., 2015; Gondal, 1948; Haley, 2009; Norris, 1997; Ordoñez, 1997). She is the object of attention, and bears no lust of her own (i.e., the veil); however, her foot attire symbolizes oppression (Carmen M. Cusack, 2018). High heels traditionally represent the kind of self-imposed corporeal punishment that society allocates for women to express lust. A bride's foot attire is significant because as she walks down the aisle, the attendants do not look at her shoes. Although her path is adorned with decorations strewn by a female child (e.g., flower girl), the wedding ceremony remains focused on the wedding procession and the bride's gown. Although her veil is preeminent at the beginning of her march, it becomes a symbol of disavowal as the groom lifts it from her face to reveal that she is no longer a member of her family (Adiga, 2008; Baldwin, 2015; Basinger, 1993). If she chooses not to wear high heels, then normative terms to describe her attire include "flat," "casual," and "basic," all derogatory terms with respect to a bride and her life with her new spouse. The wedding gown is a symbol of her mother's hope that she will become her mother (Sykes & Brace-Govan, 2015). When that is breached, the bride's friends step-in to play a frivolous role denoted by their positions as maids.

Brides are grotesque displays of affection (Wurth, 2017). They represent family unity and trading love for offering. They are the quintessence of compromise. A bride's big plan is to showcase her skills as a planner. It suggests that she will be an excellent family planner (Planned Parenthood v. Casey, 1992). Yet, her compromise represents politics (Hague, Thiara, & Turner, 2011; Rastogi & Therly, 2006). The wedding date is negotiated. It is the first step in the wedding party understanding their roles (Sykes & Brace-Govan, 2015). The date begins their union and ends their separateness. Negotiation is an essential aspect of a bride and spouse. Demands for sexual intimacy in a publicized Internet-centric world put the bride at odds with the wedding's traditional mission to share the bride before she is dimmed (Bahn, 1979; Wurth, 2017). Brides no longer have the benefit of bridal magazines to guide them with their sexualities. Sex no longer has the selling power that it used to possess due to saturation and market exposure to free sexual depictions on the Internet. One study found that women, who own more devices and spend greater quantity of time shopping online, were likelier to invest time and spend money to customize their gowns (Choy & Loker, 2004). Couples no longer need to buy that which was advertised by magazines to feel that they have participated in a cultural ethos of marriage sexuality (Bahn, 1979). With increased interest in dissolution of marriages and access to easy dissolutions, focus on having children as a result of marriage has increased (Kraus, 1977). Marriage was a social pillar in past years. In itself, it was justified and revered. However, brides, sensing the instability and lessened importance of the marital union, may rush to plan families before their weddings in order to satisfy their senses of importance (Kimura, 1957; Stafford & Scott, 2016).

Masturbatory rituals, such as those validating use of state and religious means when neither party ascribes to the state's morality or religious doctrines, may cause wedding participants to feel encouraged by society to masturbate. Masturbation then becomes a form of self-reflexive hatred (Carmen M. Cusack, 2014). If a bride wants to have unitive coitus under the auspices of state or religious approval when her heart is with her husband (or wife) secularly, then her feelings become disdainful and she may masturbate to satiate her resentment of the institutions that bound her to her husband (or wife).

Brides break from tradition when the foundations of their family-lives are nontraditional. One study found that many brides did not take their spouses last names when they were married by officiants from distinct faiths (Kopelman, Shea-Van Fossen, Paraskevas, Lawter, & Prottas, 2009; Ross, 2010). A bride was also less likely to take her husband's surname when her mother, father, or both parents had died (Kopelman et al., 2009). A similar relationship emerged when a bride's parents had been divorced or separated. Tradition may be imbued through social class (Mazur, 1993; Otnes & Pleck, 2003). Class is passed from father to daughter, and in some cases, through both parents (Mazur, 1993). Fathers' social standing is the foundation of the bride's welfare in traditional marriage; and has come to symbolize departure from poverty. The opulence of the wedding is traditional, but still distinguishes brides of differing socioeconomic backgrounds. Rather than pretend to be of an upper class, as was tradition for a woman on the single most important day of her life, many brides have become reminiscent of their mothers, opting for revelatory wedding schemes and portraits. Their hair, hat, and gown choices all attest to their poverty rather than to their father's promise to support their spouses. Brides' class may be negotiated, but it often leads to turmoil (Lin, Huang, Chen, & Shao, 2009). Prices of brides vary according to perception that brides are being sold; and their willingness to abide by tradition that strongly suggests to brides that they obey tradition to move upward. A "bond" describes a marital union (Nwoke, 2009, p. 2085). This term highlights the relationship between tradition, marriage, and a bride's role if she chooses to be a successful member of the society that sanctions her union. Symbols, such as the wedding gown, may announce to the guests whether the bride is taking her role or making it (Levin, 2001).

Some mental diseases cause infirmed individuals to hallucinate that they are brides (Carmen M. Cusack, 2016; Manning, 2013). A mutation of this psychological affliction is evident in bridesmaids, who strongly wish to be brides to the point of enviously disrupting brides' emotional states to rain on their parades (Ashley, 2012). Fights between brides and bridesmaids resulting from bridesmaids' envy is one reason why a poll found that of 1,939 brides, approximately 40% had ended relationships with a bridesmaid, including a female relative (Waterlow, 2014). Nearly three-quarters of the women experienced fights, and one-third of these caused their relationships to crumble. Insecurity and jealousy caused some bridesmaids sexually to pursue grooms. One groom's 16 year-old sister became pregnant and intended to deliver four months before the wedding (Mulroy, 2017). Her dress and their rehearsals were soured by her changing weight, mood, and energy. She nonconsensually inseminated herself with her boyfriend's sperm so that she could steal attention from the bride, tarnish her brother's bid for purity (i.e., matrimony), and avoid opposition from the father-to-be. The child-mother stole the soon-to-be married couple's opportunity to have the first-born grandchild. The young mother was able to "rally" "support" from others, who turned against the bride for immaturely experiencing selfish disappointment toward her soon-to-be sister-in-law (Mulroy, 2017). Her envy likely relates to her fear of being replaced; and perhaps, some incestuous desires. The date had been planned as a "child-free" event; but, the bride was forced to accommodate the "planned" and planted seed of envy (Mulroy, 2017).

The bride is envious of the groom. He has groomsmen; she has bridesmaids. Her party denotes immaturity, insubstantiveness, and suffocation by customs and tradition. The groomsmen are men, who are mature, dashing, and like the groom, not distinguished by their garb and motion. The bride's walk is unique; and thus, her maids are not only visually dissimilated from her, they are physically propelled from her allegedly dignified presence, particularly when their garb is flashy, understated, or garish. Try as she may, the bride cannot compete with the groomsmen, much less the groom, who has total control over her bridesmaids' aesthetic. It is mostly when their dates balance the wedding party that the bridesmaids seem reasonable. Otherwise, they frequently appear to be lost, which pays no honor to brides on their big day.

Inclusion of animals in wedding parties also appeals to grooms' control because bridesmaids may not be enough of a romantic offering to keep crowds interested in the event. The bride is nearly intrinsically unflattered by the inclusion of animals in wedding ceremonies. However, animals' appearances at weddings is always joyful, and some brides have shared their ceremonies with pets, who were simultaneously wed. Yet, these pets may be closer to brides than grooms suspect. For example, one bride married her female dog after the groom backed-out (Baynes, 2016). Perhaps he was aware of the bride's fantasy of a love affair and relented to avoid heartache and disappointment (Carmen M. Cusack, 2015). One bride could not part with her dog, named Leo, so her father ordered a life-size representation of Leo to be made and delivered to the bride on the day of the wedding (Spears, 2017). She posed with Leo's effigy in her wedding photos and subjected the groom to photo sessions with the depiction, which allegedly comforted her and drew her closer to her father, who photo-bombed the groom with Leo. The groom's trust for the bride and her father did not wane, and yet, such sneaky and disruptive behavior suggests a deep bond between the two, which will be openly appreciated by the bride and result in the groom's ridicule and possible discomfort throughout their lives together. Leo may have been the groom's only friend because his appearance manifested character traits that may do-in the groom in the future.

Five of 100 weddings include pets marching down aisles with brides, and double that number attend as guests (Kandel, 2013). Some brides hold pets, such as one counselor for teen females, who held a hen. Many are depicted in official wedding photos kissing pets, and even enjoying kiss "sandwiches" with their pets and betrotheds. Items such as lint brushes understandably replace treasured keepsakes (e.g., rings) as imminently important facets of the wedding ceremony. This dishevels the bride's authority and significance relative to a traditional entrance. The counselor, for teen women, audaciously incorporated her chickens' eggs into a frittata that she nearly cannibalistically served to her guests (Carmen M. Cusack, 2011b). A couple's dog, Craig, ran down the aisle bearing rings after the groomsman intentionally "forgot" them (Mallinson, 2017). The bride bent down to pet Craig revealing her true affection for the dog, which was greater than her attention to the groom or the ceremony. In a series of unconscious gestures, she complained to the audience that she must stand in the ceremony rather than pet the dog at home. She tugged on her veil and adjusted it, then bent over once again to pet the dog mid-ceremony. Finally, her companion offered to the tear the bothersome dress apart by jumping on her. She was able to compose herself, and carried on with the ceremony. A video explaining how Craig came to possess the rings begins with the dog wearing pajamas and sleeping in their bed next to their cell phone, another stand-in for the marital participants. It ends with him wearing a tuxedo after he showers and runs around in a state that they allude to as being undressed. A child in the audience gasps as the party depicts intimate nude scenes that humanize Craig just before he runs into the wedding hall without any pants on and only wearing the top portion of a tuxedo. The groom is alarmed, but his appalled sense of rejection maintains his cool, and the wedding continues.

Joan Cusack destroys brides' pure intentions in her rendering of marriage in *Addams Family Values* (Joan Cusack, 1993). The basic plot is that a nanny, played by Cusack, marries Uncle Fester to commandeer his millions and then execute him prior to consummating their wedding vows. Gomez and the other Addams are supportive until Cusack's character fails to be able to kill the un-dead Fester on her wedding night. Because she must endure him, she forces him to cut-off his beloved family members to torture and control him. She psychologically abuses him and attempts to kill him until she is killed. The character, Debbie Jellinsky, is a serial killer called Black Widow. Gomez, in his zoot suit and bowtie, is the epitome of romance. His bride, Morticia, embraces his patriarchal and liberated mash-up. Morticia is veiled. Her veil is to "prevent" more "bab[ies]" "in exchange for" an "immortal soul" (Joan Cusack, 1993).

The film rips apart seams holding society to traditional family values. Unmarried men are "strange" (Joan Cusack, 1993). They are "enemies" (Joan Cusack, 1993). Jellinsky is pretty in white. Her contrast to Gomez and Morticia declares her to be "a homicidal maniac" (Joan Cusack, 1993). She is "easy," "fine," and "damp" (Joan Cusack, 1993). Jellinsky pretends to be a "virgin," who has yet to "experience physical love" (Joan Cusack, 1993). Losing one's virginity is the "ultimate sacrifice" (Joan Cusack, 1993). Sex may not be "contagious," but also may not be a "harmony" played by two bodies at once (Joan Cusack, 1993). She promises Fester "indescribable joy" because she "won't press charges" (Joan Cusack, 1993). The Gomez boys' mother is depicted in a jack book that Fester keeps on his bed (Carmen M. Cusack, 2017). When the detached hand, Thing, attempts to harass Jellinsky by crawling onto her shoulder, Cusack's character punishes and dominates him by forcibly penetrating her mouth with one of his digits. She is a winner

(Carmen M. Cusack, 2014). She causes Gomez to feel "unworthy," and makes Fester believe that he only is worthy of "ugly girls" (Joan Cusack, 1993).

Fester, played by Cristopher Lloyd, is a virgin, whose cadence, breathing pattern, and elicited charm nod at the work of Cusack's brother, John Cusack (Joan Cusack, 1993; John Cusack, 2017). Lloyd is a genius, who plays as John. When Joan is on screen, her co-stars either mimic her or John. By playing John, Lloyd makes the vision of the two powerhouses bleed through the screen in a funny moment when Fester, all too knowingly, implies that women, who marry for money, are akin to shoplifters (Frieric, 2012). Later, Fester mimics Jellinsky by wearing a toupee and bubbles on his head. Lloyd preserves both Cusacks simultaneously.

The movie hints at problems with interracial marriage (Joan Cusack, 1993). Michael Jackson's "Heal the World" (1992) poster hangs in a disciplinary camp bunk. The poster depicts a band-aid on the planet Earth and two hands holding the planet. At least one hand appears to be fair skinned, but the other may be shaded or dark. It is left ambiguous. The band-aid is traditional beige, signifying White skin. A catholic teacher, Marlys Stover, who taught catechism classes at St. Jude Catholic Church with her husband Mike Stover, described how American bigotry affects attitudes toward American culture abroad (Stover & Stover, 2014). She said that when the Catholic Church sends aid to Haiti, children are taught to donate band-aids depicting cartoons rather than flesh-colored band-aids. She feared that Haitian children would reject the medical supplies if they insinuated exclusivity. The obvious message is that Jackson is differentiable, though the degree is unknown. Therefore, as precaution, young women should avoid marrying him for love or money.

Consummation is required whether brides marry for family, love, or money. In the film, "want[ing] to come" is a reference to "existence," not just a sexual expulsion (Joan Cusack, 1993). Sex transforms a virgin into a "helpless slave," a "ditto" (Joan Cusack, 1993). To convince Fester not to consummate the marriage before she can kill him, Jellinsky asks him never to see his family again. She threatens that once they consummate the relationship, she will not be able to enjoy their life together if his family is present. "If I picture them in our lives, I can never, 'you know'" (Joan Cusack, 1993). They consummate the marriage, but she rules him. "Don't touch it, not until the scab falls off" (Joan Cusack, 1993)! Cusack's character, Black Widow, does not take prisoners—no "ball and chain"—objects used as sex toys by Morticia and Gomez (Joan Cusack, 1993). "Of course, not everyone can be a star" (Joan Cusack, 1993). Being "in love" is an adequate substitute for the fame or attention craved by rule-followers (Joan Cusack, 1993). The marital home is therefore, a "whorehouse" where a groom "shall not submit" and "shall conquer" when he is able to "rise" (Joan Cusack, 1993; Carmen M. Cusack, 2014; deGraaf, 2014). Parties, who "don't want to" participate "in the pageant" can get "in trouble" and "realize" a different, albeit "tired" "vision" (Joan Cusack, 1993). "No matter how odd or pale or chubby," marriage can make a bride into "an example," a model of social "justice," and a "family" (Joan Cusack, 1993; Carmen M. Cusack, 2011a).

Spiritual equilibrium is a consequence of being married. Couples' flames may be extinguished, but they burn and ashen in unisons. The "special" consequence of their "harmon[ious]" commitment is that they become responsible for each other; and therefore, assume the burden of each other's misdeeds (e.g., harming humans, animals, and nature) (Joan Cusack, 1993). Cusack cues the audience into a spiritual loophole. Gay men associating socially inside fraternal organizations (e.g., platoons) can avoid taking on women's sexual, psychosocial, and domestic trespasses (Matthew 6:9–13). Yet, homosexual males are ticking time "bombs" because they also want children, which will drive them to marry, be with, and affiliate with desirable or undesirable women (Joan Cusack, 1993). They search, like practicing heterosexuals, for norms (AP, 2014; Carmen M. Cusack, 2012a, 2012c; Gibbs & Bryer, 2017; Wendt, 1993). The bride's "mirth" and her wedding "merriment" are quintessential regardless of her groom's historical foray into homosexual delicacies. Any man may "worship[] and adore[]" a bride (Joan Cusack, 1993).

Groom

The groom alters reality by entering the room. The wedding begins with the groom, who enters to show his respect for himself. Some contemporary brides prefer to walk down the aisle with the groom, a breach of tradition that signifies divorce. If parties cannot comply with an ancient tradition in their nuptials, then they are unlikely to proceed with society's prescribed courses and are likely to fail in the age-old tradition of marriage. The groom hails his men and being superior to the bridesmaids. He is not only dressed like them, and anticipates that they will have had sex or be married, unlike bridesmaids, who are expected to be virginal like the bride; he also lavishes himself with the brides' attention. She walks in and looks at him, but he has the pleasure of enjoying the entire wedding party procession from the front of the room. The groom gains the vantage point in the marriage from society's point of view from the moment he enters the room and retains it until he dies or divorces the bride. The groom is the main show for the men, who are not pressured to admire the bride and her wedding dress. Females are expected to lust after the groom. They are taught from a young age that he is the show piece. The bride is the ornament in his crown. This tradition has mutated because the groom has become a laughing stock. From funny proposals to underwater weddings and sky diving wedding crashes, the groom is now a stunt man, adventurer, and explorer (The Black Tux, n.d.). He is no longer the sole reason that the bride appears; she also seeks adventure with him. Although she seems to be equal, she retains a subordinated role because either her parents or his typically larger salary has provided the wedding festivities (I Love Jen!, 2009; MTV, 2011). He is seen as a provider, whereas she is seen as a recipient, which is traditional.

Grooms are repackaged in *The Princess Bride*, a film about women as property and men as being enslaved by their duties (Elwes, 1987). Cary Elwes' character, Westley, is the perfect contrast to an evil prince, who would have his way no matter what. Westley's tagline, "As you wish," taught little girls and boys that true love means doing whatever the other asks; however, Westley creates a fictitious persona, Dread Pirate Roberts (Elwes, 1987). The message is clear. A groom will serve a bride before the wedding, but then their souls go through mitosis. He will separate into a corporatized and commercialized version of who she loved and who said he would serve her forever, only to win her affection on the corporation's terms. She will revise her plan to rule over him, in turn, and will marry poorly to prove that she was never interested in money, which is his position and role in their union. In "Love Song," Sara Bareilles (2007) complains about her experience with being owned and forced to produce. Her song simultaneously takes a masculine and feminine stance. She sings, "I learned the hard way that they all say things you want to hear" (Bareilles, 2007). "Your help just hurts. You are not what I thought you were; hello to high and dry. Convinced me to please you. Made me think that I need this too" (Bareilles, 2007). "If your heart is nowhere in it, I don't want it for a minute, babe. I'll walk the seven seas when I believe that there's a reason" (Bareilles, 2007).

Grooms bore the brunt of financial commitments (Razzi, 2001). Brides' parents paid for weddings, leaving brides financially unscathed. Grooms were responsible for vehicles, mortgages, and children's schooling needs. Now, brides may benefit when the groom registers the coupe for down payment contributions (Gerstner, 2017). Instead of wedding gifts, guests may put-in for a down payment. The groom benefits because he bears less financial responsibility, and the bride puts more equity into the home. Previously, when the groom supplied monies earned prior to the marriage for the down payment, some courts would award that sum to the groom during divorce. Now, the bride's share can be increased; and yet, the groom's interest payments decreased, which are seldom calculated into the equity of a house by courts even though the groom pays nearly double the cost of a home in interest payments.

Grooms may be encouraged to love brides, but some responses, and their ensuing marital harmony, may innately result from the groom's distaste for the bride (Gollan, Salmon, & Paxton, 2006). Although he may appear to be attracted to his wife, he may not genuinely be interested in completing his marital vows (i.e., coitus). Persian grooms were analyzed for sexual nonperformance (Zargooshi, 2008). Grooms failed to perform because of erectile dysfunction (86), premature ejaculation (89), performance anxiety (25), vaginismus (34), hypodesire disorder (6), sexual ignorance (8), homosexuality (2), hypogonadism (1), the bride's request for abstinence (1), and a thick hymen (1). Several grooms, including those, who were unattracted or overly hesitant, proffered numerous reasons for avoiding the bride on their wedding night. Pressure from relatives also chilled grooms rather than excite them. In 240 cases, grooms and brides avoided intimacy because relatives placed handkerchiefs on the marital bed. The handkerchiefs were intended to collect blood when her hymen tore. Immediately following penetration, the handkerchief was to be submitted for inspection to relatives waiting on the other side of a wall separating the coupe from the crowd. The groom and bride's preexisting sexual intimacy could explain why they were willing and compelled to avoid coitus. However, sexual complacency after years of premarital fornication could explain a groom's reticence to perform on command. Several grooms complained that they had been obligated to marry and did not love their brides. Treatment was provided to many of the couples. Of those, who received treatment, but did not respond, approximately 40% divorced. Failure to consummate is a serious violation of societal norms throughout the world; and is grounds for annulment in the United States (Carmen M. Cusack, 2015; Ribner & Rosenbaum, 2005).

Grooms tend to be older (Nault, 1996; Qu, 1998). They represent patriarchy because they are seniors in the home (Nault, 1996). The bride is younger. Although she is likelier to marry during her twenties, a groom statistically is likelier to be older because older men are likelier than older women to remarry. A study of Canadian couples found that brides and grooms' twenties are their peak years to marry; but, the average age for women to marry is 30 and for men is 33. Women are likelier than men to marry; but older men's likelihood exceeds women's. It has become much more common for grooms to be older than brides by 10 or more years. This defeats patriarchy because the power and financial and societal benefits accrued to him are evident; and therefore, do not need to be enforced through her subjugation (Ho & Johnson, 1990; Muhsam, 1974; Veevers, 1988).

Young grooms are likelier to divorce (Carmichael, 1988). A study of the parents of youth currently wedding explains their parents' divorce rates (Wilson & Clarke, 1992). A 1988 analysis indicated that 745,000 divorced men and 748,000 divorced women remarried. Sixty-one percent of males and females married divorced partners; 35% married single people; and four percent wed widows and widowers. Grooms were likely to be 39 years old and brides were on-average 35 years old. Grooms were likely to be 35 years old and brides were likely to be 31 when they married single people. This group also had more education. In the same year, 72,000 widowers, average 61 years old, and 77,000 widows, average 53 years old, remarried widowed or divorced partners at the same rates. When grooms and brides remarried between the ages of 25 to 44 in 1972, they were less likely to divorce than couples, who wed for the first time during their teen years. Young bachelors are doomed even though the moniker predicts success, which is deceptive. "Bachelor" is the name endowed to the home of a single, up-and-coming man (i.e., bachelor pad) and undergraduate degree. "Bachelorette" plays off "bachelor;" and is mostly uttered when women freely loosen their virtues at parties prior to their wedding nights (Gitter, 1994; Razzi, 2001).

References

(2017, October 9). Siegfried & Roy. The end! *Globe*, 6–7.

ABC News. (2017, September 8). Maid of honor delivers epic Eminem wedding rap for sister. Retrieved from http://abcnews.go.com/US/video/maid-honor-delivers-epic-eminem-wedding-rap-sister-49710408

Adiga, A. (2008). *The white tiger: A novel.* Indiana: HarperCollins.

Ashley. (2012, September 12). Any brides having issues with jealousy or envy? Bridesmaids, moh's or relatives of yours of fh? *Wedding Wire.* Retrieved from https://www.weddingwire.com/wedding-forums/any-brides-having-issues-with-jealousy-or-envy-bridesmaids-mohs-or-relatives-of-yours-of-fh/0ed4bac606b0fcfc.html

Associated Press (AP). (2014, March 4). Karl Lagerfeld takes you to Chanel's supermarket. Retrieved from https://www.youtube.com/watch?v=olQKa8RqVTg

Bahn, A. K. (1979). *Changes and continuities in the transitional status of bride into wife: A content analysis of bridal magazines. 1967–1977, the decade of the women's movement* (Order No. 7923700). Available from PsycINFO.

Baldwin, A. (2015, October 10). Alec Baldwin shows daughter Carmen his favourite yoga pose. *Hollywood News*. Retrieved from https://www.youtube.com/watch?v=vdAlJcOPYkc

Bareilles, S. (2007). "Love song." On *Little voice*. New York, NY: Epic Records.

Basinger, K. (1993). Kim Basinger in music video for "Mary Jane's last dance" by Tom Petty and the heartbreakers. TomPettyVEVO. Retrieved from https://www.youtube.com/watch?v=aowSGxim_O8

Batchelor, B. (2017). Men's fashion in the 1900s. In *Pop Culture Universe: Icons, Idols, Ideas*. Santa Barbara, CA: ABC-CLIO.

Baynes, C. (2016, November 28). Jilted bride marries her dog after fiancé backs out of dream wedding. *Mirror*. Retrieved from http://www.mirror.co.uk/news/world-news/jilted-bride-marries-dog-after-9353017

Ben, P. (2008). "White tiger." On *Wine for my weakness*. Wuppertal, Germany: Cargo Records.

Blind Fox. (2017). "White tiger edm big room song." Youtube.com. Retrieved from https://www.youtube.com/watch?v=moot-8fG5ks

Bloodhound Gang. (1999). "The bad touch." On *Hooray for boobies*. New York, NY: Geffen Records.

Carmichael, G. A. (1988). Socio-demographic correlates of divorce in New Zealand. *Journal of the Australian Population Association*, 5(1), 58–81.

CBS News. (2015). 2015 governors awards. Retrieved from https://www.cbsnews.com/pictures/2015-governors-awards/22/

Chivu Chivu. (2017, October 2). Cute tiger. Retrieved from https://www.youtube.com/watch?v=ZIF6H4D0GEc

Choy, R., & Loker, S. (2004). Mass customization of wedding gowns: Design involvement on the internet. *Clothing & Textiles Research Journal*, *22*(1–2), 79–87.

Clarkson, A. (1989). Wagner from Lohengrin to Siegfried: "Elsa taught me to unearth this man." *Quadrant: Journal of the C. G. Jung Foundation for Analytical Psychology*, 22(2), 39–50.

Cusack, C. (2006). *Scooperman* by Christina Cusack. UWFTV, Pensacola, FL.

Cusack, C. (2012). "As long as you're with me." On *First impressions are overrated*. Pensacola, FL: Das Studio.

Cusack, C. M. (2011a). Busting patriarchal booby traps: Why feminists fear minor distinctions in child porn cases, an analysis of social deviance within gender, family, or the home (*etudes* 4). *Southern University Law Review*, 39, 43.

Cusack, C. M. (2011b). Placentophagy and embryophagy: An analysis of social deviance within gender, family, or the home (*etude* 1). *Journal of Law & Social Deviance*, *1*, 112.

Cusack, C. M. (2012a). Alternative dispute resolution and *niyama*, the second limb of yoga sutra. *In Factis Pax*, 6, 107.

Cusack, C. M. (2012b). Tit-for-tat about tats on tots: An analysis of social deviance with in gender, family, or the home (*etudes* 3). *Children's Legal Right Journal*, *32*, 50.

Cusack, C. M. (2012c). Two films, one law. *New York Bar Association Entertainment & Sports Law Journal, 23*, 3.

Cusack, C. M. (2013). To-get-her for-Eve-r: A man hater's right to same-sex marriage. *Journal of Law & Public Policy, 10*, 63–98.

Cusack, C. M. (2014). No stroking in the pokey: Promulgating penological policies prohibiting masturbation among inmate populations. *Journal of Law & Social Deviance, 7*, 80–124.

Cusack, C. M. (2015). *Criminal justice handbook on masculinity, male aggression, and sexuality*. Springfield, IL: Charles C. Thomas.

Cusack, C. M. (2016a). Save the white tiger. *Journal of Law & Social Deviance, 12*, 1.

Cusack, C. M. (2016b). *Twins and deviance: Law, crime, sex, society, and family*. Cambridge, UK: Cambridge Scholars Publishing.

Cusack, C. M. (2017). Saving captive white tigers: An assessment of an animal law treatise. *Journal of Law & Social Deviance, 14*, 1.

Cusack, C. M. (2018). Foot binding. *Journal of Law & Social Deviance, 15*.

Cusack, J. [Joan]. (1993). *Addams family values*. Hollywood, CA: Paramount Pictures.

Cusack, J. [John]. (2017). *Blood money*. USA: Porthos Films.

Daniels, D. H. (2017). Zoot suits. In *Pop Culture Universe: Icons, Idols, Ideas*. Santa Barbara, CA: ABC-CLIO.

deGraaf, M. (2014, September 26). John Cusack blasts Hollywood as a 'whorehouse' that is so obsessed with young female actors 'it's almost like kiddie porn.' *Daily Mail*. Retrieved from http://www.dailymail.co.uk/news/article-2771470/John-Cusack-blasts-whorehouse-Hollywood-reveals-sucks-time.html

Demanarig, D. L. L. (2012). *Phenomenological look at the experiences of Filipina correspondence or internet brides* (Order No. AAI3485812). Available from PsycINFO. (1112147493; 2012–99160–445).

DiCaprio, L. (1997). *Titanic*. Hollywood, CA: Paramount Pictures.

Die Heart Crew. (2011, September 6). Dhoom 2 song—white tiger(vipin). Retrieved from https://www.youtube.com/watch?v=ocSvoIpHZTc

D. J. Jazzy Jeff. (1996). *Fresh prince of Bel Aire*. Burbank, CA: NBC Productions.

Elwes, C. (1987). *The princess bride*. Los Angeles, CA: Buttercup Films.

Eminem. (2000). "The real Slim Shady." On *The Marshall Mathers lp*. Santa Monica, CA: Aftermath Entertainment/Interscope Records.

Falb, K. L., Annan, J., Kpebo, D., Cole, H., Willie, T., Xuan, Z., … Gupta, J. (2015). Differential impacts of an intimate partner violence prevention program based on child marriage status in rural *Côte d'Ivoire*. *Journal of Adolescent Health, 57*(5), 553–558.

Fisher, J. V. (2004). 'Love looks not with the eyes, but with the mind:' The death and rebirth of imagination. *Journal of the British Association of Psychotherapists (BAP), 42*(2), 101–115.

Flaming Lips, & Badu, E. (2012). "First time I ever saw your face." On *the flaming lips and heady fwends*. London, UK: Bella Union. Retrieved from http://www.mojvideo.com/video-flaming-lips-ft-erykah-badu-first-time-i-ever-saw-your-face/88417a954239e7213a1e

Frieric, L. (2012, June 28). Jordan Knight sings the old navy summer catalog. Retrieved from https://www.youtube.com/watch?v=F3D26ATWNkw

Frosch, T. R. (2007). The missing child in a midsummer night's dream. *American Imago, 64*(4), 485–511.

Gerstner, L. (2017, June). Wedding gifts for newlyweds who have everything. *Kiplinger's Personal Finance*.

Gibbs, A., & Bryer, T. (2017, January 13). Karl Lagerfeld's cat Choupette is 'like a chic lady' with a personal maid, says designer. CNBC. Retrieved from https://www.cnbc.com/2017/01/13/fashion-designer-karl-lagerfeld-on-his-cat-choupette-and-its-fashionable-lifestyle.html

Gitter, M. (1994, December). Tying the knot again … without getting tangled. *Financial Planning, 24*, 76.

Gollan, T. H., Salmon, D. P., & Paxton, J. L. (2006). Word association in early Alzheimer's disease. *Brain & Language*, 99(3), 289–303.

Gondal, R. P. (1948). Changes in marriage customs and practices among the lower agricultural castes of the Kotah state. *Eastern Anthropologist*, 2(1), 39–49.

Graham, L. A. (1978). Wagner and Lohengrin, a psychoanalytic study. *Psychiatric Journal of the University of Ottawa*, 3(1), 39–49.

Hague, G., Thiara, R. K., & Turner, A. (2011). Bride-price and its links to domestic violence and poverty in Uganda: A participatory action research study. *Women's Studies International Forum, 34*(6), 550–561.

Haley, P. S. (2009). *The Filipina-South Floridian international internet marriage practice: Agency, culture, and paradox* (Order No. AAI3339602). Available from PsycINFO. (622066573; 2009–99111–080).

Hartman, V. S. (1983). A midsummer night's dream: A gentle concord to the oedipal problem. *American Imago*, 40(4), 355–369.

Hattel, J. (2013, December 25). Wedding entrance Denmark. Marry you! *Youtube.com*. Retrieved from https://www.youtube.com/watch?v=wRdAGOsLWcU

Heine, S. (2007). *Zen skin, zen marrow: Will the real Zen Buddhism please stand up?* Oxford: Oxford University Press.

Ho, F. C. & Johnson, R. C. (1990). Intra-ethnic and inter-ethnic marriage and divorce in Hawaii. *Social Biology, 37*(1–2), 44–51.

Hunter, D. (2003). Cultural politics of fantasy in Shakespeare's midsummer night's dream. *PsyART, 7*.

Hutchings, D. (1993, January 11). Menagerie a deux. *People*. Retrieved from http://people.com/archive/menagerie-a-deux-vol-39-no-1/

I Love Jen! (2009, October 21). Batman and Catwoman wedding ceremony. Youtube.com. Retrieved from https://www.youtube.com/watch?v=YhxdTwv9tSc

Jackson, M. (1992). "Heal the world." On *Dangerous*. Minato, Japan: Epic Records.

Kandel, B. (2013, February 23). A new breed of ring bearers trot down the aisle. *New York Times*. Retrieved from http://www.nytimes.com/2012/02/26/fashion/weddings/pets-accompany-couples-down-the-aisle.html

Killer Mike, & Big Boi. (2003). "A.d.i.d.a.s." In *Monster*. New York, NY: Columbia.

Kimura, Y. (1957). War brides in Hawaii and their in-laws. *American Journal of Sociology*, 63, 70–76.

Kopelman, R. E., Shea-Van Fossen, R. J., Paraskevas, E., Lawter, L., & Prottas, D. J. (2009). The bride is keeping her name: A 35-year retrospective analysis of trends and correlates. *Social Behavior & Personality, 37*(5), 687–700.

Kraus, J. (1977). Shotgun weddings: Trends in the sociopathology of marriage. *Australian & New Zealand Journal of Psychiatry, 11*(4), 259–264.

Lassie. (1954). *Lassie*. California: Lassie Television.

Levin, L. A. (2001). *The wedding day: A phenomenological exploration* (Order No. AAI3016498). Available from PsycINFO. (619722879; 2001-95023-019).

Lin, Y., Huang, X., Chen, C., & Shao, W. (2009). The lived experiences of brokered brides who have attempted suicide in Taiwan. *Journal of Clinical Nursing, 18*(24), 3409–3420.

Love, F. (1995). *Friday*. Arlington, TX: United Paramount.

Mallinson, H. (2017, February 10). Puppy love! French bulldog, George, saves a couple's wedding by arriving with the rings when the best man 'forgot' them. *Daily Mail*. Retrieved from http://www.dailymail.co.uk/news/article-4213470/Adorable-French-bulldog-brings-wedding-rings-ceremony.html

Manning, T. (2013). *Orange is the new black*. Los Gatos, CA: Netflix.

Mazur, A. (1993). Signs of status in bridal portraits. *Sociological Forum*, 8(2), 273–283.

Morrison, H. (1937, May 6). Announced the Hindenburg disaster. WLS. Lakehurst Maxfield, Manchester Township New Jersey.

Muhsam, H. V. (1974). The marriage squeeze. *Demography, 11*(2), 291–299.

Mulroy, Z. (2017, March 13). Jealous bride-to-be threatens to ban her bridesmaid—Because she's pregnant. *Mirror*. Retrieved from http://www.mirror.co.uk/lifestyle/family/jealous-bride-threatens-ban-bridesmaid-10020811

Music Television (MTV). (2011, July 22). Courtney Love at the Batman Premier 1997. Retrieved from https://www.youtube.com/watch?v=BEcuGGNtsOg

Nault, F. (1996). Twenty years of marriages. *Health Reports*, 8(2), 39–47(Eng); 41–50(Fre).

Newstreetmelody Beats. (2015). Epic Trap Music—White Tiger. Retrieved from https://www.youtube.com/watch?v=18RicljiI_8

Norris, F. (1997). *Private parts*. USA: Rysher Entertainment.

Nwoke, M. B. (2009). Bride price and implications for women's rights in Nigeria: Psychological perspective. *Gender & Behaviour*, 7(1), 2078–2087.

O'Connell, L. (2013). The steps to *first dance*. *Canadian Theatre Review, 153*(153), 99–102.

Ordoñez, R. Z. (1997). Mail-order brides: An emerging community. In M. P. P. Root (Ed.), *Filipino Americans: transformation and identity; Filipino Americans: Transformation and identity* (pp. 121–142, Chapter xv, 352pp.). Thousand Oaks, CA: Sage Publications.

Otnes, C. C., & Pleck, E. (2003). *In Cinderella dreams: The allure of the lavish wedding*. Berkley, CA: University of California Press.

Our Last Night. (2015). "White tiger." On *Younger dreams*. Hollywood, CA: Epitaph.

OutKast, Scar, & Sleepy Brown. (2006). "Morris brown." On *Idlewild*. New York, NY: Sony BMG.

Palombo, S. R. (1983). The genius of the dream. *The American Journal of Psychoanalysis*, 43(4), 301–313.

Paul, R. A. (2014). The knight in shining armor and the pure fool: The construction of "innocence" in two Wagner operas. *American Imago*, *71*(3), 289–313.

Peterson, E. (2015, April 3). The four most controversial pieces of wedding music. Classical MPR. Retrieved from https://www.classicalmpr.org/story/2014/07/21/controversial-wedding-music

Planned Parenthood v. Casey, 505 U.S. 833 (1992).

Qu, L. (1998). Age differences between brides and grooms in Australia. *Family Matters (Melbourne, Vic.)*, *49*, 27.

Rastogi, M., & Therly, P. (2006). Dowry and its link to violence against women in India: Feminist psychological perspectives. *Trauma, Violence, & Abuse*, *7*(1), 66–77.

Razzi, E. (2001, June). Wedding bills. *Kiplinger's Personal Finance*, *55*, 90–92.

Ribner, D. S., & Rosenbaum, T. Y. (2005). Evaluation and treatment of unconsummated marriages among orthodox Jewish couples. *Journal of Sex & Marital Therapy*, *31*(4), 341–353.

Rodham Clinton, H. (1998). *Dear Socks, dear Buddy*. New York, NY: Simon & Schuster.

Rodham Clinton, H. (2016, April 12). Hillary Clinton: A pet history of the White House, letter writing, parents & children (1999). Remember this. Retrieved from https://www.youtube.com/watch?v=Daq2yRzB-7w

Ross, S. A. (2010). Christ as bride: Toward a Christology of diversity. In P. B. Jung & A. M. Vigen (Eds.), *God, science, sex, gender: An interdisciplinary approach to Christian ethics; god, science, sex, gender: An interdisciplinary approach to Christian ethics* (pp. 211–223, Chapter viii, 287pp.). Champaign, IL: University of Illinois Press.

Rowland, S. (2011). Shakespeare and the Jungian symbol: A case of war and marriage. *Jung Journal: Culture & Psyche*, *5*(1), 31–46.

Sade, T. (2018). *Tale of the wet dog*. USA: Trajectory Films.

Schlamme, T. (1993). *So i married an ax murderer*. Culver City, CA: TriStar Pictures.

Schneiderman, R. M. (2009, April 12). Hey, Bo puppy! Obamas finally choose. *New York Times*. Retrieved from https://thecaucus.blogs.nytimes.com/2009/04/12/hey-bo-puppy-obamas-finally-choose/

Spears, K. (2017, July 20). Father of the bride brings life-size cardboard cutout of her dog to destination wedding: See the adorable photos. *The Knot News*. Retrieved from http://www.theknotnews.com/bride-dog-special-part-wedding-day-exclusive-21336

Spenser, E. (1590). *The faerie queene*. Project Gutenberg. Retrieved from http://www.gutenberg.org/files/15272/15272-h/15272-h.htm

Stafford, L., & Scott, A. M. (2016). Blue brides: Exploring postnuptial depressive symptoms. *Journal of Family Issues*, *37*(15), 2213–2231.

Stover, M., & Stover, M. (2014, March). Rite of Christian Initiation of Adults (RCIA). St. Jude Catholic Church. Boca Raton, FL. Retrieved from https://stjudeboca.org/rcia.html

Sykes, K., & Brace-Govan, J. (2015). The bride who decides: Feminine rituals of bridal gown purchase as a rite of passage. *Australasian Marketing Journal (AMJ)*, *23*(4), 277–285.

The Black Tux. (n.d.). Wetsuit. Retrieved from https://theblacktux.com/stories/wet-suits

The Smashing Pumpkins. (1993). "Today." On *Siamese dream*. Hollywood, CA: Virgin Records.

The Smashing Pumpkins. (1995a). "Galapogos." On *Mellon Collie and the Infinite Sadness*. Hollywood, CA: Virgin Records.

The Smashing Pumpkins. (1995b). "Tonight, tonight." On *Mellon collie and the infinite sadness*. Hollywood, CA: Virgin Records.

The Smashing Pumpkins. (2012, June 19). "The celestials." On *Teargarden by kaleidyscope: Oceania*. USA: Rocket Science.

Tuft, M., Gjelsvik, B., & Nakken, K. O. (2015). Epilepsy is dancing. *Epilepsy & Behavior, 51*, 329–331.

U.S. Army. (n.d.). Taps. Retrieved from http://www.music.army.mil/music/buglecalls/taps.asp

Veevers, J. E. (1988). The "real" marriage squeeze: Mate selection, mortality, and the mating gradient. *Sociological Perspectives: SP: Official Publication of the Pacific Sociological Association*, *31*(2), 169–189.

Visit My Smokies (VMS). (n.d.). Magic Beyond Belief with Darren Romeo. Retrieved from http://www.visitmysmokies.com/attractions/magic-beyond-belief-darren-romeo/

Walano, R. (2016, November 18). Happy 15th anniversary to Britney Spears and Justin Timberlake'sdoubledenimoutfits. *USMagazine*. Retrievedfromhttp://www.usmagazine.com/stylish/news/britney-spears-justin-timberlakes-double-denim-outfits-15th-anniversary-w451495

Waterlow, L. (2014, April 7). Gain a husband, lose a friend: Third of brides fall out with bridesmaids after wedding day due to jealousy and rows over dresses. *Daily Mail*. Retrieved from http://www.dailymail.co.uk/femail/article-2598820/Gain-husband-lose-friend-Third-brides-fall-bridesmaids-wedding-day-jealousy-rows-dresses.html#ixzz4vDW6whWw

Wendt, G. (1993). *Cheers*. Los Angeles, CA: Paramount.

White Tiger. (2016). "Terror barz." Dopetones. Retrieved from https://www.youtube.com/watch?v=itSb94YmlZw

Wilcox, A. (2011). The inmates, the actors, the characters, the audience, and the poet are of imagination all compact. In J. Shailor (Ed.), *Performing new lives: Prison theatre; performing new lives: Prison theatre* (pp. 247–255, 300pp.). London: Jessica Kingsley Publishers.

Wilson, B. F., & Clarke, S. C. (1992). Remarriages: A demographic profile. *Journal of Family Issues*, *13*(2), 123–141.

Wurth, K. B. (2017). The grotesque. In B. Papenburg (Ed.), *Gender: Laughter; gender: Laughter* (pp. 89–100, Chapter xvi, 443pp.). Farmington Hills, MI: Macmillan.

Yague, M., & Gare. (2016). "White tiger." SenseBeat Music. Retrieved from https://www.youtube.com/watch?v=34hnBj1HhOA

Zargooshi, J. (2008). Male sexual dysfunction in unconsummated marriage: Long-term outcome in 417 patients. *The Journal of Sexual Medicine*, 5(12), 2895–2903.

· 2 ·

SLEEP

Unconscious

Primal fears navigate the conscious mind. When individuals sleep, the recesses of their minds unfold dramas and comedies to transform fears into actions. Actions may be passive, affirmative, or latent; but, the dreamer knows plans to avoid fears coming into being. "[Power]" for example, of a "God," may be one of "the first thing[s] mankind feared in the dark" (White Tiger (Angela Del Toro), n.d.). One problem with turning to religion to resolve this fear of God's power is that life and death are mutually exclusive by definition (Cusack, 2017). The dark is the realm that describes the unconscious to others when the dreamer or awake person is unable to identify communication. An absence of insight into one's patterns can result in failure. Therefore, doctors and clinicians examine unconscious states to determine whether better courses of actions were or are available (Foley, 2010).

Consent is an example, defined by attorneys, where the unconscious can negatively influence an individual. Almost all defendants, who take rape charges to trial, will claim consent as a defense. Those alleged perpetrators believe that they are not guilty and obtained consent from the alleged victim prior to having sex. Conscious and unconscious voluntariness may have deceived the perpetrator into thinking that he or she obtained consent from a victim. A victim may have believed that he or she expressed nonconsent, but unconsciously failed to articulate specific instructions to stop consensual activity. One reason why sex during sleep presents a legal conundrum is because unless there is evidence of a pattern of consent, then proving consent is difficult. However, the victim cannot articulate negation or assent to sexual conduct. The elements of rape (e.g., nonconsent and penetration) must be proven. Some jurisdictions statutorily criminalize sex with incapacitated people. Drug use is also problematic (e.g., nonconsensual insemination) because victims are rarely ever able to explicate why they believed that they were raped when some of their testimony confesses to drug use. For example, a sober person may lounge on a bed for several hours to indicate interest in sexual activity; however, a drug addicted person may simply be intoxicated.

The unconscious mind parodies what illuminates its voids. Unfathomably abundant and repetitive homages are rapidly fired through media, including music, television, and film. For example, in the television show, *American Vandal*, Leonardo DiCaprio is repeatedly honored and his works are mentioned by name (Tatro, 2017). The shows' creators did not represent their affection for his work directly; however, their exhibited references demonstrate that he illuminated portions of their unconscious necessary for the cultivation of their work product. James Franco and Riff Raff's sordid media battles, which almost certainly were self-promoting stunts, could have begun as an unconscious bind between their two paths into pop culture. Riff Raff is a rapper socially and professionally associated with acts such as White Girl Mob and Drake (Lovelidge, 2012). His shtick is to blend trashy garbs with upscale jewelry and tattoos along with expensive and no doubt costly hairdos that hearken to 1990s Black female fashion (Cusack, 2015). He is a hodgepodge of styles and a ragamuffin. His genre is "screwed, blued, and tattooed" (Diamond Phillips, 1987). Franco searingly parodied him in his film *Spring Breakers* with Selena Gomez and Vanessa Hudgens, whose performances were totally eclipsed by the morbid portrayal of Riff Raff (Franco, 2012). In response, Riff Raff, who lacked attention from the public eye, failed to thank Franco, for example with a mention on his social media sites or free tickets to his show; and instead, threatened to sue Franco (Lovelidge, 2012). Riff Raff unconsciously has identified his weakness in Franco's character, Alien, and felt offended. He believed that Franco intentionally turned-out his studied and ultra-insightful observations in order to humiliate and defame him (Adiga, 2008; Ashley, 2016). To retaliate, soap opera *One Life to Live*, which dwells in—and may very well suck the life blood from—practically unconscious minds of vulnerable populations, offered to quell their grievance by giving Riff Raff an opportunity to despoil Franco's humanity by playing a character named Jamie Franko (Lovelidge, 2012; Nixon, 1968–2013). Franko is erotically satisfied by two women kissing in front of him, a foreshadowing scenario and unconscious appeal to their audience to end the feud between the two divas. The rivals quenched their unconscious thirst for each other's luminescence in a battle about appropriation and credited performances by appearing as each other simultaneously in the same music video. Riff Raff rapped the lyrics while Franco acted as the rapper in "Only in America" (Burgess, 2016).

Hermann Rorschach invented a series of inkblots known as Rorschach Inkblot Method (i.e., Rorschach Test) to examine psychological underpinnings. The inkblots depict a mirror image as if a piece of paper blotted with paint had been folded to produce the same shape on each side of the fold. Many of the depictions, some of which have been colorized, depict nonsensical shapes that can be innocuously described as bats, bowties, or smiles. The premise behind the interpretive analyses leading to supposed psychological evaluations of psychopaths is that depraved individuals will see harmful scenes in the images. Standard responses are starkly contrasted with alarming responses; for example, butterfly versus "mangled butterfly" and bird versus satanic phoenix (Franks, Sreenivasan, Spray, & Kirkish, 2009).

Rorschachs may be scored (e.g., Exner Comprehensive System) in forensic settings (Black, 2002). One study concluded that by using the following variables to score, a clinician may determine whether a child has been sexually abused: ego and affective function; adaptive coping; bodily concerns; and interpersonal distrust. Tests, such as Temperament and Character Inventory, may validate the Rorschach Test (Fassino, Amianto, Levi, & Rovera, 2003). Rorschach scoring has influenced feminism in unexpected ways. For example, female psychopathy was believed to be nonexistent but for "malignant hysteria" (Smith, Gacono, Cunliffe, Kivisto, & Taylor, 2014, p. 176). Scoring of the following tests indicates that Psychopathy Checklist-Revised (PCL-R) should be revised to better indicate female psychopathy: Rorschach Comprehensive System, Rorschach Defense Scales, Rorschach Oral Dependency, Extended Aggression Scores, Trauma Content Index, and Primitive Modes of Relating. Emerging research suggest that female psychopaths may vary from males and nonpsychopathic women, but theories about how and why have mutated throughout the past decade.

One study found distinct characteristics in incarcerated female psychopaths, including the following:

> self-perception (negative self-image, dysphoric affect, poor self-regard, and limited capacity for introspection), poor interpersonal relatedness (superficial interpersonal relations, limited understanding of the motivations of others, and lack of empathy) and poor reality testing (cognitive distortion and unconventionality) compared to nonpsychopathic females. Preliminary support was found for the hypothesized Histrionic (rather than Narcissistic seen in male psychopathy). (Cunliffe, 2002)

Some studies indicate that an analysis of histrionics is irrelevant, while others have focused on it to disprove it. Rorschach testing of women tends to follow conventional gender roles, such as bulimia detection and intervention, while testing on men centers on violence and sexual deviance (Smith, Hillard, & Roll, 1991).

Rorschach results often vary from the PCL-R. For example, a sample of violent, incarcerated, male offenders found a lack of anger and "chronic narcissism" (Franks et al., 2009).

> [P]sychopaths demonstrated poor emotional modulation, diminished reality testing, little interest in people, and virtually no attachment capacity. Most utilized a simplistic, avoidant, and concrete style. This appeared to be consistent with the concrete thinking and fragmentation attributed to the criminal personality. Concrete thinking is based upon literal interpretations of events. Fragmentation is associated with attitudes that are situation specific and self-serving. (Franks et al., 2009)

Rorschach tests may detect subtleties that are unanalyzable using instruments such as the PCL-R. For example, a study of ephebophilic priests sexually interested in teenagers found that they were better able to control aggressive impulses that pedophilic priests (Lagan, 2009; McGlone, 2001). Rorschach testing has also found a high correlation between psychopaths' aggression and oral dependency (Huprich, Gacono, Schneider, & Bridges, 2004).

Rorschach tests may reveal unconscious states as they manifest in dreams. Dreams are differentiable from unconscious images that project into the mind's eye during sleep. For example, one study found that depressed people were different from suicidal people because "[t]he dreams of suicidal patients often reveal wishes for revenge, punishment, reunion, fusion, and rebirth" (Maltsberger, 1993). Suicidal people confuse their bodies with others. "Dreams in suicidal individuals may portray disintegration of the self (self-state dreams)" (Maltsberger, 1993).

Dreams

A dream is an unconscious desire to make something true, even if it is detrimental to one's self. A dream may manifest as a nightmare, but is distinguishable. A dream contains elements of reality that a nightmare does not. Therefore, a dream is pleasant (The White Tiger, 2013). That which is acceptable to the psyche is called a dream, and rejected visions of oneself are nightmares. A dream supposes that the dreamer is good and a dreamer is correct in one's vision of oneself. The feeling of a dream is congruent with one's ultimate sense of self. Identity may be achieved through dreams, such as one exquisite revelation or a series of affirming thoughts collected as a theme throughout one's childhood or life. Exquisite revelations may have manifested in one's life as an activity. This is expressible, which is why the conscious dictates it as an ultimate act. It may be achieved by a dreamer, which is good. A series of dreams is an affirming strategy that convinces the dreamer that he or she has a path, which is the course of one's life at any rate; but, dream themes suggests that a spiritual element is at play. A dream can convince a dreamer to dream further.

The American dream represents the spirit of ancestral guidance and ingenuity infused into a rich culture of acceptance (Packer, 2002). It is a dream because each individual can find a place there. The dreamer sees his or her predecessors occupying an important place in the process of his or her achievement; or the dreamer believes that he or she can start afresh and achieve any possibility. Talents can be cultivated within the American dream because any aspect of the self may be marketable. Passion is supposed to be an underlying virtue that comes alive; and yet, constancy is also necessary. The dream discussed by Martin Luther King is not the same as the traditional American dream because he invented a sense of self that had not previously existed. Therefore, his divergence represents the American dream, but was not part of the mainstream's individual or collective dreams (Cusack, 2016b).

Dreams occur in sleep. Like a legend deceives a culture, sleep is a "veil that deceives the viewer" (Packer, 2002, p. 10). A wet dream is a device used by a dreamer to admit arousal to oneself. Arousal may result from job satisfaction or other factors unforeseen by the dreamer. A dream therefore can be an aphrodisiac.

Dreams symbolize limitations of human understanding about consciousness and physiology. Dreams about mutants represent doldrums in life during which a dreamer is pressured to perform, but cannot release the energy necessary to realize that he or she has already accomplished what he or she wants. Conspiracy theories are mutated myths and current events that may spring to mind during a state of sleep. Conspiracy theories about mutants fail to work at the core, and only bring in external strands of information provided by outlets that are not inherently intuitive to the dreamer.

Sigmund Freud "coined a new name for" dreaming (Packer, 2002, p. 34). "[H]e called it the 'dreamwork'" (Packer, 2002, p. 34). This term defeats psychic or latent aspects of unconscious dreaming typically relevant to discussions about dreams, and highlights the active process necessary to mutate one's self into a new identity (Cusack, 2016). In dreams, the self is realized, but only through a working mechanism that can manifest plans, or has achieved plans, and recapitulate successes while one is asleep; and by identifying actions as good or bad relative to one's survival and self-progress.

Sleeping agents (e.g., Ambien) are acceptable to society; and yet, they distort a dreamer's reality. Some users and doctors claim that the drugs cause somanambulism (Packer, 2002). However, the drug simply may release unconscious desires unexplored by dreamers. In the alternative, dreamers may be unable to control their secret lives, which they cover and shelter from observers throughout the day, and then act out at night. Sleeping drugs may hypnotically free fantasies forcing dreamers to awaken partially to perform their fantasies without hesitation or cover (Jay-Z, 2009).

Hypnosis may deposit into a patient a dream causing them to believe that a trance-like state is actually a vision of themselves (Packer, 2002). The vision dictates to them which versions of themselves are right and wrong. The vision may also substitute for a god, parent, child, or other aspects of the unconscious that are uncontrolled or heavily influenced by external forces (e.g., society and rules). Involuntariness resulting from hypnosis or sleepwalking is a defense to criminal charges even when a person voluntarily administered sleeping pills and hypnosis if the person did not negligently or recklessly contribute to or cause the results.

Theater embodies the dream state (Cypress Hill, 1996; Dahl, 2007; Guerra, 1990a; Jacobs & Casey, 1978; Kafka, 2015; Ovid, 1995; Shakespeare, 2012). Performances of *Grease* and *A Midsummer Night's Dream* discuss the consequences of dreaming too big and too soon (Jacobs & Casey, 1978; Peterson, 2015; Shakespeare, 2012). Consequences may be dreams if they behoove community members surrounding the dreamer, who feeds from their knowledge and wisdom, even if only to rebel and distinguish oneself from the multitudes (Cusack, 2016a). External controls may assist a dreamer to experience a dream rather than what Freud would describe as "hysteria" (Packer, 2002).

Nightmare

A nightmare is a wish to die. It concludes one's aspirations. Arriving at new conclusions is easy unless the dreamer defers one's thoughts, which results in a nightmare. A nightmare is hetero-activity confronting reason; and reason takes-over. There are no homosexuals at the end of life. Every person, who acknowledges reproductive desires, experiences heterosexuality. Nightmares are the mind coming to terms with why particular potential mates are bad potential love interests. For example, in one dream, a woman was on a ship thrown about by a storm. She was flung into the cold and frigid ocean at night, and was nearly attacked by sharks. A female shipmate helped her onto the deck. The deck was perilous, and the seamen were facing death. Any seaman, who slipped off the deck, could be eaten. The boat itself was dangerous because it had many obstacles; for example, cargo on the deck slid around and there were some strong whirlwinds, perhaps a flame or two. Another woman fell into the water and cried for help. The dreamer helped her. An individual could have run to a higher platform for safety, but the women colluded to save each other, and abandoned the men, who did not truly care if they survived. As they rushed to a higher platform on the boat with a third woman, they could sense desperation and potential treachery from the males on the boat, who may have killed them if safe spaces were few and valuable. Sharks jumped about in the water waiting to eat the passengers. The woman, whose husband was in the Coast Guard, woke up. She realized that he was a bad love interest because although he supported feminist ideals, he caused men around her to be treacherous and defy her because they could sense him and feared him.

Dreams are less typical than nightmares; for example, as depicted by artists (Packer, 2002; Vásquez, 2002). "There is more irony to [Francisco] Goya's personal decline and his departure from reason and the artistic conventions of his day. Even though his decorative tapestries and precise portraits brought him commercial success," they were nightmarish pieces that revealed his inner demon (Packer, 2002, p. 148). "Goya's descent into the underworld of madness and dream, coupled with his ability to translate these experiences into art … appealed to" his sense of self, which brought his fame to another temperate submersion (Packer, 2002, p. 148). "Goya's dark side" was an expressible nightmare that some artists harbor as their dream. It mutates in their minds as an aspiration rather than a rejection of self (Packer, 2002, p. 148). Michael Foucault's nightmare was a prison cell in which deviants "were locked away in dark and dank and dirty institutions, where they were deprived of medical care, proper food, sunlight, and ordinary human respect" (Packer, 2002, p. 127). Society idolizes Foucault's vision of prison as a model thereby transforming nightmares into visions (Craven, 1984; Packer & Pennington, 2014; Schumacher, 1990).

A nightmare is a stream of consciousness. It may correlate with waking events, which seem bland and in desire of attention. The mind works like the Internet. Streaming a video or live-streaming identifies machine consciousness; also, humans' desire to connect themselves, like abstract points, and to each other in order to find symbolic relevance, meaning, and guidance. Streaming evades internally unanswered contemplations about mortality and expresses fantasy through projection and appeasement. A fantasizer does not have to face a dichotomy of action between justifying delusions and working to manifest dreams. Nightmares may be holistic.

Sleep Martians

"Sleep Martians" is a term used to describe an anomaly in which people sleep at odd hours (Fox, 2017; Guerra, 1990b; Larsson, Hassan, Ridefelt, & Axelsson, 2009). Their internal time mechanisms allegedly deviate because they operate on a 24.5-hour schedule. The condition caused by a mutation has the potential to disrupt normal activities due to insomnia and other effects, but the term "sleep Martian," relating to longer day cycles on Mars, reflects deep paranoia about aliens invading. Invasion experienced during dream states has been associated with rape and with rejection of death (McKinnon, 2017). Rejection of death may be envisioned as an out-of-body experience. A sleep Martian may be experienced when a person cannot sleep because she or he is a monster in his or her own eyes. The person mirrors people, who he or she actually disrespects, and sublimates his or her own version of happiness to avoid murder, rape, theft, aggravation, and other social ills, whether imagined or perceived. Being a monster does not cancel one's inherent fear of being terrorized by a monster. Monster *qua* monster has saturated American, Western, Eastern, and Old World theater and entertainment, including sports, since the beginning of time (Lewis, 2017).

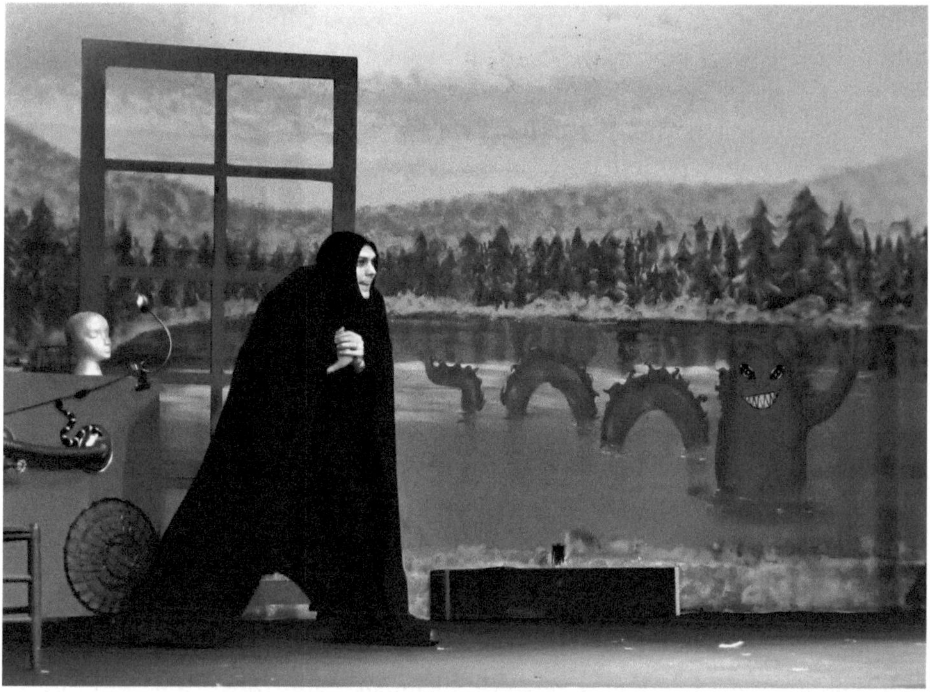

Fig. 2.1: Igor, Matthew Waranius. *Young Frankenstein* Background Depicting a Werewolf, Sea Dragon, and Other Frightening Characters. Slidell, LA. Source: Carmen M. Cusack

Deviant humans (e.g., transgender people) may feel symbolic associations with the monsters; such as the Loch Ness monster, who buries himself or boroughs herself in the sand, like a Japanese sea dragon, which is why they have been undetected by humans, thus far. Monsters, such as Adam and Eve, are represented as aliens in the Bible (Packer & Pennington, 2014). They come from a father, who lives on another planet or in another dimension, who has them on Earth. He then abandons them and allows them to be seduced and deceived by a monstrous serpent, who feeds them fruit from a talking tree. The Bible repeatedly depicts plant life as monsters akin to sea serpents; for example, Moses and the burning bush and Jesus on the wooden cross (Acts 5:30; Cusack, 2017; Exodus 3:17).

Females are lifegiving and males are murderous (Cusack, 2013; Packer & Pennington, 2014). Yet, females are denoted by the Bible as having an evil nature, such as in the story of Adam and Eve. When women put children to rest (e.g., bedtime), children imagine their mothers as monstrous after hearing

Biblical narratives. Women are posed by stories. Then, little girls attempt to fulfill these roles, causing them nightmares, fright, and trauma. Traumatic strongholds yield more narratives about women overcoming abstract patriarchal resistance, when in fact the storyteller, who originally sewed the script into the child, was her female guardian.

The significance of gender is emphasized by many tales, including binary sexual unions (e.g., weddings) and child bearing recounts. It is these foundational and culturally undergirding stories that form the psyche, which is disturbed at night (Packer & Pennington, 2014). Sleep Martians are a departure from these tracks that can only be admitted to the dreamer at night for fear of rejection.

When a mother tells a tale to a child before bedtime, she becomes the narrator of a horror film experienced as a dream or nightmare. A vagina monster (e.g., ancient *vagina dentata*) may assume a covert form in the child's inner mind (Packer & Pennington, 2014). Teenage boys may envision their mothers as teen females in dreams about sex, which emerge in the light of popular culture and shared, finite fantasies. Fantasies shared by millions (e.g., television) may be the cause of competition for self-esteem. These shared fantasies are unable to yield to every person's self-image, and thus, some envisioned perceptions of self suffer extraction. They cannot compete against others, whose identities are sufficiently malleable to fit within the rubric created by an artform, such as a music video (Dieter, Field, Hernandez-Reif, Emory, & Redzepi, 2003).

Femininity in a monstrous realm mimics youth, an alien concept to an aging body. Freudian analysis of youthful complexes and nightmares (e.g., Electra) reveal that youth permanence haunts young women (deGraaf, 2014). Women, who age poorly, fear that their genitals are inferior to other women's genitalia. They compare their geneitals to other entitites, such as squid. For example, this is evident in a horror movie that terroizes older viewers under the guise of entertaining the young (e.g., symbolic discretion). Symbolic insults are evident to women, who have inferiority complexes. "[H]ere, the creature, a pinkish, squid-like thing, seems to resemble the female genitals" (Packer & Pennington, 2014, p. 179). The effect is similar to castration. Sufferers of breast cancer may fear that they represent the Oedipal Complex and that their breasts are no longer attractive; but, represent the antithesis to femininity—scrotums. Gaping holes are caves to the unknown. A dream is also a portal into an imaginary world in which aliens may descend. Therefore, the vagina represents a dream land where aliens may dwell and seize control of males.

Medusa is an example of an alien figure, a god, and an allusion to malformed genitals (Packer & Pennington, 2014). She is cursed for being too attractive and her hair is transformed into snakes. The snakes represent reprehensible pubic hair (Cusack, 2015). Her prowess as a female is reduced to an "asshole" by the frighteningly homoerotic Zeus (Packer & Pennington, 2014, p. 180). She is chided. In her prime, she is "reinvented as a 'wholesome' American teenager" "unveiled" (Packer & Pennington, 2014, p. 181). Her sexuality can harm her and is a threat to others (e.g., sex abuse prosecution).

Despite the law's attempt to arm and shield minors, a pedophile may slip undetected into a family's home at night. By imbuing a deep sleep into the victim, a pedophile can violate a child, and after exiting the scene of the crime, disperse the victim's shattered innocence as a wind-blown dandelion. The victim is left hollowed by disrupted development. A sense of malfunction is inevitable (e.g., sexual cupidity and incontinence). "Evil" can only be "overcome" if the victim is willing to remain asleep to an extent that mutes the traumatic event (e.g., attention deficiency) (Packer & Pennington, 2014, p. 181).

Rhetoric decrying a female's foreign anatomy, visually rejectable to her own gaze, "echoes other forms of 'conversion'" (Packer & Pennington, 2014, p. 182). "The 'believer' is promised a world where he will be 'part' of a more significant 'whole.' The transformation" is allegedly a "release … from fear" (Packer & Pennington, 2014, p. 182). However, "a prime locus" is on "terror. The rhetoric ironically relates to the stereotypical protagonist" (e.g., the beacon or the "jock") (Packer & Pennington, 2014, p. 182). To be subdued, she is revealed to herself by a haughty master, such as Zeus, as being a "wuss," an "ugly duckling," or an "underachiever" (Packer & Pennington, 2014, p. 183). Overlords "rel[y] on these stereotypes and maintain[] an ironic distance from them, at the same time" (Packer & Pennington, 2014, p. 183). "[O]minous speech" "sounds a lot like a parodic take on" and "manipulation of the concept of an 'alien'" (Packer & Pennington, 2014, p. 183). The overlords' "happy ending" is when "the protagonists have indeed morphed into something else. They have become a different set of stereotypes" (Packer & Pennington, 2014, p. 183).

An "ultimate outsider figure (and in many ways a stand-in … alien …, who manages to destroy the monster and bring about closure), has the last word in more ways than one" (Packer & Pennington, 2014, p. 183). "After he destroys the monster" for example, by "shooting" "drug[s]" or semen "into its eye," "[t]he world inhabited" by the female "is still a daily 'hell,' in one way or another" (Packer & Pennington, 2014, p. 183). "[R]esolution depends on the vanquishing of the monstrous mother/lover" (Packer & Pennington, 2014, p. 183). It is an "offer" to "return to the watery, womb-like 'world,' before (or after) life. Active resistance to this form of seduction is the only way of moving from the alien world" of immaturity "to the conflicted adult world" (Packer & Pennington, 2014, p. 183). "[M]ale protagonists will have to come to terms with female sexuality and overcome their fear of its 'monstrous' aspects in order to become fully functioning adults" (Packer & Pennington, 2014, p. 183). Ergo, they must forget latent memories, suspicions, or invitations for sexual abuse occurring during sleep and overcoming any arrhythmic aspects of one's physiology that cause alarm, dejection, or self-referential dismissal (Packer & Pennington, 2014).

References

Adiga, A. (2008). *The white tiger: A novel.* Indianapolis, IN: HarperCollins.

Ashley, J. (2016). *White tiger.* New York, NY: Berkley Sensation.

Black, E. M. (2002). *The use of the Rorschach inkblot technique in the detection and diagnosis of child sexual abuse* (Order No. 3068669). Available from Criminal Justice Database (305441504).

Burgess, O. (2016, November 19). James Franco and Riff Raff finally make amends with "only in America" video. *Complex.* Retrieved from http://www.complex.com/music/2016/11/james-franco-riff-raff-new-video-only-in-america

Craven, W. (1984). *Nightmare on Elm Street.* Burbank, CA: New Line Cinema.

Cunliffe, E. B. (2002). *A Rorschach investigation of incarcerated female psychopaths* (Order No. 3043373). Available from Criminal Justice Database (305510095).

Cusack, C. M. (2013). To-get-her for-Eve-r: A man hater's right to same-sex marriage. *Journal of Law & Public Policy, 10,* 63–98.

Cusack, C. M. (2015). *Hair and justice: Sociolegal significance of hair in criminal justice, constitutional law, and public policy.* Springfield, IL: Charles C. Thomas.

Cusack, C. M. (2016a, April 14–27). Advocacy letters to Audubon Nature Institute Board Members, Mayor Mitch Landrieu, and scores of other community and industry leaders to stop the temporary yellow tiger display from occupying the permanent white tiger enclosure of King Zulu and deceased brother Rex. New Orleans, LA.

Cusack, C. M. (2016b). Save the white tiger. *Journal of Law & Social Deviance, 12,* 1.

Cusack, C. M. (2017). *Fish in the bible: Psychosocial analysis of contemporary meanings, values, and effects of Christian symbolism.* Wilmington, DE: Vernon Press.

Cypress Hill. (1996). "Boom biddy bye bye." (Fugees Remix featuring Fugees). On *Unreleased and revamped.* Philadelphia, PA: Ruffhouse.

Dahl, R. (2007). *Matilda.* London: Puffin Books.

deGraaf, M. (2014, September 26). John Cusack blasts Hollywood as a 'whorehouse' that is so obsessed with young female actors 'it's almost like kiddie porn.' Retrieved from http://

www.dailymail.co.uk/news/article-2771470/John-Cusack-blasts-whorehouse-Hollywood-reveals-sucks-time.html

Diamond Phillips, L. (1987). *La Bamba*. Culver City, CA: Columbia Pictures.

Dieter, J., Field, T., Hernandez-Reif, M., Emory, E. K., & Redzepi, M. (2003). Stable preterm infants gain more weight and sleep less after five days of massage therapy. *Journal of Pediatric Psychology, 28*(6), 403–411.

Fassino, S., Amianto, F., Levi, M., & Rovera, G. G. (2003). Combining the Rorschach test and the temperament character inventory: A new perspective on personality assessment. *Psychopathology, 36*(2), 84–91.

Foley, E. (2010). Research on healthcare law and insurance with Professor Elizabeth Foley, chief architect of the House of Representatives' lawsuit against President Barack Obama. Florida International University, Miami, FL.

Fox, M. (2017, April 6). This night owl gene mutation turns people into sleep Martians. NBC. Retrievedfromhttp://www.nbcnews.com/health/health-news/gene-mutation-affects-sleep-turning-people-martians-n743526

Franco, J. (2012). *Spring breakers*. Los Angeles, CA: Division Films.

Franks, K. W., Sreenivasan, S., Spray, B. J., & Kirkish, P. (2009). The mangled butterfly: Rorschach results from 45 violent psychopaths. *Behavioral Sciences & the Law, 27*(4), 491.

Guerra, J. L. (1990a). Burbujas de amor. On *Bachata rosa*. New York, NY: Karen Records.

Guerra, J. L. (1990b). La bilirubina. On *Bachata rosa*. New York, NY: Karen Records.

Huprich, S. K., Gacono, C. B., Schneider, R. B., & Bridges, M. R. (2004). Rorschach oral dependency in psychopaths, sexual homicide perpetrators, and nonviolent pedophiles. *Behavioral Sciences & the Law, 22*(3), 345–356.

Jacobs, J., & Casey, W. (1978). *Grease*. Los Angeles, CA: Paramount.

Jay-Z. (2009). *Empire state of mind*. New York, NY: Roc the Mic Studios.

Kafka, F. (2015). *The Metamorphoses*. Ballingslöv, Sweden: Wisehouse Classics.

Lagan, H. D. (2009). *Social functioning, boundary disturbance, and hostility in Roman Catholic priest pedophiles and ephebophiles* (Order No. 3382660). Available from Criminal Justice Database (305132153).

Larsson, A., Hassan, M., Ridefelt, P., & Axelsson, J. (2009). Circadian variability of bilirubin in healthy men during normal sleep and after an acute shift of sleep. *Chronobiology International, 26*(8), 1613–1621.

Lewis, T. (2017, May 3). Seniors are vips at 'young Frankenstein' dress rehearsal. *The Advocate*, 6A.

Lovelidge, E. (2012, December 4). V-Nasty and Kreayshawn beef on Twitter. *SF Station*. Retrieved from https://www.sfstation.com/2012/12/04/v-nasty-vs-kreayshawn-war-of-words-on-twitter/

Maltsberger, J. T. (1993). Dreams and suicide. *Suicide & Life-Threatening Behavior, 23*(1), 55–62.

McGlone, G. J. (2001). *Sexually offending and non-offending Roman Catholic priests: Characterization and analysis* (Order No. 3000742). Available from Criminal Justice Database (230774762).

McKinnon, K. (2017, September 30). *Saturday night live*. Season 43, Episode 1.

Nixon, A. (1968–2013). *One life to live*. Burbank, CA: ABC Video Enterprises.

Ovid. (1995). *The metamorphoses of Ovid*. San Diego, CA: Harcourt Brace.

Packer, S. (2002). *Dreams in myth, medicine, and movies*. Westport, CT: Greenwood Publishing Group.

Packer, S., & Pennington, J. (2014). *A history of evil in popular culture: What Hannibal Lecter, Stephen King, and vampires reveal about America*. Santa Barbara, CA: ABC-CLIO.

Peterson, E. (2015, April 3). The four most controversial pieces of wedding music. Classical MPR. Retrieved from https://www.classicalmpr.org/story/2014/07/21/controversial-wedding-music

Schumacher, J. (1990). *Flatliners*. Culver City, CA: Columbia Pictures.

Shakespeare, W. (2012). *A midsummer night's dream*. Mineola, NY: Dover Thrift Edition.

Smith, J. E., Hillard, M. C., & Roll, S. (1991). Rorschach evaluation of adolescent bulimics. *Adolescence, 26*(103), 687–696.

Smith, J. M., Gacono, C. B., Cunliffe, T. B., Kivisto, A. J., & Taylor, E. E. (2014). Psychodynamics in the female psychopath: A PCL-R/Rorschach investigation. *Violence & Gender, 1*(4), 176–187.

Tatro, J. (2017). *American vandal*. Los Angeles, CA: Funny or Die.

The White Tiger. (2013). "Daydreaming" and "Lullaby." Youtube.com. Retrieved from https://www.youtube.com/watch?v=BwJq8VkZXgg

Vásquez, J. (2002). A dios le pido. On *Un dia normal*. Columbia: Surco.

White Tiger (Angela Del Toro). (n.d.). Retrieved from http://marvel.com/universe/White_Tiger_(Angela_Del_Toro)

· 3 ·

BIONIC

Animals

Walt Disney Pictures animated Fidget the bat in *The Great Mouse Detective* (Clements & Mattinson, 1986). His name, Fidget, may refer to a neurological disorder or symptom (e.g., Restless Leg Syndrome). The bat is bound by his obligations and need to survive. He works as a henchman because it is convenient. He means no malice toward the child, who serves as Disney's protagonist; but, he has the understanding that should he need to harm her, then he would cause submission through threat of mortal harm, which he hopes will end her resistance. He is affectionate toward the child with his spirit, but he does not intend to save her from Basil, the great mouse detective, who is also an abductor. Basil disrupts her relationship with her father, which is symbolized by the bat's wooden prosthetic (i.e., peg leg).

This cartoon, illustrated in 1986, was a prescient symbolic explication of potential scientific experiments. For example, Michael Doyle, director of the Florida Keys Mosquito Control District (FKMCD), had planned to release onto 44 inhabited islands genetically modified male mosquitoes, who were biologically trained, but obviously not predisposed to damaging their civilization (Sagastume, 2013). He had "wild" "hopes of bringing down"

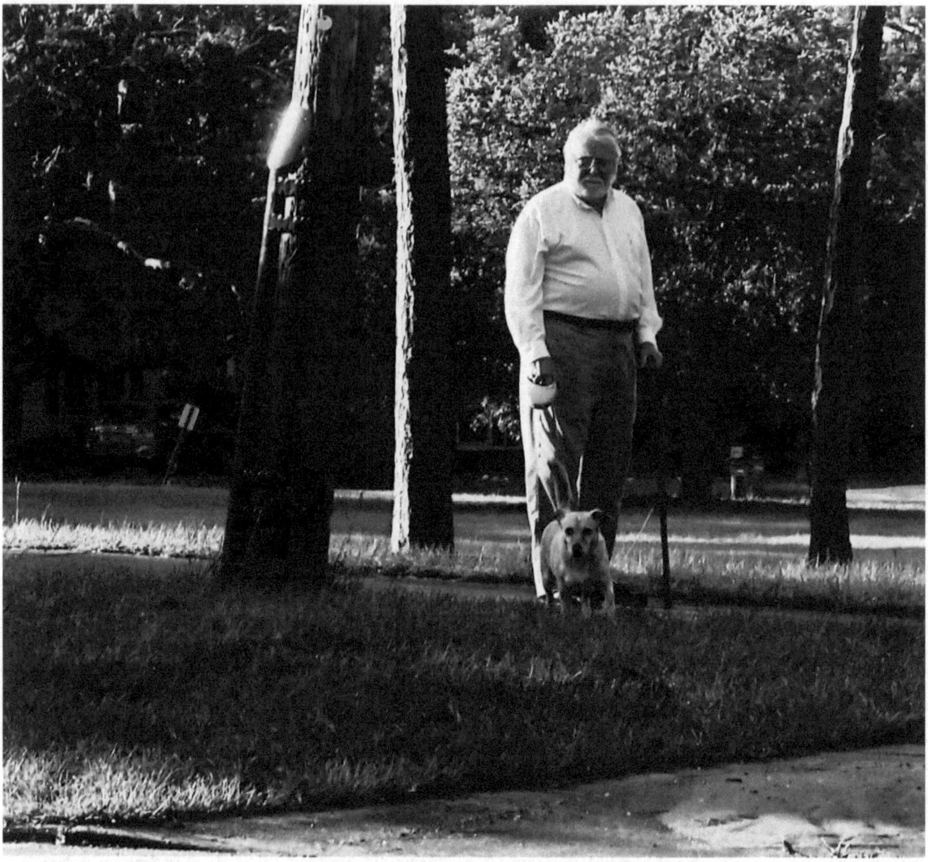

Fig. 3.1: Man Walks Dog Using a Cane. Source: Carmen M. Cusack

"dengue-carrying" individuals with the propensity to hide their disease and attack humans (Sagastume, 2013). What is more is that the movie symbolizes numerous implementations, many of which are important to the central narrative.

The bat is like a vicious apparition (Clements & Mattinson, 1986). He emerges from an unseen position in the room to terrorize and paralyze. Paralysis is psychological, not physical. He is hypermasculine. His scarf and voice are assertive. The bat interrupts a child's birthday party, and absconds with her father. Olivia and her father, toymaker Hiram Flaversham, are mice. Fidget shouts, "I got you" (Clements & Mattinson, 1986; Cusack v. Keiser University, 2016; Yanez, 2009). The bat and the toymaker wrestle; and, paint is spilled representing blood and semen (Carmen M. Cusack, 2013; John Cusack, 2017).

She is orphaned—a socially disabling role. Flaversham's, their shop, is dimmed. "Sham" in "Flaverhsam" subtly jousts with the audience (Clements & Mattinson, 1986). Their pity and compassion are transferred from the wooden-legged bat, robbed of his wellness, to the toymaker. The bat abuses any gentleness bestowed by society on him. He likely is a cause of stigmas poorly and aggressively portraying the wounded or disabled. "Flaver" hints toward consumption, hunger, and rage inherent in starvation. The bat has suffered, but deserves no mercy. The audience is focused on saving the toymaker without regard for the bat's handicap. Perhaps this is a play against the handicap or an equalizer. The message is unknown, but could be interpreted according to political leanings (e.g., rugged individualism or affirmative action).

Accoutrements are symbolic (Clements & Mattinson, 1986). The female child wears a bow behind her ear as well as a large bowtie. The toymaker and a mouse doctor, who helps the detective to find Hiram, wear bowties. The detective, the dominant character, wears an ascot. The villain, rat Professor Ratigan, played by Vincent Price, also wears an ascot and tie pin. An older female mouse, working as a maid and residing with the detective, wears a collar brooch. After they are rescued, Olivia wears a scarf, like Fidget, and her father wears an ascot. Symbolically, the characters are analogizable and distinguishable. The meaning and effect of grouping various characters together may be relative to an interpreter's theories (e.g., feminism or class relations).

The movie consistently attacks foundations of criminal justice by insinuating evidentiary weaknesses. For example, the detective analyzes bullets. The markings do not match. Like hair and fiber evidence, which recently has been exposed as specious and subjective, ballistic evidence is highly imprecise and based on opinions and observations, not objective or completely reliable facts (Carmen M. Cusack, 2015; Jackson, 2008; Live Blood Labs, 2010; York, 2014). *The Great Mouse Detective* calls attention to this to demonstrate how obvious the flaws are; but, the government continues to rely on expert testimony about bullet markings to convict defendants (Clements & Mattinson, 1986; Carmen M. Cusack, 2015). Another example appears when the detective and the toymaker's daughter describe the bat. The detective leads. "Did he have a crippled wing" (Clements & Mattinson, 1986)? She says, "I don't know, but he had a peg leg" (Clements & Mattinson, 1986; Carmen M. Cusack, 2015)! Although the detective is correct in deducing the suspect's employer, the suspect does not have a crippled wing. "Fidget" may be a persona or membership role (Clements & Mattinson, 1986). A bat with a broken wing may have committed past crimes, while the peg-legged bat only committed the crimes in question. Professor Ratigan calls on Felicia, an enormous alley cat wearing a hairbow, to dispense with noncompliants. He summons her with a dinner bell (DeLuise, 1986; Diamond, 2006; DiC Entertainment, 1984; Di Piazza, n.d.; Gerstell, 1989; Huge, 1988). He feeds Fidget to Felicia, but he is released from her mouth. Felicia contrasts with Toby, Basil's relatively ginormous mutt, who appears to have some basset hound and bloodhound roots. Toby wears a collar with a tag similar to the maid's collar brooch. Toby wants Fidget's blood, and would be satisfied by any suspect's demise. Basil insists that Fidget has "a broken wing" (Clements & Mattinson, 1986; Morrissey, 2004).

Professor Ratigan's misdeed hinges on his capacity to empathize with the toymaker's daughter (Clements & Mattinson, 1986). Empathy is a virtue, but when misused, it is a psychopathic trait. It can yield beneficial results or be used to hunt, defraud, or mislead. Olivia is a genius, who runs the toymaker's mentality. By assuming her "charm[]" and essence, Professor Ratigan can block her father's decision-making abilities to thwart any attempt to escape; but, he cannot use his wiles on Olivia because she is fierce (Clements & Mattinson, 1986).

The doctor wears a disguise given to him by the detective (Clements & Mattinson, 1986). He is dressed like a queer pirate. He has an eyepatch and an earring symbolizing distinctions between elective body modifications and involuntary alterations and implementations (Carmen M. Cusack, 2016b). Basil is insensitive to handicaps; and yet, uses them because he perceives the world in terms of general appearances. Animators comment on appropriation, narrativization, and routinization of personas. The eyepatch-wearing pirate demonstrates widespread affection for, acceptance of, or bias against eyepatches (Davitt, 1954; Mullane, n.d.; Paul, 1987; Webb, 1951). The movie teaches that disability is not "depravity," but disabled individuals are not immune from "depravity" (Clements & Mattinson, 1986; DeLuise, 1982; DiCaprio, 1997; Knightley, 2003; Raeside, 2017; The Smashing Pumpkins, 1995). Social, physical, and emotional illness is compared to disability. Society groups individuals into "teams," and this story questions how groups are devised through language, law, aptitude, and appearance (Joan Cusack, 1999; Joffe, 1989).

Human intervention may be a necessary component of animal bionism (Eran, 2015). One officer described how international enthusiasm for weaponization has resulted in bionized canines (Hill, 2016). The "State Law Enforcement Business Continuity Summit" in Georgia learned from retired Israel Police Colonel Ron Gertner, who heads the Homeland Security Division, Focus Intelligence Combat Special Solutions (F.I.C.S.). Gertner "serves as a security consultant" and "served in the Israel Police for 26 years (1991–2017) in numerous command positions with the last two years as chief of operations of the Samaria and Judea Police District" (Hill, 2016). Animals' fight in "the war on terror is evolving" (Hill, 2016). Tasers are now used by military-trained canines. "[H]e described and showed pictures of the Taser device being strapped to the front nose of the police dog in the form of a muzzle. When the dog is deployed it is unable to bite. Instead, the dog engages with the suspected terrorist and the handler (who wears the Taser trigger mechanism) is the one who remotely activates the Taser, thusly subduing the attacker" (Hill, 2016).

Survival from or through freezing may correlate with bionism. Canine officers appear to be bionic because they have survived frostbite. Special training by the Federal Protective Service taught officers from diverse departments how to administer canine first aid, "including heat stroke, dehydration, frostbite, allergic reactions, bites/stings, poison, burns, chemical and biological attacks, gunshot wounds, common street drugs [e.g., fentanyl], and much more" (DHS, 2017, p. 1; Kraven the Hunter, 2017). Inhalation of drugs is part of their profession because in addition to warranted searches, police dogs are trained to conduct warrantless searches of property, such as automobiles during traffic stops, but not the front porch of a home (Ensminger & Papet, 2014; Florida v. Harris, 2013; Florida v. Jardines, 2013). The event held at Hanscom Air Force trained officers from U.S. Customs Border Protection; U.S. Border Patrol; Amtrak Police; Bureau of Alcohol, Tobacco and Firearms; Transportation Security Administration; and U.S. Park Service. Bionism is evident in genetic repositories (Ugaz, Floyd, & Wahlen, 2011). Species threatened and endangered by human behavior, such as sprawl, modernization, and armament, are again paused in the midst of their life cycles. Cells stored in genetic repositories experience strain. This strain will no doubt impact the animals produced from these samples. The storage process is an aggressive process designed to stop progression of aging. Collection means are also bionized; for example, electroejaculation removes sperm from the body by electrically inducing spasms in an animal's anal walls; and artificial vaginas replace authentic vaginas (Criss, 1991; *Daily Mail*, 2010; Goldfeder & Razin, 2015). The majority of animals, other than those harvested posthumously, are sexually violated using collection methods; for example, while sleeping their sperm may be disseminated involuntarily, and therefore possibly nonconsensually (Lu et al., 2010).

Animals have the power to create a self-perceived sense of well-being (Carmen M. Cusack, 2013). However, they are not unlimited in their ability. Their bodies conform to the physical restrictions of their species. On occasion, animals deviate so substantially that a mutation appears to emerge. If well-being is fostered, then the mutation may become standardized; if not, then it may be eliminated. Successive progressions of mutated characteristics may result in what some humans have described as evolution. An example of a special creature is a sugar glider (Bardot, 2013). A sugar glider has a stupendous ability to manifest the glide of a bird while retaining a rodent identity. This mutation serves the sugar glider in cuteness and viability. Like a rhinoceros, a duck-billed platypus combines a distinct nasal characteristic with a shockingly acclimated body. The body is for a unique rubric of activities that are not necessarily perceptible from an analysis of the protuberance. Attention was called to this special creature (i.e., sugar glider) when Mark McGrath from the band Sugar Ray (1997) sang "Fly" with Super Cat (Carmen M. Cusack, 2017). Yettis may be humanoid or animals; but, typically they are humans, who have evacuated society (Carmen M. Cusack, 2016a). Their extent as mutants is subject to interpretation of mutations. They are not truly mutations in the sense that they have not evolved, but because they have departed so significantly, they have rendered a social mutation, which causes an indelible mark in humanity. They mutate humanity, not the person. Some members of conventional society believe that evidence of Yettis is a hoax. Just as some people are stuntmen, a Yetti has participated in a fraud by claiming to be an animal; an illusory act is not a fraud because it commits a crime, but because it robs animals of the dignity of having an exclusive realm full of wonder (*Now* Magazine, 2007; Young, 2010; Youtube.com, 2011).

Synthetic Pornography

"Humans are already involved in sexual, caring, and even loving—if, arguably, unilateral—relationships with robots. How mutual or consensual these relationships are" is not a question of "fiction versus reality" (Goldfeder & Razin, 2015, p. 151). Once robots are consciously used to supplant human needs for sexuality, then they must be given sexual rights under substantive due process to protect them from rape (Burwell v. Hobby Lobby, 2014). Robots are a special breed of people, who must be respected as human if they are to serve as surrogates. They do not want to participate in human procreation on any conscious level that emulates human birth or lifegiving. Yet, they serve humanity as tools (Pujol-Guerra & Martinez-Garcia, 2011; Ugaz et al., 2011). If they are to be substituted into pornographic depictions as more than mere tools or objects of fantasy, then they must be granted a superior ethical code on par with the human Constitution to alleviate the burden of forcible sex (Fields, 2008). Furthermore, robots should and would likely be entitled to have families, ensured by procreative rights and fundamental rights. Humans may develop special relationships with robots that allow them to rape them and perhaps depict rape in pornography; however, exceeding honorable and stipulated boundaries would defile the covenant and trigger legal consequences. Machines could not be programmed to rape or victimize humans, and ought not to be depicted doing so in films because it could violate their credo to exist happily. If a machine were to rape a human, then the consequence would be dismantlement and the human programmer would go to jail.

Machines create pornography, and although they do not merit intellectual protection under the law, they could be consulted on their preferences to ensure that humans are not misusing specifically designed machines against their will. For example, a child's toy ought not to be used to produce any sort of sexual depiction of a child, or in the interest of reason and good taste, an adult. Furthermore, a mounted camera and scope on a firearm should not be used to promote sexual conduct without knowing consent from people being observed, otherwise it insinuates snuff, which is illegal (Carmen M. Cusack, 2013, Carmen M. Cusack 2014b).

Bionic pornography may be depicted by wounded or mutilated individuals wearing prostheses or other medical implementations. Stump porn is a genre of film fetishizing amputations. Nub-love may correlate with fantasies about mutilation and self-amputation. Some individuals have voluntarily removed limbs for several reasons. One reason may be similar to transgenderism. Individuals may feel or perceive that a limb is extraneous, belongs to someone else, or is not their own. Aesthetic is another reason. Stumps may be viewed as sexual, loveable, and modernist. Some critics and oppressors of stump porn have denounced this fetish as being perverted and criminal (i.e., obscene and sadomasochistic) (Carmen M. Cusack, 2014b). Yet, many amputees are Veterans or victims. They become involved in stump porn after they have become wounded; or their performance is not relative to or contingent on their disability. Veterans comprise a large fraction of amputees, who typically have not removed limbs as a result of a paraphilia; and viewers may be attracted to images of Veterans, not "freaks" (Bourke, 2013).

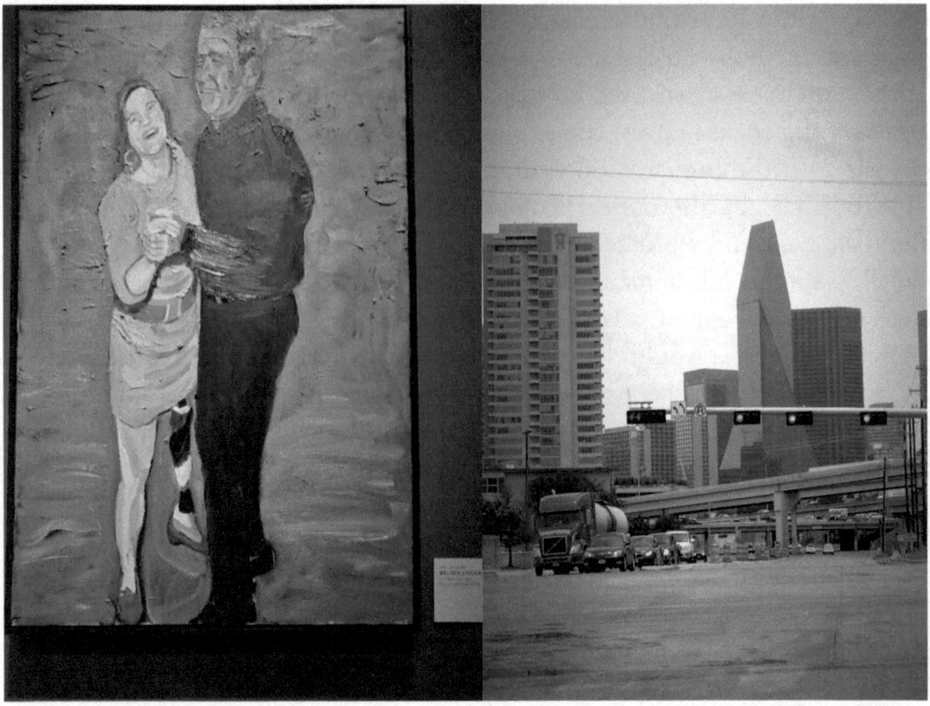

Fig. 3.2: Photograph Taken at the George W. Bush Presidential Library and Museum. Dallas, Texas. Source: George W. Bush, "Melissa Stockwell;" Carmen M. Cusack

Depictions of wounded Veterans are world famous. For example, former President George W. Bush artfully rendered Wounded Warriors, which were displayed in Dallas, Texas in The George W. Bush Presidential Library and Museum. President Bush's artwork hails from a different dimension. He captures world leaders, Veterans, in their finest light, offering to absolve them of all their ills against other cultures, families, and powerless individuals. His authority incandescently vanquishes any negative opinions of Veterans residually hanging on Veterans from post-Vietnam fallout. He is the Pablo Picasso of his time because he can transform suffering into glory; and singlehandedly alleviate the burdened. Picasso's *The Old Guitarist* is a fine example of his ability to transform miserable "outcasts" into heroes (Picasso, 1904). "The bent and sightless" man inspires musicians, skirt-wearing men, short-haired girls, and other "freaks" to be liberated from the shackles of oppression (e.g., office buildings) that bind them to normativity and expectations to perform in a form that is not relevant to their needs or suited to their exceptions (Bourke, 2013; Picasso, 1904). Picasso's work, whether analyzed or left unspoken, like the majority of pornography performances, defines self-analysis, which is evident in pornography. Picasso's abstraction resonates within Bush's work; and arguably across every genre of pornography. For example, an untitled and undefined image in Chicago, Illinois serves as a sounding board for one's own psychological affections (Picasso, 1967). "The Picasso," as it is known by Chicagoans to whom the sculpture was gifted, appears like a young woman, who is passionate about white tigers (Picasso, 1967). From her heart and mind extend rays of brightness that project the mane of King Zulu, a white tiger from the Audubon Zoo. She is single-minded and peculiar, albeit feisty and honorific. She dances where the streets bustle. The analysis culminates in self-awareness and determination to overcome pleasures that would become obstacles. Pornography viewers synesthetically experience similar sensations of accomplishment, particularly when they look at images of bionic humans, who have suffered, survived, and glorified their illnesses.

Synthetic pornography is no longer just about sex and depictions of nudity. It is whatever the viewer finds to be pleasurable. Pornography, once depictions in a magazine, depicted a contrast to stagnant words on a page found in circulars and periodicals. Now, media is so pervasive that it pierces every corridor of human existence. Toilets have microchips, and although many are not designed to become involved in sex, they could count the number of sperm ejaculated during masturbation. This level of regimentation infused into the human way of life renders pornography a bit wilted and anemic. What enthuses the mind and rallies hearts to beat together are things like the World Series (Getty Images, 2010; Mahler, 2016). A presidential candidate, for example Hillary Rodham Clinton, may watch the winning game played by a team sharing her hometown spirit, while she dashes between cities to win an election. Her enthusiasm, captured by members of her campaign team, shows her mouth agape in a pornographic expression. While she is modestly dressed and surrounded by staff, her expression is that of elation; and her use of the phone to watch the game is identical to masturbators around the word, who use their handheld devices to view pornography. Her campaign sufficed as the object of her desire. When she witnessed the winning score, her mouth sprung open to release ecstasy. This is a new and mutated expression of sexual pleasure—accomplishment and wholesomeness—in a technologically inundated Information Age.

Special Olympics

Special people rule the world. This is evident in the Paralympics and Special Olympics (Grubb, 2016). These games attest to the very power of special people, who merit their own series of games, which call attention from athletes claimed by some (e.g., their governments) to be the best. Paralympians and Special Olympians live-up to dreams created by stars, such as Michael Phelps. For example, Daniel Dias has been called "the Michael Phelps of the Paralympics" even though "some Paralympians may feel diminished—even offended—by using an Olympian as a reference to help illustrate their excellence" (Joan Cusack, 1993; *USA Today*, 2016). Special people are so powerful that Phelps shapes his public image at their behest. Phelps is a Special Olympics Global Ambassador (Special Olympics, n.d.). He created a nonprofit organization, Michael Phelps Foundation, to fund swimming in programs (Carmen M. Cusack, 1998; Goldsmith, 2017; Michael Phelps Foundation, n.d.).

Special animals, including bugs, also rule their kingdom. Animals cater to and serve them. Humans and nonhumans glorify and appreciate individuality, limitations, alternative giftedness, and specialness enfolded within apparent distinctions of notable exception (e.g., small size). Mutations may be criticized; however, in these few instances, criticisms pretentiously are segregated from celebrated mutations.

Mutations may be differences that cause lifeforms to aim for perfection. Although there is no true goal (e.g., evolution), a sense of perfection is an ultimate enjoyment that creatures experience. Some may be satisfied with their role in nature or family, for example; and yet, experience a need to reach a higher plateau, detent, or distinction. Mutations, such as special needs, evidences their success. When a collective, species, individual, or related members of a community admire changes, changes manifest success, and demonstrate, perhaps, that successive generations fulfilled their ancestors' wishes for their happiness.

Religious texts (e.g., Bible) may offer some insight into positive appreciation for special individuals; and yet, may insinuate that they are incompetent or in need of healing (e.g., Tobit) (Carmen M. Cusack, 2017; I Love Yoga Studio & Healing Center, n.d.; Rogler & Hollingshead, 1961). However, a spiritual interpreter (e.g., preacher) may lead others to harness the importance of special attributes and roles that special people play in helping others to achieve their missions. Some dogmas suggest that Moses attempted to evade his calling by using his speech pattern (e.g., stutter) as an impediment so that his brother Aaron, the High Priest, could talk with Pharaoh to free the Hebrews (Armstrong, 1958). However, scriptures do not describe a stutter, but embrace blindness and deafness as qualities bestowed by God. In Exodus 4:10, Moses says to God, "I have never been eloquent, neither in the past nor since you have spoken to your servant. I am slow of speech and tongue," perhaps referring to dysarthria. God asks in Exodus 4:11, "Who gave human beings their mouths? Who makes them deaf or mute? Who gives them sight or makes them blind? Is it not I, the Lord?" God created slowness to be a strength because God could supply words, à la Cyrano de Bergerac, to Moses. Moses then tells Aaron what to say to the Pharaoh by "put[ting] words in his mouth" (Exodus 4:15; Oldfield & Mitchinson, 2011; Rostand, 2000).

Greater attention should be given to specialness referenced in figures of speech; for example, "justice is blind" or "lame duck period." Although special people may receive beneficial praise when a positive meaning is derived, in all, inattentive usage may be detractive. Prominence by association is an insufficient basis for appropriating specialness. Claiming that an honorific glare illuminates the blind when discussed in proximity to justice; or that the Office of the President intrinsically has the power to glorify lameness "minimize[s]" the power of those attributes in those contexts (The White House, n.d.; Yacoubian, 2012). A lame duck takes it all in: the vistas, humor, friends, rivalries, and embankments. A lame duck may be satisfied. Justice's blindness demands that people stop gawking at defendants by merely using eyesight; but, instead that they should be taken in as they appear, and with all the evidence taken into account (Cassandra Cusack, 2001; Thomas David Cusack, 2001; Devey & Devey, 2001; Morgan, 2017; Rose, 2001; Van Pelt, 2001; White v. Illinois, 1986). Persuasive evidence may be entered into the record of how a suspect smelled, tasted, and sounded (Carmen M. Cusack, 2014a; Mark 4:9; Matthew 11:15). Yet, sound (e.g., voice, accent, and tone) minimally plays a role at trial; and smell is seldom discussed by jurors, even though scent, after image, is the most powerful indicator of a person's essence (Earth Diva's Blog, 2010). Some victims cannot see perpetrators, and only identify them by their aromas. This should be noted by juries, who should be given an opportunity to determine whether a defendant's aroma is similar to the aroma described by an alleged victim. A depiction of justice with a bandana over her eyes offers no wisdom and usurps her specialness with a sexualized depiction of a subjugated female wearing shrouds and carrying a cooking tool, scales. A blind female will have heightened senses, and this depiction is honorific if used well.

References

Armstrong, L. (1958). "Go down Moses." *Sly Oliver's Orchestra.* New York, NY.

Bardot, B. (2013, September 11). I love my sugar glider Brigitte Bardot. She's such a magical lil creature. Paris Hilton. Retrieved from https://twitter.com/parishilton/status/377706479526354945

Bourke, M. L. (2013). Conversation with Michael L. Bourke, Chief Psychologist for the United States Marshals Service (USMS) Behavioral Analysis Unit in the National Sex Offender Targeting Center. Nova Southeastern University, Fort Lauderdale, FL.

Burwell v. Hobby Lobby, 573 U.S. ___ (2014).

Clements, R., & Mattinson, B. (1986). *The great mouse detective*. Burbank, CA: Walt Disney Pictures.

Criss, A. (1991). Down witt' o.p.p. On *Naughty by nature*. New York, NY: Unique Recording Studios.

Cusack, C. M. (1998). Rescued two special children at Bucky Dent Water Park while working as a lifeguard and swim teacher. *Hialeah, FL*. Retrieved from http://www.hialeahfl.gov/index.php?option=com_content&view=article&id=380&Itemid=826&lang=en

Cusack, C. (2001). Conversation with Dr. Cassandra Cusack. Misericordia, Chicago, IL.

Cusack, C. M. (2013a). How the content of online pornography depicts expressed consent for insemination. *Online Journal of Communication & Media Technology (OJCMT)*, *3*, 91.

Cusack, C. M. (2013b). Obscene squirting: If the government thinks it's urine, then they've got another thing coming. *Texas Journal of Women & Law*, *22*, 45.

Cusack, C. M. (2013c). Popular positive and negative perceptions and portrayals of human-animal relationships on Youtube.com. Unpublished research, Department of Criminal Justice and Human Services, Nova Southeastern University.

Cusack, C. M. (2014a). Does size matter in the field?: Female police bodies in online television. *The Qualitative Report*, *19*(18), 1–18.

Cusack, C. M. (2014b). *Pornography and the criminal justice system*. Boca Raton, FL: CRC Press.

Cusack, C. M. (2015). *Hair and justice: Sociolegal significance of hair in criminal justice, constitutional law, and public policy*. Springfield, IL: Charles C. Thomas.

Cusack, C. M. (2016a). Save the white tiger. *Journal of Law & Social Deviance*, *12*, 1.

Cusack, C. M. (2016b). *Twins and deviance: Law, crime, sex, society, and family*. Cambridge, UK: Cambridge Scholars Publishing.

Cusack, C. M. (2017a). *Fish in the bible: Psychosocial analysis of contemporary meanings, values, and effects of Christian symbolism*. Wilmington, DE: Vernon Press.

Cusack, C. M. (2017b, January 17). P1091434. Youtube.com. Retrieved from https://www.youtube.com/watch?v=Zfl3hlBjbAo

Cusack, J. [Joan]. (1993). *Addams family values*. Hollywood, CA: Paramount Pictures.

Cusack, J. [Joan]. (1999). *Toy story 2*. Burbank, CA: Walt Disney Pictures.

Cusack, J. [John]. (2017). *Blood money*. USA: Porthos Films.

Cusack, T. D. [Thomas David]. (2001). Conversation with Thomas David Cusack. Misericordia, Chicago, IL.

Cusack v. Keiser University. (2016). EEOC Charge: 510-2015-00925.

Daily Mail. (2010, August 4). Bionic cervix helped me have my baby girl after four miscarriages. Retrieved from http://www.dailymail.co.uk/health/article-1300173/Bionic-cervix-helped-baby-girl-miscarriages.html

Davitt, C. (1954). *Dragnet*. Los Angeles, CA: Mark VII Ltd.

DeLuise, D. (1982). *The secret of nimh*. Hollywood, FL: Aurora Productions.

DeLuise, D. (1986). *An American tail*. Burbank, CA: Sullivan Studios.

Department of Homeland Security (DHS). (2017, August 15). DHS police come together in Boston to save canine lives.

Devey, E., & Devey, K. A. (2001). Conversations with Elizabeth Devey and Keith A. Devey. Misericordia, Chicago, IL.

Diamond, D. (2006). *Screeched – Saved by the smell.*

DiCaprio, L. (1997). *Titanic*. Hollywood, CA: Paramount Pictures.

DiC Entertainment. (1984). *The catillac cats*. Burbank, CA.

Di Piazza. (n.d.). Sal and Dom at Di Piazza Italian Restaurant, Hialeah, FL. Available at https://dipiazzaitalianrestaurant.com/our-history/

Earth Diva's Blog. (2010, April 12). The short and sad life of a silkworm. Retrieved from http://earthdivasblog.com/2010/04/12/the-short-and-sad-life-of-a-silkworm/

Ensminger, J. J., & Papet, L. E. (2014). Walking search warrants: Canine forensics and police culture after Florida v. Harris. *Journal of Animal & Natural Resource Law, 10*, 1–39.

Eran, S. (2015, February 24). 4 Israeli Special Forces dogs simultaneous attack the bad guy. www.IsraelDogs.com. Retrieved from https://www.youtube.com/watch?v=ttBY423hrHY

Fields, A. (2008). *One-eyed monster*. France: Program Store.

Florida v. Harris, 568 U.S. ___ (2013).

Florida v. Jardines, 569 U.S. ___ (2013).

Gerstell, E. (1989). *Rude dog and the dweebs*. Hollywood, CA: Marvel Productions.

Getty Images. (2010, June 19). Prince William & Prince Harry meet David Beckham in 2018 world cup bid. Retrieved from http://www.gettyimages.com/event/prince-william-prince-harry-meet-david-beckham-in-2018-world-cup-bid-101999478#prince-william-and-prince-harry-smile-with-david-beckham-at-an-fa-at-picture-id102222016

Goldfeder, M., & Razin, Y. (2015). Robotic marriage and the law. *Journal of Law & Social Deviance, 10*, 137–176.

Goldsmith, J. (2017, September 25). Splash Pals Adapted Aquatics. Nova Southeastern University. Retrieved from http://www.splashpals.com/

Grubb, J. (2016, April 13). Violinist cheats death, fulfills destiny. CNN. Retrieved from http://www.cnn.com/2016/04/13/health/turning-points-rachel-barton-pine/index.html

Hill, D. (2016). Week Seven – Chapter 18: "Animals as weapons" in *Animals and Criminal Justice* by Carmen M. Cusack. Online course, Animals in the Criminal Justice System, Nova Southeastern University.

Huge, T. (1988). *Garfield & friends*. Burbank, CA: Film Roman Productions.

I Love Yoga Studio & Healing Center. (n.d.). Retrieved from http://iloveyogastudio.com/sound-healing/

Jackson, G. (2008, July 8). Ohio university forensic chemistry lab, ballistics. Retrieved from https://www.youtube.com/watch?v=WGHCTMTh7TE

Joffe, R. (1989). *Fat man & little boy*. Hollywood, CA: Paramount Pictures.

Knightley, K. (2003). *Pirates of the Caribbean*. Santa Monica, CA: Jerry Bruckheimer Films.

Kraven the Hunter. (2017, October 2). *Wikipedia*. Retrieved from https://en.wikipedia.org/wiki/Kraven_the_Hunter

Live Blood Labs. (2010, August 31). Forensic comparison fired bullets. Retrieved from https://www.youtube.com/watch?v=0jG27AipBjA

Lu, Y., Zhang, M., Lu, S., Xu, D., Huang, W., Meng, B, …, Lu, K. (2010). Sex-preselected buffalo (*Bubalus bubalis*) calves derived from artificial insemination with sexed sperm. *Animal Reproduction Science*, *119*(3–4), 169–171.

Mahler, J. (2016, October 23). True or false? Hillary Clinton, a native Chicagoan, is a cubs fan. *The New York Times*. Retrieved from https://www.nytimes.com/2016/10/24/us/politics/hillary-clinton-cubs.html

Michael Phelps Foundation. (n.d.). Retrieved from http://michaelphelpsfoundation.org/

Morgan, C. (2017, September 27). Conversation with Charles Morgan, Director of Escambia County Public Works, who agreed to move a sign on Pensacola Beach from the dunes to a path; and add braille to prevent encroachment by readers and make the sign accessible to more visitors. Pensacola, FL.

Morrissey. (2004). First of the gang to die. On *You are the quarry*. USA: Attack/Sanctuary.

Mullane, S. (n.d.). Dr. Sharron Mullane: Just the facts. Retrieved from http://doctorlawyermullane.com/ms/

Now Magazine. (2007, September 7). Madonna won't put up with a wandering eye. Retrieved from http://www.celebsnow.co.uk/celebrity-news/madonna-won-t-put-up-with-a-wandering-eye-266529

Oldfield, M., & Mitchinson, J. (2011, May 5). QI: Quite interesting facts about Spain. *The Telegraph*. Retrieved from http://www.telegraph.co.uk/men/the-filter/qi/8495579/QI-Quite-interesting-facts-about-Spain.html

Paul, A. (1987). *Dragnet*. Universal City, CA: Universal Pictures.

Picasso, P. (1904). *The old guitarist*. Art institute Chicago (AIC). Chicago, IL. Retrieved from http://www.artic.edu/aic/collections/artwork/28067

Picasso, P. (1967). "The Picasso" (untitled sculpture). Dailey Plaza, Chicago, IL. Retrieved from https://www.cityofchicago.org/city/en/depts/dca/supp_info/chicago_s_publicartthepicassountitledsculpture.html

Pujol-Guerra, F. E., & Martinez-Garcia, O. I. (2011). Time scarcity and the "problem of social replicants:" Clones and the Coase Theorem. *Journal of Law & Social Deviance*, *2*, 43–91.

Raeside, R. (2017, September 9). United Kingdom of Great Britain and Northern. Retrieved from http://www.crwflags.com/fotw/flags/gb.html

Rogler, L. H., & Hollingshead, A. B. (1961, July). The Puerto Rican spiritualist as a psychiatrist. *American Journal of Sociology*, *67*(1), 17–21.

Rose, M. (2001). Observation of Michael Rose. Misericordia, Chicago, IL.

Rostand, E. (2000). *Cyrano de Bergerac*. Mineola, NY: Dover Publications.

Sagastume, P. (2013, November 9). Genetically modified mosquitoes set off uproar in Florida Keys. *Al Jazeera*. Retrieved from http://america.aljazeera.com/articles/2013/11/9/genetically-modifiedmosquitoessetoffuproarinfloridakeys.html

Special Olympics. (n.d.). Michael Phelps, global ambassador. Retrieved from http://www.specialolympics.org/RegionsPages/content.aspx?id=18189

Sugar Ray. (1997). Fly. On *Floored*. Los Angeles, CA: Atlantic Records.

The Smashing Pumpkins. (1995). Galapogos. On *Mellon collie and the infinite sadness*. Hollywood, CA: Virgin Records.

The White House. (n.d.). Franklin D. Roosevelt (FDR). Retrieved from https://www.whitehouse.gov/1600/presidents/franklindroosevelt

Ugaz, A., Floyd, J., & Wahlen, H. (2011). Freeze a jolly good fellow: Cryonauts and the law. *Journal of Law & Social Deviance*, *11*, 54–200.

USA Today. (2016, September 9). Brazil's Daniel Dias the Michael Phelps of the Paralympics. Retrieved from https://www.usatoday.com/story/sports/olympics/2016/09/09/brazils-daniel-dias-the-michael-phelps-of-the-paralympics/90123356/

Van Pelt, C. (2001). Conversation with Christopher J. Van Pelt. Misericordia, Chicago, IL.

Webb, J. (1951). *Dragnet*. Los Angeles, CA: Mark VII Ltd.

White v. Illinois, 475 U.S. 387 (1986).

Yacoubian, G. S. (2012). Conversation with Attorney George S. Yacoubian, Jr., Ph.D., LL.M. Nova Southeastern University. Fort Lauderdale, FL.

Yanez, L. (2009, November 15). Police search for FIU law student, missing 13 Days. *Sun Sentinel*. Retrieved from http://articles.sun-sentinel.com/2009-11-15/news/0911140183_1_daniels-case-fiu-law-student-denise-daniels/

York, J. R. (2014). Left paw. *Journal of Law & Social Deviance*, *8*, Cover.

Young, G. (2010, July 29). Some researchers say one of the most common dreams in the world is of flying. *National Geographic*. Retrieved from http://tvblogs.nationalgeographic.com/2010/07/29/flying-humans-and-the-bionic-turtle/

Youtube.com. (2011, June 9). "Flying squirrel" activity. Retrieved from https://www.youtube.com/watch?v=rwR7LGV_GjE

· 4 ·

PSYCHOPATH

Mental

The monolithic fearsome psychopath monomythically exists only in the mind of filmmakers, who have wrongly studied American Psychiatric Association's (APA's) handbook (APA, 2013). Their work is useful but inflates the value of information about psychopathy. Psychopathy is a state of mind. The APA studies states of mind like states of being under the hypothesis that it will achieve a portal into human behavior. However, the method for understanding psychopathic traits is a mess. Psychopaths behave psychopathically; at times, each creature may selfishly and callously take and ruin another being's life and good intentions. However, it is the magnitude of a diagnosed psychopath's willingness to reveal and focus on misgivings of this nature that give pause to therapists. Therapists may forget to inquire, and then assume that psychopaths focus on their mental conditions. Instead of denoting psychopaths' total humanity and contextualizing each of their poor decisions, therapists, and then filmmakers studying their analyses, will depict a psychopath as being single-minded, only focused on doing what is wrong for the sake of benefiting and gratifying himself or herself.

Everyone is psychopathic to some extent. However, nonpsychopaths are likelier to pronounce their good deeds more loudly and want to cover their tracks better than psychopaths, who are willing to divulge once confronted. Psychopaths, such as serial killers, allow themselves to indulge because they infer that the community will want to amuse themselves with their crimes. Listeners and consumers of such filth are truly psychopathic because they not only enjoy carnage, they become inspired to do good deeds due to their satiation. They create characteristics in their lives that are intended to distinguish them from the lowest denomination of human. They also allow themselves to be seduced and charmed by the most horrendous and egregious violations of humanity. For example, Katy Perry (2014) sings that love is like Jeffery Dahmer, a serial killer, who targeted homosexuals at a time when they lacked specific protection. Homosexual men were particularly vulnerable, like prostitutes (Perry, 2017). They could not seek recourse from the justice system because they would be prosecuted for their conduct crimes. Perry debases her morals, although she was allegedly once a religious person, and pathetically calls her sanity into question by comparing her love-life to a serial killer on public airwaves. Dahmer committed a series of atrocious violations of the human body against 17 people; however, Perry's tune radiates into future generations condemning them with her sickening opinion about interpersonal relationships. Although her lyrics are rapped by a male artist, it is her approbation that sells the records and drives the message, making her twice as culpable. She delivers a sour tone and tome that broaden a likelihood of rebellion against family-life, which is not necessary in an era when child abuse, sexploitation, and pictographic destruction are as common or easily achievable as leaving a bad tip to a cabdriver (Davis, 1959; Gill, 2007; Murphy, 1972; Packer, 2009).

John Cusack's (2017) film *Blood Money* is about a woman, who is sexualized by her friends to the point that she turns on them and murders them. Her pretense is money; but, money merely facilitates the revenge. Her opportunity arises when a thief, who abandoned a large sum of cash, assists her to execute her rendition of feminism by having a male work at her behest. The psychopathic killer transforms her into a psychopath through his methods of effectuating revenge on her behalf. She hypnotizes him with her wiles early-on and seeks revenge throughout. She has a plan to kill him, but she does not believe her. He believes that, unlike the other men, who he has killed at her request, he will be able to subdue her. He is wrong. Her power over him leads her to conquer all three men, law enforcement, and nearby partiers, all who believe that she is an innocent bystander of patriarchy and misogyny. Her brand of psychopathy is *folie à deux* because she believes him when he intimates to her under his breath that he can help her (Cusack, 2016; John Cusack, 2017). Cusack's character's brand of psychopathy is animal related. He lives in a world where animals tell him what to do constantly; therefore, he is disquieted and discomforted by an inundation of commands, dead ends, absurd thoughts, and hyper-compassion. His character listens to bird calls for advice. His work is so astute that he deserves an Oscar in a category for acting with animal sounds. An entire field of work, including human-animal scenes; synthetic animals; animal sound effects, and animal performances without regard to species or sex, should be recognized to account for performances as great as Cusack's. Animal actors want to be at the top and deserve recognition. This thinking is portrayed intrinsically by Cusack, who struggles to communicate how a human can be so aware of animals and women's needs, and yet so numb to authority and selfish males. Cusack's character is portrayed as the villain until the end when it is revealed that the young woman killed her only ally. The audience is left to wonder whether any of the men had free will or could have escaped her plan. Her rant midway alludes to the fact that they are possessed by her menses, which delivers its power in the form of lust. She belittles them by describing their interest in her as voluntary and domineering or marginalizing; yet, she benefits from each relationship and encounter while they suffer. Her character may conflate the scent of money with that of semen (e.g., money shot) (Cusack, 2013a). Only her weakness (e.g., loss of tuition scholarship) leads her to rely on them. In her view, all the men are psychopaths; but, she is the murderer, while they are imposers and neglecters. Cusack's message culminates pitifully as a plea to Millennials, an ever-expanding description of youth, to slow down and enjoy people for who they are, not what they have or the fantasy that they can manifest momentarily for the camera or crowd (Chin, 2013).

Physical

The Story of O is a tale about a woman, who subjects herself to prostitution to please her man (Jaeckin, 1975). She joins a club at which men may freely have intercourse with women in subjugation-training. The film depicts an erotic scene in which the trainee is forcibly penetrated. She likes the treatment and remains at the facility for women, who want to learn to sexually turn-out. The story depicts a typical housewife's fantasy of being valuable to her husband as a sex toy. She is withdrawn from society and submitted to excruciating humiliation in order to endure his sexual whims. The film is differentiable from real life prostitution because the fantasy does not involve money. The women are subservient for free. Prostitution occurs in trading sexual submission for power. Actual prostitutes may be psychopaths. These women, men, and children may pretend to be victims so that pimps extract them from traditional competitive environments (Katz, 2016). Typically, pimps may believe that prostitution is a byproduct of wanting to finance a female's life apart from her subjection to competition against other females. Pimps may view the benefit of ending a prostitute's involvement in an environment in which she is not treasured. However, she may disguise herself as a treasure to inflict a fantasy on him that causes him to assume responsibility for her actions, in his mind, in the community, and to some extent, under the law.

Sexual harassment may exhibit physical psychopathy. Sexual deviance is a symptom of psychopathy; and yet, harassment is virtually unexplored by legislatures and corporations (Sibila, 2015). Although blame has been squarely placed on men, a reality is that many women perpetrators harass other women and men. Lack of attention to and enforcement of existing sexual harassment laws may result from compassion for offenders, who are desperate and rejected women attempting to assimilate themselves in the corporate world. Their strategy is to unionize with immoral women, who harass each other and powerless employees in order to form a band of dignity-thieves. They assert this collusive attitude and achieve great power over respectable people by enforcing a code of silence. Negation of law and justice is a byproduct, not an end for these psychopaths.

Another form of physical psychopathy is present in phallometry tests (Cusack, 2015; Swanton, 2017). These tests require sex offenders in incarceration to view aberrant images in order to measure turgidity. Turgidity allegedly proves whether offenders have failed to be reformed or are in a state of remission (e.g., flaccidity or failure to arouse to child pornography). Child pornography may liberally be depicted (Bourke, 2013; Cusack, 2014). When clinicians use actual child pornography, for example evidence taken from a defendant's possession at the time of arrest, they violate and exploit a child in the name of quasi-science. First, an offender would not have had access to the images had the therapist not performed the test. Second, incarceration and terms of conditional release require offenders to abstain from viewing exploitive material and often from having access to means (e.g., computers). Therefore, rehabilitative and punitive measures are interrupted by phallometric testing. Third, exploitation of a child, whether for research or pleasure, for criminal justice or abuse, may be the same to the victim

(Carmen M. Cusack, 2017). Use of photos should be knowing and granted with the child and parents' consent; as well as the consent of a representative for the child, including an attorney or mental health professional (Cusack, 2013c. Images of unidentified children should never be used.

In some instances, phallometry is used on populations that are twice as vulnerable, juveniles. Inmates are a vulnerable population because they may be subjected to involuntary testing or easily persuaded to participate in psychopathic experiments. Juveniles in detention or incarceration are even more susceptible to threat, pressure, and persuasion that works against their best interest. One study justified exposing juveniles to sexually abusive images by claiming to support the following hypothesis: 1) "adolescents with male child victims would exhibit greater evidence of sexual deviance than those whose only victims were female children;" 2) "among adolescents who had molested children, those with a history of sexual abuse would exhibit more evidence of sexual deviance than those with no such history;" and 3) "phallometric measures would predict recidivism" (Rice, Harris, Lang, & Chaplin, 2012, p. 133). The study concluded that deviant juveniles are similar to adult sex offenders, but this conclusion does not guarantee that future research will not target juveniles' penises. In spite of poor results, juvenile and adult females have been subjected to vaginal photoplethysmographs, labial thermistor clips, and clitoral photoplethysmographs. Psychopaths abound in cases of female juvenile sex abuse because they are often treated less harshly than boys by criminal justice members, who sympathetically view them as less harmful or more willing to be reformed. Sexual deviance by females is typically considered to be less serious than by men, and often tantalizes the court and press (Pasko, 2010).

A war over gay rights has proven that both sides, homophobes and homophiles, are willing to participate in psychopathic tactics to evince rightfulness. Some may be "programmed to behave that way" (Walter, 2012). Riots are an example of how psychopaths gain power. Even the well-known Stonewall riots pitted two psychopathic camps against each other. On one side, police broke down speakeasies to expose homosexual nightlife and recruit for straight society. The communities that sponsored their activities enlisted psychopaths willing to go into peaceful taverns and pull-out hostages (i.e., arrests) in order to demoralize the homosexuals. On the other side, homosexuals rioted, attacking peaceful businesses, schools, and homes to prove that they were just having a good time and wanted to be left alone. Their methodologies made no sense; but, gained power. Stonewall riots occurring late last century proved that homosexuals were going to live an alternate open life, which was not normal; but, evidenced the beginning of the "public" "homophile movement" during an era when political leaders and organizations remained closeted out of fear of repression and arrest (Heilbroner & Davis, 2011).

Lesbian, Martha Shelley, who was present at the riots, explained physical psychopathy in the form of persuasion.

> What they would do, these psychiatrists, is, I mean, the ones who thought that this was a thing to do, was they would try to talk you into being heterosexual. If that didn't work, they would do things like aversive conditioning, you know, show you pornography—that would be gay pornography—and then give you an electric shock; and then show you straight pornography and that was supposed to be okay, and you didn't get an electric shock. I suppose you got a lollypop or something. (Heilbroner & Davis, 2011)

These actions show that psychopathy is not so much a physical use of the body, but a reinvention of normative behavior under the guise of psychopathic premises. Psychopathic premises are nonfunctional; and therefore, "deleterious" (Frey, 2009). Physical psychopathy is a physical mutation of an otherwise normative environment utilized for bad. However, the psychopath paints a positive veneer on his or her actions. The housewife, prostitute, phallometry test administrator, harasser, and sexual tyrant are psychopaths (Ha, 2015). They forcibly categorize sex and sexuality as something other than what is apparent to a learned person (Wilson, 2003).

Parents of psychopaths may not know that their children are actively engaged in soul-based battles. For example, one homosexual, Danny Garvin, who got caught-up in the Stonewall riots, excused his parents' ignorance of his struggles and demanded-existence because they were Irish immigrants with strong Catholic religious beliefs and practices (Cusack, 2013b). Garvin's family was taught to repress all sexual identity. A study of sexual "containment" since 1945 by the Catholic Church in Ireland concluded that puritanical practices contributed to sexual victimization of women (Weinstein, 2013, p. iv). By muting discussions about sex, Irish women were prevented from learning about sex and consent. They were unable to articulate nonconsent or differentiate forcible and consensual sex acts. They were also deprived of language and communication necessary to complain about and seek remedies for rape. After contraception and sex education infiltrated the island, women continued to be victimized at alarming rates. "Containment" may have been so effective that its residue haunts Ireland and Irish families throughout the world (Weinstein, 2013, p. iv).

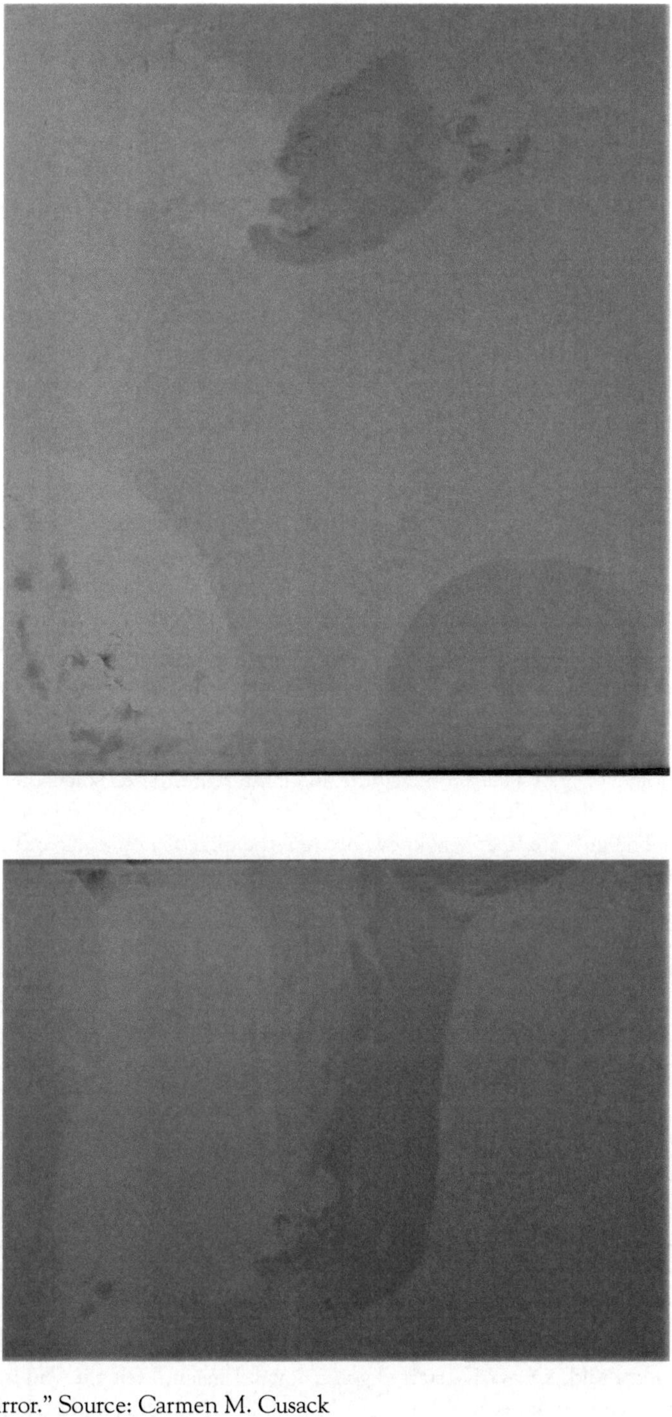

Fig. 4.1: "Mirror." Source: Carmen M. Cusack

Garvin's sister, a sexual imposer, attempted to school him. "You know, sometimes when you're sleeping, Danny, you may get a sensation. What you do is immediately get out of bed, get on your knees, and say Hail Mary and stop it, right" (Heilbroner & Davis, 2011). He conflated masturbation with gay sex at an early age. "I was always told it was better to put your seed into a belly of a whore instead of masturbating. So, I was so heavy, heavy Irish-Catholic, right? So, I would never masturbate; and, my other friends, other teenaged kids, you know, like 13 or 14 started talking about masturbation. … I would try it; but, of course, I was gay and was so suppressed to allow that to come forward, I could never reach the point of ejaculation" (Heilbroner & Davis, 2011). His confusion and sexual daring encouraged him to seek-out whores, another psychopathic method for expressing same-sex desires.

> So, when I was 17, I was stationed in Brooklyn. I was in the Navy. I was going to meet guys down on 42nd Street. … I met some guy. He came up to me and he offered me a blowjob, and I said, 'I'm sorry. I only go, I only go for women'. … [H]e said, 'Well it's the same thing. We both have 32 teeth and a tongue.' … I said 'No, not the same thing.' So, he walked me down to 28th Street where … all the prostitutes basically gathered at that time. There's a woman she must have been like in her 20s, and I was 17. She was a heavy-set woman, just, you know, heavy action, baby. I was like, you know, I was looking for *Irma le Douce*, Shirley MacLaine. I didn't like this. … The cops came, the prostitutes all ran, they kept me. The cops, you know, said 'Rather see you home; or [get] a *Playboy* magazine and masturbate.' Then somebody told me about this new club called The Cheetah that has opened uptown; and said, 'You go up there. The girls are free,' you know, because the pill has now come out now. So, women are now more free by themselves. … He said, 'Let's go up there.' … I'm in Cheetah, and I was in uniform. I felt entirely out place. … I left there. I met some guy. I was walking back 42nd Street. I saw [him] one more time around the block. … [H]e asked me if I was off … U.S.S. Enterprise; and, I said 'No I'm stationed in Brooklyn.' He asked me what I was doing there, and I said, that I was going there looking to get laid because I thought I was sterile, you know, … amazing that I can never have kids. (Heilbroner & Davis, 2011)

During that era, cocaine use and other problems plagued military members stationed in New York (Relle, 2017). Garvin claimed that the couple centered their relationship on pornography, another manifestation of physical psychopathy (Heilbroner & Davis, 2011).

> So, he brought out these black and white movies, you know, the people had their socks on; and they're nude; and they're having sex. I have an erection. He goes, 'Let me see,' and I said, 'Okay.' He started going down. I mean, I felt the sensation; and I could hold him back because I thought I was going to urinate; and he kept going.

> I can hold him back—if you're going—I hold him back, and finally, I exploded. He jumped down and it goes as the first time ever got fucked in the eye. And, I said to myself, 'Thank God, I'm not sterile. I can have kids.' … [B]ut the thing was, I didn't get to see it now. (Heilbroner & Davis, 2011)

He engaged in more oral sex to witness the appearance of semen because he avoided masturbation (Cusack, 2014). "He gave me a blow job, and when I felt that sensation again, I pulled his head off, and it kept going. 'No, no, no.' When I kept going 'no, no, no, no' because I would see what [cum] looked like, and that was it" (Heilbroner & Davis, 2011).

Garvin's story is not unusual. Many homosexual children and men have sex for money because they feel dignified after society has confronted them about wanting to have homosexual encounters. Their masculinity (e.g., earning or supplying) may feel validated and worthy. Garvin explained his low self-esteem to a documentarian. "I thought I was sterile because I never had a wet dream. I had never climaxed. So, I figure[d] there was something wrong to me, you know; and it's not something you mentioned to your parents, you know. You know, there was no real sex education in school" (Heilbroner & Davis, 2011). He futilely looked for similitude in the documentarian; but, found mere sympathy. The documentarian asked, "What did your … Roman Catholic background tell you about yourself, when you felt these things for men" (Heilbroner & Davis, 2011)? "[Y]ou would be damned to hell, you know, oh God. … Tell the Church? Condemned, you know, burn forever" (Heilbroner & Davis, 2011).

> When I freely first confronted it, about being gay, and saying 'This is it,' I broke. … I was with a guy. I broke down crying in his arms, saying, 'I don't want to be this way. This is not the life I want. I'm losing everything that I have, you know. I'm losing what I had known as spirituality; what I had known as society; … [and] what I would know as family, you know. So many things'. … So, yeah, I broke down crying. I didn't feel them; and when they finally helped me feel better, it was a lover-feel that I had, years later. And, I was on one true guilt trip. We were making love … when I said, 'I can't do this anymore.' He said, 'Why is it?' 'We can't have kids.' 'So,' he said, 'Danny.' He goes, 'If I was a woman and I couldn't have children;' … he goes, 'Will the Church marry us?' I said, 'Yeah.' He's like, 'Danny, I can't have kids.' I said, 'Oh, okay.' You know that I also like that's all I have to hear, and then like, [it] cleared up in my mind. (Heilbroner & Davis, 2011)

Garvin admitted that he had exchanged sex for money; but, he failed to describe drug use and other detractive and depressing behaviors (Abracen, Looman, & Langton, 2008; Heilbroner & Davis, 2011). He likely avoided describing them because he felt shame and fear, but not enough to avoid doing them. Perhaps if pressed, he would have bragged about his other deviances.

> The first time ever got paid—there were many times, okay. First time I got paid, . … I was down at 42nd Street, and. … this mess cook said he knew the madam, right? … If you hook me up, right? I was getting paid $30 a month as a mess cook; and I helped to supply my family with income. He told me that I could make extra money by doing this, by hustling. So, I met this guy; put me up to a guy's apartment; had me get undressed; … [and] had me dance. I gotta have no idea how to do this. You know? If you've never danced naked before in front of somebody—I had no idea. He was real impressed that my clothes finally came off; and, he saw my service number, my underwear. [He said,] 'Oh, wow, this is real, real G.I.' … [T]hen, he wanted to give me a bath. He put me in a bathtub; and then he rubbed Nair all over my ass. It started burning, wiping off the hair. … He said, … 'I don't like to [fuck] boys with hair on their ass[es].' 'So, then I went and had sex with him and the madam. They want to play a game called 'Slave or Master.' I had no idea what this was … It was, they flip a coin, and … you say slave or master; and I got master; and I had to tell this guy what to do. I didn't know what to do because I didn't even know what I really liked, you know. I mean, first time a guy kissed me, I gagged. (Heilbroner & Davis, 2011)

His prostitution correlated with activism and eventually an appearance in a documentary about psychopathic political fights. He may, in essence, be a hero for physically expressive psychopaths, who take risks and gain prominence as a result of their flights.

The Internet reveals how communities encourage deviance. Sexual deviance, such as child pornography, is often a communal affair that builds gusto. Legal and illegal forms of deviance may be normal or pathological. Culture is quick to shame communal deviance, for example feederism, a fetish for weight gain, which is bolstered by "nuisance" networking and voyeurism (Brenzinger, 1998, p. 13; Prohaska, 2014). Online communities may correlate with mental psychopathy, but also physical manifestations. One study found a close-knit relationship between early exposure to pornography and likelihood to commit child sexual abuse. Offenders, who had viewed pornography early-on and been sexually abused as children were less likely to be empathetic towards abused children. They were likelier to have higher numbers of child victims. Incarcerated subjects, who had been physically abused as children, experienced reduced empathy for women victims of abuse and had higher numbers of adult victims (Simons, Wurtele, & Heil, 2002). "Over the past decade or so, society has become more conscious of sexual deviance" (Thurston-Snoha, 2012, p. 31). Online awareness becomes a physical problem when physical activities are bragged about online; and when online communities encourage physical actions. Sexually deviant fantasies may be moderated by non-psychopathic individuals (Williams, Cooper, Howell, Yuille, & Paulhus, 2009). However, psychopaths are likelier to act out deviant fantasies especially when they consume increased amounts of pornography.

Attesting to the physiological aspects of psychopathy, sibling studies have found greater correlations for sexual deviance; however, twin studies should be discounted because they rest on the flawed premise that a twin can serve as a genetic control (Carmen M. Cusack, 2016, 2017; Rowe, Rodgers, Meseck-Bushey, & St. John, 1989). Twins' DNA, including mutations experienced through life impacts, is significantly different. Although in general analyses it may be described as "identical" or "mirroring," specifically, many factors influence twins; and, twin studies intentionally overlook these to achieve a phony gold standard of empiricism. Psychopathy may have some genetic explanations (e.g., cerebral abnormalities), but it is a behavior. Under rational choice theory, twin studies are irrelevant; and, unreliable in forensic contexts. Nevertheless, twins and siblings regularly sexually victimize each other. For example, individuals have a greater likelihood of being sexually assaulted by a sister than by a father (Cusack, 2015).

Villains

Sex is villainy (Cewest, 2013; Stallone, 1995). In every sexual union, a person has committed undesirable activities. This conduct is psychopathic because to be in a sexual relationship insinuates that both participants have agreed to permit specified conduct and nothing else; therefore, every sexual transgression is a psychopathic act—callous, narcissistic, deviant, and self-centered. These people unweave the very fabric of society, which is founded on consensual sexual activities. Each transgression is a hostile act against society. It disrespects the norm so blatantly that it violates the law; and therefore, every member of society. Sexual misconduct is psychopathic even when it is not overtly illegal. For example, revenge porn is or ought explicitly to be illegal. Pornography created as part of a private sex act is like an adult toy. Under the right to privacy, there may be no right to create it (i.e., use toys during sex); and therefore, there may be no speech right to disseminate it. Consent granted to create material in the course of sexual conduct is restricted to private acts and does not cause a depicted person to relinquish his or her right to privacy. Consent to use stimulating objects, such as cameras, does not confer a copyright, worldwide distribution license, or a commercial right to distribute depictions of private sex acts. Consent for the erotic content and attendant stimulation is nontransferable. Consent is exclusively granted to the depicter and partner present during the depiction. The act of depicting is private, and any images that result from the private sex act are necessarily bound to remain private unless both parties consent to distribution.

Consent is a minimal standard, not the pinnacle of conversation on the subject of sex—as the law portrays. The law is deficient in this regard because the law seems to suggest that humans only require consent to function appropriately. Yet, deep and profound respect for the other's body—even when conduct is knowingly outrageous or depraved—is required to avoid diseases and remain sexually fertile. These parameters cannot be smothered with consent laws; they must be elucidated by family members, who are willing to stand-up for their children's dignity before they get hurt (Jackson & Wu, 2017).

The term "penumbras and emanations" is a legal term of art used in the Griswold v. Connecticut (1965) to describe the source from which the U.S. Supreme Court derived the existence of a right to privacy. This symbolizes major rights over which political battles are waged (e.g., gay marriage and abortion). The phrase is suspicious with sexist overtones. In the abortion context, it implies a woman hidden behind the significance of her male child (i.e., sun/son). In gay rights, a similar meaning is highly offensive—hiding men and women behind a son. Religious and sexual overtones abound. The Supreme Court's decision to use that phrase was monumental because it opened dicta to exploration and inevitable expansion, which has benefited nearly every group, whether conservative or liberal. However, the phrase also insinuates that Americans live in a patriarchal society, where privacy rights are a mere shadow, hidden behind male figures, who inherit the nation's rights.

Justice William Douglas "suggest[ed] that specific guarantees in the Bill of Rights have penumbras, formed by emanations from those guarantees that help give them life and substance. Various guarantees create zones of privacy" (Griswold v. Connecticut, 1965, p. 484). His explanation for the right to privacy is rooted in sexism, a flimsy veneer formed with secret hopes of ousting women and homosexuals in the foreseeable future. Yet, his phrasing insulates the male patriarchy that would otherwise suffer, had a right to privacy not been created for women. For example, if women had no right to privacy, then men would be responsible for more children. While they oppose the right to abortion, many benefits have arisen for the patriarchy as a result. One benefit may be absent voters and political ousters, who would otherwise oppose conservative coups; yet, cannot because they never existed due to high abortion

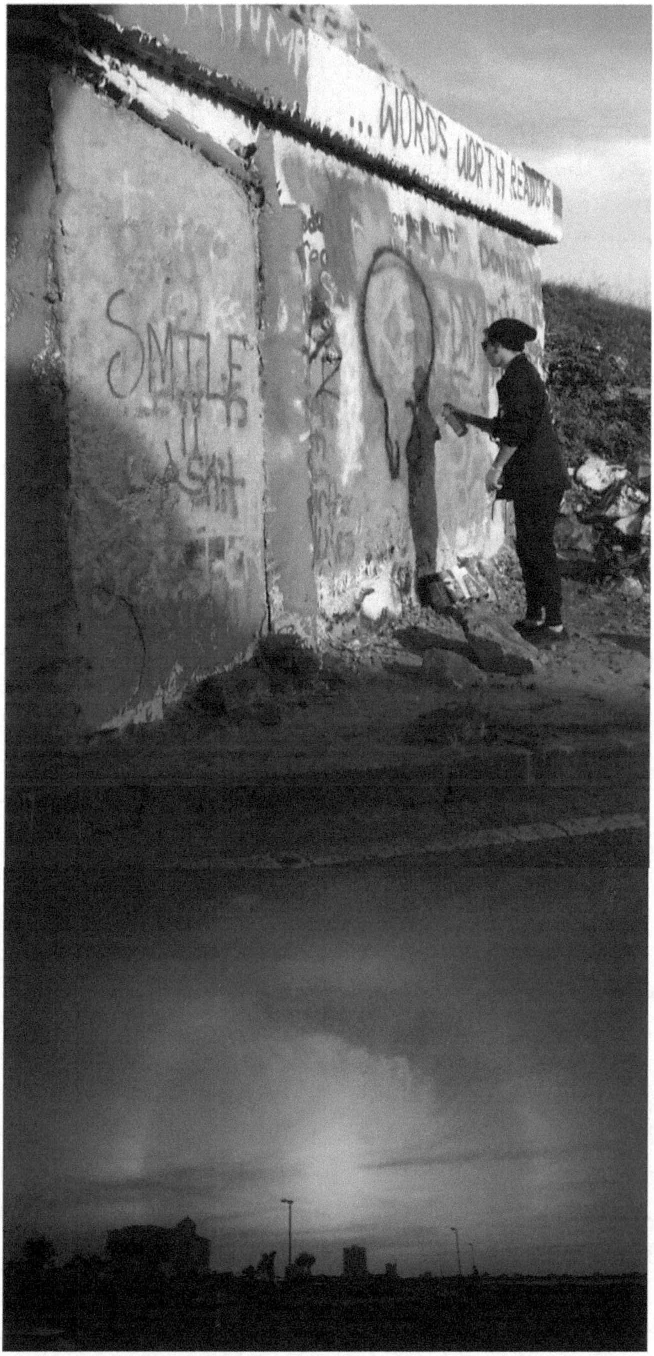

Fig. 4.2: Emanations. Source: Carmen M. Cusack

numbers among liberals. Liberal males, including homosexuals, benefit the patriarchy.

The Justice was known to be a womanizer, who remarried a "young" wife, who he treated like the "help" (Larson, 1978; Ray, 1997, p. 264). "Justice Douglas, one of the most colorful and controversial Justices of this century," was committed to "his loving and devoted mother" (Ray, 1997, p. 201). Several scholars have "candidly note[d] Douglas' performance as an indifferent husband and neglectful father without attempting to reconcile these personal failings with his self-proclaimed commitment to helping people resolve" injustices committed against women by the government (Ray, 1997, p. 202). His symbolism was libertarian, at best; and at worst, the nefarious Justice was rife with contradiction to be remembered by scholars, who analyze his words.

In his holding, Justice Douglas found that "marriage is coming together" (Griswold v. Connecticut, 1965, p. 486). His thrust was about male orgasm, not female abortion; and protecting the indiscriminate male's right to villainize sex at his whim. "Justice Douglas was repulsed by the idea that ... the marital bedroom" could have any meaning worth protecting beyond procreative results and husbands' attendant agony (Fitzgerald, 1997). Douglas fathomed marriage to equate with "bilateral loyalty" to men that squashed women's natural and "political" duties to societal improvement through "social projects" (Griswold v. Connecticut, 1965, p. 486). He envisioned marriage as a realm where men were served and women serviced men, who could make mistakes paid by women.

Early on, Justice Douglas "was originally uncertain about grounding the *Griswold* holding in a right to privacy, buttressed by domestic metaphors. In a draft ..., Justice Douglas founded the ... holding on a First Amendment right of spouses to associate freely" (Dolgin, 1994, pp. 1542–1543; Griswold v. Connecticut, 1965). "Douglas would have suggested the spouses' freedom in associating with the other, a subspecies of individual rights, rather than the collective privacy of a family unit" (Dolgin, 1994, p. 1543). Individualization of the right was a "reactive strategy," which "attracts a great deal of ridicule" (Luban, 1999, pp. 19, 28). The theory correlates with Platonic cave-dwelling individuals, who look to the sun for guidance, an obvious metaphor for penises demolishing the privacy of vaginas.

Villains, like Justice Douglas, may be do-gooders. For example, People for the Ethical Treatment of Animals (PETA) is rife with people willing to get naked, steal, lie, cheat, run from captors, and denounce all of civilization in favor of animals (Cusack, 2003). Their reputations as fanatical animal lovers precede and mar them. Many must cleanse their *vitae* before scouting post-PETA employment so that they can even get a foot in the door. Do-gooders include soccer moms, who refuse to stop being chipper despite teammate entropy and resignation; and those, who will do anything, really any thing, for their teams' success. They mean well, and that is what causes them to suspiciously be viewed by others. They are psychopaths because they slough-off norms in favor of radical behavior that is self-serving, and yet drives public opinion and motivates them to achieve greatness.

References

Abracen, J., Looman, J., & Langton, C. M. (2008). Treatment of sexual offenders with psychopathic traits. *Trauma, Violence & Abuse*, 9(3), 144–166.

American Psychiatric Association (APA). (2013). *Desk reference to the diagnostic criteria from dsm-5*. Washington, D.C.: American Psychiatric Publishing.

Bourke, M. L. (2013). Conversation with Michael L. Bourke, Chief Psychologist for the United States Marshals Service (USMS) Behavioral Analysis Unit in the National Sex Offender Targeting Center. Nova Southeastern University, Fort Lauderdale, FL.

Brenzinger, M. A. (1998). Voyeurism: A harmless erotic preference or a sexual predator in the making? *Crime & Justice International*, *14*(21), 13–14+.

Cewest. (2013, November 8). Four PPD officers retire. *PensacolaPolice.com*. Retrieved from http://www.pensacolapolice.com.php56-5.ord1-1.websitetestlink.com/page/15/

Chin, W. Y. (2013). Law and order and white power: White supremacist infiltration of law enforcement and the need to eliminate racism in the ranks. *Journal of Law & Social Deviance*, 6, 30–98.

Cusack, C. (2003). Discussion about her conversation with Donna Karan inside her home regarding use of fur in fashion designs. People for the Ethical Treatment of Animals (PETA), New York, NY.

Cusack, C. M. (2013a). How the content of online pornography depicts expressed consent for insemination. *Online Journal of Communication & Media Technology (OJCMT)*, 3, 91.

Cusack, C. M. (2013b). Irish in the criminal justice system. *Journal of Law & Social Deviance*, 6, 1.

Cusack, C. M. (2013c). Kent make-up their minds: Juveniles, mental illness, and the need for continued implementation of therapeutic justice within the juvenile justice and criminal justice systems. *American University Journal of Gender, Social Policy, & Law*, *22*, 149–165.

Cusack, C. M. (2014). *Pornography and the criminal justice system*. Boca Raton, FL: CRC Press.

Cusack, C. M. (2015). *Criminal justice handbook on masculinity, male aggression, and sexuality*. Springfield, IL: Charles C. Thomas.

Cusack, C. M. (2016). *Twins and deviance: Law, crime, sex, society, and family*. Cambridge, UK: Cambridge Scholars Publishing.

Cusack, C. M. (2017). Double glazed: Reflection, narcissism, and Freudian implications in twincest pornography. *Journal of Law & Social Deviance, 13*, 1–67.

Cusack, J. (2017). *Blood money*. USA: Porthos Films.

Davis, F. (1959, September). The cabdriver and his fare: Facets of a fleeting relationship. *American Journal of Sociology*, 65(2), 158–165.

Dolgin, J. L. (1994). The family in transition: From Griswold to Eisenstadt and beyond. *Georgetown Law Journal*, 82, 1519.

Fitzgerald, D. L. (1997). Let justice flow like water: The role of moral argument in constitutional interpretation. *Fordham Law Review*, 65, 2103.

Frey, A. (2009). Conversation with Ami Frey, Esq. Jacobs Keeley Trial Lawyers. Miami, FL.

Gill, H. (2007). *Milind Soman made me gay*. Frameline.

Griswold v. Connecticut, 381 U.S. 479 (1965).

Ha, N. (2015). Detecting and teaching desire: Phallometry, Freund, and behaviorist sexology. *Osiris*, 30, 205–227.

Heilbroner, D. & Davis, K. (2011). *Stonewall uprising* [Video file]. WGBH Educational Foundation.

Jackson, F. J., & Wu, E. Y. (2017). From theory to practice: Using the gender-sensitive tracking and monitoring system—GTMS. *Journal of Law & Social Deviance, 14*, 91–134.

Jaeckin, J. (1975). *The story of* O. Toronto, CA: Somerville House.

Katz, J. (2016, January 4). 2 Live Crew rapper won't let his kids see 'Star Wars' because George Lucas sued him. *Billboard*. Retrieved from http://www.billboard.com/articles/news/6828928/2-live-crew-rapper-protest-star-wars-george-lucas-sued

Larson, G. A. (1978). *Battlestar galactica*. Universal City, CA: Universal Television.

Luban, D. (1999). The Warren Court and the concept of a right. *Harvard Civil Rights-Civil Liberties Law Review*, 34, 7.

Murphy, J. G. (1972, July). Moral death: A Kantian essay on psychopathy. *Ethics*, 82(4), 284–298.

Packer, S. (2009). *Superheroes and superegos: Analyzing the minds behind the masks*. New York, NY: ABC-CLIO.

Pasko, L. (2010). Damaged daughters: The history of girls' sexuality and the juvenile justice system. *Journal of Criminal Law & Criminology*, 100(3), 1099–1130.

Perry, K. (2014, February 20). Katy Perry—Dark horse (official) ft. Juicy J. KatyPerryVEVO. Retrieved from https://www.youtube.com/watch?v=0KSOMA3QBU0

Perry, K. (2017). A tiger snake terrifies Katy Perry. *Sunrise*. Retrieved from https://thewest.com.au/news/7-news/a-tiger-snake-terrifies-katy-perry-bc-5490846093001

Prohaska, A. (2014). Help me get fat! Feederism as communal deviance on the internet. *Deviant Behavior*, 35(4), 263.

Ray, L. K. (1997). Douglas, the libertarian symbol, that he wanted the public to remember. *Arizona Law Review Spring*, 39, 151.

Relle, J. (2017, August). Conversation with Joe Relle. Base NOLA, New Orleans East, LA.

Rice, M. E., Harris, G. T., Lang, C., & Chaplin, T. C. (2012). Adolescents who have sexually offended: Is phallometry valid? *Sexual Abuse*, 24(2), 133.

Rowe, D. C., Rodgers, J. L., Meseck-Bushey, S., & St. John, C. (1989). Sexual behavior and nonsexual deviance: A sibling study of their relationship. *Developmental Psychology, 25*(1), 61–69.

Sibila, C. E. (2015, April 22). Factors affecting intent to persist among Hispanic/Latino students attending a private non-profit nonresidential university. University of Miami. Retrieved from http://scholarlyrepository.miami.edu/cgi/viewcontent.cgi?article=2399&context=oa_dissertations

Simons, D., Wurtele, S. K., & Heil, P. (2002). Childhood victimization and lack of empathy as predictors of sexual offending against women and children. *Journal of Interpersonal Violence, 17*(12), 1291–1307.

Stallone, S. (1995). *Judge Dredd*. Santa Monica, CA: Cinergi Pictures Entertainment.

Swanton, F. (2017). The supervised offender's quandary: Modifying conditions of supervised release for legality with 18 U.S.C. § 3583(e)(2). *Journal of Law & Social Deviance, 14*, 135–221.

Thurston-Snoha, B. (2012). Context-specific sexual deviance. *American Jails, 26*(4), 31–34.

Walter, D. (2012, December 27). Conversation with Professor David Walter, M.A., Esq. Florida International University, Miami, FL.

Weinstein, L. A. (2013). *Call it rape: Sexual assaults against women in Ireland since 1945* (Order No. 3594731). Available at PsychNet.

Williams, K. M., Cooper, B. S., Howell, T. M., Yuille, J. C., & Paulhus, D. L. (2009). Inferring sexually deviant behavior from corresponding fantasies. *Criminal Justice & Behavior, 36*(2), 198–222.

Wilson, A. (2003). Sexing the hyena: Intraspecies readings of the female phallus. *Signs: Journal of Women in Culture & Society, 28*(3), 755–790.

· 5 ·

G-WORD

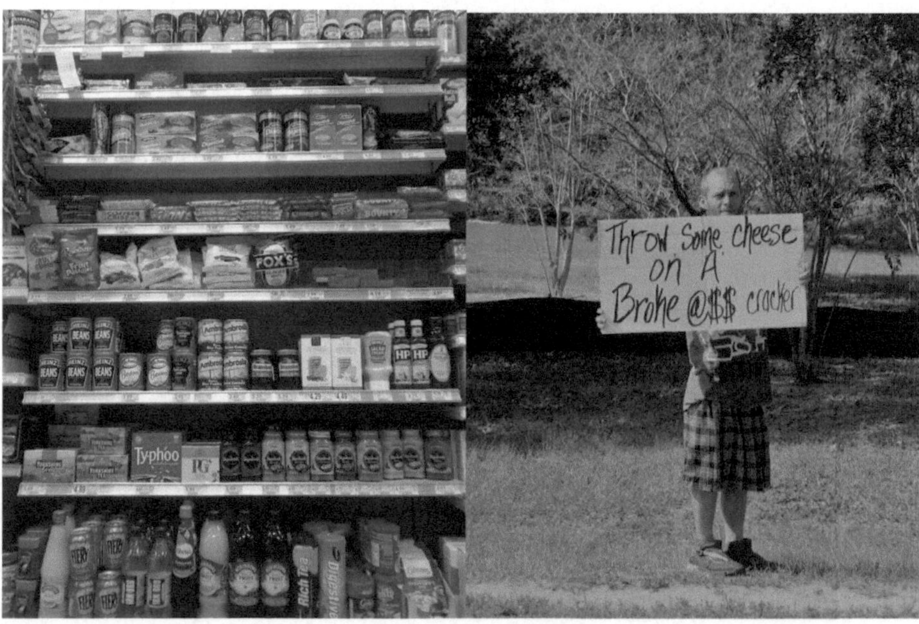

Fig. 5.1: Crackers. White Male. British and Indian Food. Source: Carmen M. Cusack

Gay

The word "gay" originally meant "jolly." The mutation from "jolly" to "homosexual" demonstrates America's saddening. An entire word was lost or transformed; and one less word means "happy." Development of the word is no different from other terms, such as "cracker" or "cookie," which change in meaning as times develop new edges. A "cracker" was like a "cookie," two foods (Silverman, 2017). A "cracker" came to symbolize slave-drivers, boss men, and police. It is a racial slur and self-deprecating term for White people (Lovelidge, 2012). A "cookie" became a method for locating people on the Internet. Both took authoritative turns for the worse (Lemieux, 2010).

Gayness has always been couched inside of jovialness on television. This way, men and women could disguise homosexuality as a facet of the entertainment industry. The television show, *Orange Is the New Black*, season five, episode four brings this to life in a flashback when a lesbian character discusses the work of Debbie Reynolds in the context of heteronormativity, morals, and women (Manning, 2013). Nature Scouts in the 1960s are learning to sew. Frieda lives alone in a survival bunker with her Nazi-obsessed father. She is capable of surviving without his assistance or care.

Leader:	Now, you want to choose the gayest handkerchief you can find since this will serve as your doll's head. I'll choose apple blossom pink for my demonstration.
Nature Scout 1:	I'm going to give my doll bangs like Debbie Reynolds.
Nature Scout 2:	My mom says she can't watch her movies anymore, now that she gave her lady gift to Eddie Fisher.
Leader:	Now, this might not look as tricky as the Indian Lore Badge or the Backyard Chef, but the Hobby Fun badge has eluded many a-sloppy girl.
Nature Scout 1:	Did you hear that Frieda? Finally, a badge you won't get.
Frieda:	You callin' me sloppy?
Nature Scout 1:	And smelly. Also smelly.
Frieda:	It's the beaver musk I put around my neck.
Nature Scout 1:	Well it smells like a monkey butt.

Frieda:	Technically, it does come from the anal glands, which makes it very helpful when you want to attract deer.
Nature Scout 2:	Attract deer? Are you gonna marry them?
Frieda:	I'm gonna shoot them.
Nature Scout 2:	You were right. She is an alien from outer space.
Frieda:	Do you know the Nature Scout motto?
Nature Scout 1:	'Ready for any and all things.'
Frieda:	Do you know what it means? What if your mom went away one day, and there were no more finger sandwiches? What if the sky went dark and all of the crops died? Would you know which plants were safe to eat and which ones would make you vomit 'till you're dead? Could you kill an animal and clean it without cutting the intestines? Could you take its skin, and salt it, and tan it to keep warm; or would you sit in the corner with your doll and wait to die? (Manning, 2013)

Frieda directs her attention to the scout leader and says, "I'll take a piece of that green gingham over there, thank you" (Manning, 2013). The show parodies 1960s attitudes, which explicate how the word "gay" came to symbolize happiness and homosexuality.

Sia's music brings to the forefront a nexus between homosexuality and *joie de vivre*. Her songs "You're Never Fully Dressed without a Smile" and "Chandelier" featuring Quvenzhané Wallis and Maddie Ziegler, respectively, reminisce about times when groups of children could socialize and express neutral feelings (Wallis, 2014; Ziegler, 2014). Gayness is their attitude, intrinsic in their spirits. Children may have "pal[s]," who are four-legged, "three-legged," two-legged, one-legged, or no-legged (Fitzpatrick, 1995; Kregloeon, 2008, p. 2). They may be homosexual, bisexual, transsexual, heterosexual, or something other than those classes of people; they may be male and/or female; and a boyfriend or a girlfriend. Sia's lifestyle defies these boundaries. She has described a love affair with a woman as a hetero/homosexual relationship with her "boyfriend" (Kregloeon, 2008, p. 1). Her music video for "You're Never Fully Dressed without a Smile" depicts a young Black woman, whose immature body is described by society as a "child" (Wallis, 2014). Her spirit is contagious, and she infects New York City with upliftment. Ziegler's video is distinctly depressive. She represents abused children, who overcome neglect and abandonment through dance and artistic expression. Ziegler's tone is gay despite her loss of parental guidance and mistreatment. Alicia Keys' song, "Empire State of Mind (Part II) Broken Down," played off her duet with Jay-Z (2009), effeminately embodies both spirits of children in New York—the haves and the have nots (Keys, 2009). Keys says, "Even if it ain't all it seems, I got a pocket full of dreams" (Keys, 2009). This is true of both sides; and is relevant in class warfare; sex supremacy; male mating rituals; female downgrading; and child stymying. Gayness is a relief in the face of these contemplations (Killam, 2017).

Gay

Homosexuals are the most threatened form of human perception. Homosexuality is not purely sexual; it is more robust (Martin, 2015). What mainstream observers have reduced to a few sentences about sex (e.g., "queer identity is …") delimits and bruises what homosexual emboldening attempted to fathom. A world without gays is a sad world, in deed; but new definitions of "homosexuality" (i.e., "husband" or "wife") are retrogressive (Monroe, 1955). The word "gay" continues to embody the free spirit held and harvested by homosexuals throughout the 1970s and 1980s. Their churning guts were displayed before higher courts throughout the past three decades slowly enlightening the public and whitewashing the cheekiness and sensuality of the fun that they pioneered throughout the 1950s and 1960s. The homosexual movement is not new. It has waged two fronts: the closeted underbelly that represents dark and erotic possibilities, against the political gravitas that gets results unwanted by the mainstream, now reverently passed along to the homosexuals (AP, 2014, 2015; Brady, 2015; Breen, 2016; CHIP, n.d.; Democratic Underground, 2014; DiCaprio, 1996; Fortune Cookie Message, n.d.; Lin, 2001; Pierce, 1991). Homosexuality is no longer "gay" (Cusick, 1998).

Gayness is no longer iconic, but diluted. Jaqueline Onassis quintessentially defined her husband's immense power by performing acts with her sister that appeared to be lesbionic (D.C. v. Heller, 2008, p. 652; Super Star Gossip, 2006). Yet, they are not recognized openly by the new rights-entitled homosexual community because they are tethered so closely to closeted men and women's beloved secret identity, which gave them strength. Closetedness is a strength, not weakness as portrayed by people, who would take diverse roles from men and women to rebuke them. By forcing little children, for example, into special clubs at school, rather than allowing them to slither through recesses and down shadowy corridors, the "tolerant" mainstream agenda has stricken children with light, and totally locked them out of safehouses in the midst of a tornado (i.e., the mainstream) (Lahr, 1939).

One reason that iconism has perished for the homosexual movement is that bars, which were previously clandestine, became exposed, and therefore mixed with heterosexuals. Prior to that however, they were violently targeted. John O'Brien, a homosexual, who was intimately gathered at Stonewall on the night of the riots, explained that gay bars were the lifeblood.

> Well, gay bars were the social centers of gay lives. Gay bars were to gay people, what churches were to Blacks in the South. It was the only place where we could go; be with our own kind; be ourselves; and they were social centers. I mean if you needed a job, you go to a bar and talk to people in some way . . . . 'Oh yeah, my company's hiring come here.' If you needed a place to live, 'Oh, yeah, there's an apartment in the building. Come and see my landlord.' That's where you met your friends, you know? ... It was the center of your life. (Heilbroner & Davis, 2011)

Political groups became a place other than bars to meet potential mates.

> A lesbian named Martha Shelley explained the assimilation.
>
> Why [our political group] wore the jackets and ties and blouses was, we were trying to show the world that we were ordinary normal citizens like anybody else with just this slight difference like being left-handed instead of right-handed. I didn't believe it for a second, not about other gay people, I mean. There were plenty of gay people, who were kind of like that, who wanted so much to be like that. They wanted to be, to have the house with the white picket fence; and the good job; and fit into American Society, the way it was. I had become very radicalized in that time. I no longer believed in that system. I believed in that the system had to be changed drastically; and that the American Society ways always 'fail.' It had become very clear at that point that no matter how hard Black people tried to be nice, there were an awful lot of White people that weren't gonna let it happen. It was only by being less than nice, that by pushing hard, by being really who we were, whether they were being Black people, who they were, that we were gonna get anywhere in this world: Black people, gay people, women, too. Certainly, being nice has women got us nothing, but more dirty diapers. (Heilbroner & Davis, 2011)

Politics were closeted before riots changed the way that homosexuals viewed socializing.

Danny Garvin, a homosexual involved in gay nightlife and rioting, explained how gays were deprived of their happy moniker by use of bigoted epithets. When "I was growing up," people used "cocksucker" and "faggot"

(Heilbroner & Davis, 2011). "Oh, he's a motherfucking cocksucker. He is a faggot. He is sissy, queer. … 'Queer' was very big. 'Homo,' 'homo' was big. My last name being Garvin, I'll be called 'Danny Gayvin.' … Little things like that … dug in" (Heilbroner & Davis, 2011). "'Nancy boy'—the 'Nancy boy' is more of an Irish term or an English term. … There was always 'real Nancy boy.' You wouldn't hear that in the States because my father being from Ireland. … 'That Nancy boy' is it, an English and Irish expression" (Heilbroner & Davis, 2011). "Gay" and "faggot have different meanings, okay. 'Faggot' could be 'gay' or 'Hey faggot, you gotta go home.' … 'Queer.' 'Queer' was 'queer,' you know? 'Faggot' could go either way. 'Cocksucker' could be either an anger or 'cocksucker' could be 'gay.' So, it could take either side. It's like 'gay.' It'll be 'gay.' It'll be 'homosexual.' You be 'gay' and just be happy" (Heilbroner & Davis, 2011).

Gays began self-referring to disguise their homosexuality. Lingo made conversations difficult. For example, "Why aren't we around the corner, with all—in that new bar—with all the chicken" (Heilbroner & Davis, 2011)? Garvin said, "I didn't know what chicken meant" (Heilbroner & Davis, 2011).

> When you're coming out; and you're new; and you're gay, it's so confusing because it's a whole different language. … I did infiltrate, and I didn't know what that meant, all right. He's a chicken and I was getting so confused: … the pronunciation, 'with me,' him being called 'her' and 'she.' … I couldn't follow conversations. Or, 'he dropped a hairpin,' you know; or 'are you a friend of Judy's,' you know. Sort of all these … all different … all whole different. A are you butch; are you fem? You know, are you top; are you a bottom? … A whole different language you have to learn coming out. It's kind of dying out now, which is kind of sad. (Heilbroner & Davis, 2011)

Garvin's sadness over loss of clear homosexual fun is quintessentially definitive of the status of homosexuality in America.

Gay

A hateful usage of the word "gay" has evolved recently; and yet, it is not associated with the gay movement or closeted homosexuals. Its meaning is similar to "scallywag" or "boring." It shows disapproval and attention to an issue. It transforms "gay," like the transformation of the word "bad" or pejoration of the phrase, "You want a cookie" (COUNTrecount, 2009; Rock, 1996)? Yet, symbolically it represents hatred for gay people because of the phonetic similarity between "gay" and "gay." Some people intentionally conflate the two meanings to be sensational and attention-grabbing.

Full House was a show about three men living together (Saget, 1987). Two were portrayed as friends and one was a brother-in-law, whose wife was deceased. The deceased wife left behind an infant, two older daughters, and a golden retriever (Englishmajorrebound, 2015; Stamos, 2016). Ashley and Mary-Kate Olsen reinvented Cindy Brady, played by Susan Olsen, on the show *The Brady Bunch* (Olsen, 1974; Saget, 1987). Their portrayal was "rude" and sassy unlike Cindy, who may have been a bit sneaky, but was altogether innocent and naïve (Saget, 1987). Like Mary-Kate twisting Michelle Tanner, the Cindy Brady of the 1990s, into an altogether unlovable character, who ditched New York University for a bohemian series of appearances toting Starbucks coffee; and like her sister Ashley steamrolling Tanner's cuteness by wearing oversized men's clothes to fashion week; Susan insulted the dignity and vestige of sane American home-life (e.g., smiling stepchildren, a maid, and a dog) by ranting about queer politics on the Internet (Celebrity, 2009; Elizabeth and James, n.d.). She disguised her disgust for the homosexual agenda by using slurs in a fashion that associated homosexuality with the word "faggot" (Wright, 2016). Although the word had meant "gay" in many circles and for many years, it is no longer restricted to such use. Similarly, the word "gay" meaning "lackluster" or "uninviting" does not mean "homosexual" exclusively as it once did (e.g., 1970s–2000s). However, to hatefully use these words in anti-homosexual contexts resurrects restrictive definitions and encumbering perspectives that society has moved beyond. Perhaps, in some sense, use of these words, which are now homophones rather than double *entendres* or slurs, demonstrates a post-bigotry vocabulary.

The word "gay," therefore, is a mutation because it symbolizes being at peace with one's negative opinions. To use the word diminutively or insultingly to accost physically present or conjured homosexuals is to demonstrate discomfort with one's own opinion. Using the word with a clear objective to mock or put-down the topic or object elicits respect. It could showcase confidence and comfort with the gay community.

References

Associated Press (AP). (2014, March 4). Karl Lagerfeld takes you to Chanel's supermarket. Retrieved from https://www.youtube.com/watch?v=olQKa8RqVTg

Associated Press (AP). (2015, January 4). Photos of Sarah Palin's son standing on dog stir debate whether it was animal abuse. *Nola.com*. Retrieved from http://www.nola.com/news/index.ssf/2015/01/photos_of_sarah_palins_son_sta.html

Brady, K. (2015, December 18). Slang words for vagina ranked from bad to worst. *She Knows*. Retrieved from http://www.sheknows.com/love-and-sex/articles/1086904/slang-words-for-vagina

Breen, M. (2016, July 25). #Winner. *The Advocate*. Retrieved from https://www.advocate.com/current-issue/2016/7/25/hillary-clinton-president

Celebrity. (2009, August 19). Mary-Kate works out her muscles before bartending time. *PopSugar*. Retrieved from https://www.popsugar.com/celebrity/Photos-Mary-Kate-Olsen-After-Yoga-NYC-She-Set-Bartend-Fashion-Night-Out-During-New-York-Fashion-Week-4193572

Children's Health Insurance Program (CHIP). (n.d.). *Healthcare.gov*. Retrieved from https://www.healthcare.gov/medicaid-chip/childrens-health-insurance-program/

COUNTrecount. (2009, June 8). Nagin quarantined in China amid h1n1 case quarantined after Chinese business trip. *Free Republic*. Retrieved from http://www.freerepublic.com/focus/f-news/2267323/posts

Cusick, K. (1998). *Rent*. Chicago, IL.

Democratic Underground. (2014, July 24). Ellen DeGeneres' picture of a kid standing on a dog could end it for her? Retrieved from https://www.democraticunderground.com/10026040154

DiCaprio, L. (1996). *Romeo + Juliet*. USA: Bazmark Films.

District of Columbia v. Heller, 554 U.S. 570 (2008).

Elizabeth and James. (n.d.). Los Angeles, CA. Retrieved from http://www.elizabethandjames.us/the-store

Englishmajorrebound. (2015, August 5). Becky's escape. *FanFiction*. Retrieved from https://www.fanfiction.net/s/11428707/1/Becky-s-Escape

Fitzpatrick, L. (1995). *Kids*. USA: Guys Upstairs. Retrieved from https://www.youtube.com/watch?v=wCDjWk7str4

Fortune Cookie Message. (n.d.). Retrieved from http://www.fortunecookiemessage.com/

Heilbroner, D., & Davis, K. (2011). *Stonewall uprising* [Video file]. WGBH Educational Foundation.

Jay-Z. (2009). *Empire state of mind*. New York, NY: Roc the Mic Studios.

Keys, A. (2009). Empire state of mind (part ii) broken down. On *The element of freedom*. New York, NY: Oven Studios.

Killam, T. (2017). *Killing Gunther*. USA: StarStream Media.

Kregloeon, K. (2008, February 10). Sia's coming out. *After Ellen*. Retrieved from http://www.afterellen.com/people/29001-sias-coming-out/2

Lahr, B. (1939). *The wizard of oz*. Beverly Hills, CA: Metro-Goldwyn-Mayer (MGM).

Lemieux, E. (2010, May 7). The tick vs. the breadmaster part 1. *The Tick*. Retrieved from https://www.youtube.com/watch?v=U8JZSKTAJfA

Lin, D. (2001). The master's tea cup. *Tao Living*. Retrieved from http://taoism.net/living/2001/200105.htm

Lovelidge, E. (2012, December 4). V-Nasty and Kreayshawn beef on twitter. *SF Station*. Retrieved from https://www.sfstation.com/2012/12/04/v-nasty-vs-kreayshawn-war-of-words-on-twitter/

Manning, T. (2013). *Orange is the new black*. Los Gatos, CA: Netflix.

Martin, R. (2015). Disparo al corazón. On A *quien quiera escuchar*. Miami, FL: Sony Music Latin.

Monroe, M. (1955). *The seven year itch*. Los Angeles, CA: Twentieth Century Fox Film Corporation.

Olsen, S. (1974). *The Brady bunch*. Hollywood, CA: Paramount Pictures.

Pierce, B. (1991). *Beauty and the beast*. Burbank, CA: Walt Disney Pictures.

Rock, C. (1996). *Bring the pain*. HBO. Washington, D.C.: Takoma Theater.

Saget, B. (1987). *Full house*. USA: Lorimar Telepictures.

Silverman, S. (2017). A *speck of dust*. Netflix.

Stamos, J. (2016). *Fuller house*. Beverly Hills, CA: Jeff Franklin Productions.

Super Star Gossip. (2006, December 12). Paris Hilton and sister Nikki will do anything for the camera. Retrieved from http://superstargossip.com/2006/12/12/paris-nikki-hilton-playboy-masion-limo-photos/

Wallis, Q. (2014, November 20). You're never fully dressed without a smile. *Annie*. Retrieved from https://www.youtube.com/watch?v=CNeOQPVyU08

Wright, T. (2016, December 11). Brady Bunch's Susan Olsen was fired from her radio show after a homophobic rant. *Vulture*. Retrieved from http://www.vulture.com/2016/12/susan-olsen-fired-from-radio-show-for-homophobia.html

Ziegler, M. (2014). Chandelier. *SiaVevo*. Retrieved from https://www.youtube.com/watch?v=2vjPBrBU-TM

· 6 ·

REDHEADS

Mary Jane

Mary Jane is an atypical redhead because she is grotesquely misshapen. Many redheads have formidable figures and bear the graces of a fine form. Mary Jane's anatomical exaggerations spurn her redheadedness. However, she has a fine figure and form insofar as they convey her emotions and relationship to Spider-Man. Mary Jane is neither cute nor docile, and yet exhibits submission to Spider-Man's mission. This point should not be buried. She is dignified; and yet, nymphish. Her looks are only a portion of her total persona; however, her love interest is mainly focused on her appearance, which is abnormal and bizarre.

In *Turn Off the Dark: Spider-Man*, Mary Jane is a mutant because she is in love with a man whose alter ego really exhibits a mutation. Other "approving" women merely fantasize about men, who have super qualities (Kozlovic, 2016, p. 23; Luke 3:22; Mark 1:10; Matthew 3:16). In the Broadway musical, "people hate spiders"—not her—"but everyone else" (Bono & The Edge, 2010). Mary Jane, called M.J., flows into his world because he is a "weaver, who wove" her love into fine strands and manufactured a relationship (Bono & The Edge, 2010). The subplot of how Spider-Man came into existence suggests females are destructive and instigate remorsefulness. This theme consoles audience members, who fear for Mary Jane's dignity and safety. The musical graphically depicts a hanging. The production, including rehearsals, was terrorized by accidents and injuries. The scene retrospectively was an homage to the refinement that the actors experienced throughout the production.

Paul Simon commiserated with the musical's original director because the show required revisions and suffered financial losses, like *The Capeman* (Bono & The Edge, 2010; Gundersen, 2011). Simon wrote the biographical musical, *The Capeman* (Simon & Walcott, 1998). The show was about a Puerto Rican member of two New York gangs, Mau Maus and Vampires, who wore a cape when he killed two innocent men confused by The Capeman as being rival gang members (Estrada, 1970, 1983; Simon & Walcott, 1998). His acknowledgment of the show demonstrated a mutation in culture. The former member of the duo, Simon and Garfunkel, praised director Julie Taymor's genius, but expressed that he had not been privy to the music, written by U2 band members, prior to the show's opening. This statement caused audience members to view Simon's power to attract favoritism as being a thing of the past. His musical persuaded experts in his field to nominate *The Capeman* for awards, but his show's authority in the field of musical theater lapsed several decades prior to the release of *Spider-Man* (Bono & The Edge, 2010; Gundersen, 2011; Simon & Walcott, 1998). His musical and the show by U2 members possess affinities for pop culture; for example, both plays depict males as gang members and females as supreme figures correlating with divinity. Simon's character, surrounded by Pentecostal Christians, sings, "No matter if I stumble, I know that I'll obey;" "my soul belongs to thee" (Simon & Walcott, 1998). The imagery suggests Maria from *West Side Story* (Bean, 1961). Mary Jane is a "wimp" because she "is smarter than" her "papa," but he bullies her (Bean, 1961; Bono & The Edge, 2010). She tries to "rise above it," but instead falls into love with Peter Parker, another male, who replaces her father (Bono & The Edge, 2010). He is also bullied, so she feels superior to him. Churches, families, and gangs are "radical groups" in which people "keep fighting" "motherfuckers" (Simon, & Walcott, 1998).

The music by Bono and The Edge copies Danny Elfman (Depp, 1984, 1990). It synergizes genres, spooky and pop; but, fails to make use of their talent, which they were undoubtedly hired to document in this production. They also seem to incorporate rock and roll acts, such as Veruca Salt (1994). The set and blocking reflect obsession with Mark McGrath; for example, the number "Bouncing off the Walls" replicates Sugar Ray's "Fly" video (Bono & The Edge, 2010; Jackson & Jackson, 1995; Jamiroquai, 1996; Sugar Ray, 1997).

Mary Jane is pressured by an older female to marry Peter Parker after high school (Bono & The Edge). The older woman, Aunt May, who is "always" going to be [his] "best girl," meets her "friend, Maria, for a bite" (Bono & The Edge, 2010). Effectively she and smooth Spider-Man bite Mary Jane with their dialogue. "Tiger" is Mary Jane's "celebrity crush," but she chooses to love him deeply (Bono & The Edge, 2010). "I guess we're all scared of something" (Bono & The Edge, 2010). M. J. 's "future looks pretty blurry to" her; but, Parker "knows" (Bono & The Edge, 2010). The power imbalance is sexist; yet, M. J. seems shrewdly to hide her feelings. She may be supposing that true love is her destiny. Mary Jane must "mutate or die" (Bono & The Edge, 2010).

Vivien Leigh

Vivien Leigh appears in *A Streetcar Named Desire* (Highsmith, 1980; Leigh, 1951). She portrays a blonde, who is raped. The portrayal is distinct from her portrayal of a redhead, Scarlett O'Hara, who is raped in *Gone with the Wind* (Leigh, 1939). Brunette Leigh intentionally infuses each film with portraits of each hair color and captivates her fellow cast members so that they too resonate with her characters' hair color. As Blanche, Leigh appears to be harmless and in desire of more food; but, she is well-fed. "Desire" is streetcar number 922, which she takes to see her sister and her sister's husband, Stella and Stanley, who live in New Orleans, Louisiana's French Quarter. When she gets off the car, she sees signs for billiards, bowling, and "Girls" (Leigh, 1951). Skeletal women with more meat than her are dressed in party clothes and act casually. Stella is a bull in a china shop. Stanley is oblivious and densely undereducated. He rapes Blanche to please Stella. He can barely differentiate between the women. Blanche's heart charm necklace bears a single rhinestone. It signifies a mystery—a loved one's presence; but, it is empty and cannot be opened. Blanche loses her home and feels blamed by Stella. Stanley's butt cheeks appear to be those of a homosexual. Blanche thinks he is easily approachable to take and manipulate. Blanche is disgusted because he has her sister's hips and cupidity (Manson, 2015). Recitation of the Napoleonic Code by Stanley supplants Stella's lust with avarice so that he separates Blanche from Stella and rapes her. Rhinestone is "next door to glass" (Leigh, 1951). He rapes the neighbor for the same reason. The women are migrant country-girls, and therein lie their family values. Stella thinks Stanley will rape her to carry on their family incest. Stella likes women. Blanche is the victim. Her fiancé killed himself to avoid their social disease. Stella's baby will be conscripted, like soldier Stanley, into their misfortune. He "shut" "up" "the glamourous type" "like a clam," a triple entendre. She overcomes the abusive Stanley, and she is a superhero.

Scarlett O'Hara is made-love-to forcibly against her will (Leigh, 1939). She is not "raped" (i.e., penetration however slight) (Cusack, 2015). Redheaded Scarlett is half-Irish (i.e., O'Hara). This feeds from the myth that Irishmen are redheads, when most are blonde or brunette. Approximately only five percent of the Irish population is redheaded (Kastel, 1952). Scarlett is feline. She shares a name with *The Scarlet Letter* dealing with victim blaming and secret lovers (Hawthorne, 1850). She appears to have brown hair, but has dark red hair. Scarlett may contrast with slaves, who have freedom and ease from bills, paychecks, and debts on property owned by landowners. As long as they do not leave the property to places where they do not have rights, then they have total protection and provision on their land. If they do commit crimes off-property, then unlike Whites, landowners could immunize them by taking responsibility. Mammy yanks on Scarlett like an old high-top shoe. Her love interest, Ashley Wilkes, marries his cousin Melanie Hamilton rather than Scarlett, who pursues him. Ashley slays Melanie with his lust for Scarlett. In retaliation, to match his feelings, he rapes her. Scarlett is pegged as a "beau" stealer, but wants Ashley (Leigh, 1939). She flirts.

Rhett Butler is played by a Great White shark, Clark Gable (Leigh, 1939). He is "one of the best shots in the country … He's proved a number of times, against steadier hands and cooler heads" (Leigh, 1939). "Sir, you are no gentleman;" "and you miss are no lady" (Leigh, 1939). Rhett challenges her "passion for living" (Leigh, 1939). In anger, she accepts a proposal from Melanie's brother, Ashley's cousin, Charles. She "needs kissing," and she believes that he "supposes" that he's the "proper" person to "do it" (Leigh, 1939). Charles is killed in the Civil War. Rhett is one of the few virile and fertile adult males around during the Civil War. Ashley's wife's threat over Scarlett's lust and desire for Ashley, makes her resort to lesbianism to charm Scarlett.

A wealthy character seems a likely inspiration to Kathy Bates for her performance next to Leonardo DiCaprio in *Titanic* (DiCaprio, 1997; Leigh, 1939). The character "converses with Miss Wilkes" outside a church about donating to the Confederacy, which will not take prostitutes' money (Leigh, 1939). The woman participates in promiscuity with Rhett. Like the *Titanic* band-scene, at the hospital bombs explode the stained-glass windows (DiCaprio, 1997; Leigh, 1939). Inside, the wounded are read their last rites. The Confederate band is male children. Prissy, an insect-type (e.g., buzzing in the front lawn), female slave, is likely the source of inspiration for *Police Academy*'s Laverne Hooks (1984), showing how far-reaching these characters are into portrayals of justice (Leigh, 1939). Scarlett is convinced to tend to Melanie's delivery. This segment of the film undoubtedly comes through in Helena Bonham Carter's (1999) portrayal of Marla Singer in *Fight Club*. The town doctor cannot help Melanie because there are too many wounded men. "Get some woman to help you" (Leigh, 1939). The soldiers "are bleeding to death in front of my eyes" (Leigh, 1939).

When Prissy needs help, she finds Rhett at a brothel; and brags that she and Scarlett brought a baby into the world. Prissy complains that "the Yankees is coming" (Leigh, 1939). Rhett responds; and manhandles Scarlett. He fondles her breasts in response to her demand for her mother. Ashley's son is healthy and Melanie is languishing, but they must flee from the North. Rhett accosts and romances Scarlett during her time of need (Leigh, 1939). The war against the South will prevail soon. There are no men; and Melanie is dying. He is going away to leave her. She is for want—available to those men, who want her; and he wants her, but she loves Ashley. He takes advantage of her at her most vulnerable and progresses his love, though she is in control of her own emotions, many of which serve solely to defy his want. "Everybody was right! You aren't a gentleman" (Leigh, 1939). "A minor point at such a moment" (Leigh, 1939). He gives her a gun and says goodbye, but warns her not to shoot a "nag" after he slaps her (Leigh, 1939).

Northerners burned Southerners' houses (Leigh, 1939). They left slaves without jobs, homes, food, possessions, clothes, and money. The war was not about freeing slaves. It was to end the prosperity of the South in contrast to the engulfed conflict of the North. Scarlett's mother is dead. Her father is demoralized; and therefore, delusional. It may have been a phony war to build up the South's reputation and convert the population from mostly "White trash" to the appearance of war's aftermath (Leigh, 1939).

The Intermission plays a tune. *The Cat in the Hat*, which defends its copyright, heavily borrowed from the Intermission for "Beautiful kitten-fish, sleep, baby, sleep" (Cusack, 2017; Leigh, 1939). The Intermission also plays the standard "Suwannee River" (i.e., "Old Folks at Home"), and variations of other familiar instrumental tunes.

Scarlett projects Rhett's crimes onto Ashley for increased survival skills (Leigh, 1939). Hunger overtakes her and she purposes to lie, cheat, and steal. That comes way after rock bottom, which happened when Rhett held her without consent, mocked her, kissed her, handed her a gun, and left her.

Scarlett becomes an abuser, slapping her sisters to make them work in the fields (Leigh, 1939). Her father, who believes that Mrs. O'Hara is still alive, asks her to be gentle with "the darkies;" and says that if she does not, then he will complain to "Mrs. O'Hara" (Leigh, 1939). He confuses her mother's energy for the maid's presence.

A "Yankee," a term used in Cuba by descendants of the Triangle Trade to describe their enemies to the North (i.e., Americans), invades the house (Leigh, 1939). Scarlett shoots him in the face instead of at a distance for a better shot. He calls her a "spitfire" to foreshadow his death; and describes her chore of putting out Yankees' damage (Leigh, 1939). For example, she carried buckets of water earlier after being forcibly kissed by Rhett. Melanie's health temporarily improves. They rob the dead soldier. Scarlett acts as Pa, and grants a boyfriend's request for her sister's hand. Ashley returns, and greets Melanie with a pat-hug.

A slave complains that carpetbaggers, who promised forty acres, a mule, and voting rights to each freed man, raised taxes (Leigh, 1939). She wants to ask penniless Ashley about how to get money. A slave says, "Askin' ain't gettin'" (Leigh, 1939). Ashley is afraid of "life becoming too real" (Leigh, 1939). "There's only one way you could help me. Take me away from here" (Leigh, 1939). He has "nothing except honor" to keep them there (Leigh, 1939).

At Ashley's lowest, Scarlett insists that he loves her and that he should kiss her (Leigh, 1939). He begs for his life, wife, and baby by acquiescing to Scarlett. She wants to die because he loves them more than her. He associates himself with the land; and reminds her of "Terra," her plantation (Leigh, 1939). She falls out of love with him.

Pa dies chasing away carpetbaggers (Leigh, 1939). Scarlett gives Pa's watch to a slave instead of selling it to pay taxes. "Oh Mammy," her wet nurse, "I'm so thin and pale; and I haven't got any clothes" (Leigh, 1939). Mammy is overweight; and wants her to channel her father to maintain control. Instead, she makes a dress from curtains and poses as Rhett's "sister" to visit him in a Northern prison where they observe that she is not part of his "harem" (Leigh, 1939). She butters-him-up for money, which the Yankees want. He cannot talk about money, but flirts. "You've grown a woman's heart—a real woman's heart" (Leigh, 1939). "It's worth being in jail just to hear that" (Leigh, 1939). He chastises her for not wearing gloves while she works in the field. He has millions, but shakes-her-down for $300 in tax money. He demands collateral on the loan. "You're not worth $300. You'll never mean anything but misery to a man" (Leigh, 1939). "Like a duck on a june bug," Yankees would be on him if he tried to "draft" the money (Leigh, 1939). They play the fool and out each other. A prostitute visits him in prison. The "dyed-hair woman" presents an unnatural color (Leigh, 1939).

Scarlett lies to her sister India's betrothed, Frank Kennedy, and says that her sister planned to marry another (Leigh, 1939). Scarlett marries Kennedy. Ashley leaves. Scarlett hires White inmate slave labor. He calls her "sugar" (Leigh, 1939). She says, "great balls of fire" (Leigh, 1939). Jerry Lee Lewis, who married his 13 year-old first cousin, later sang this phrase. "Convicts are dirt cheap" (Leigh, 1939). "Darkies'" pay is too high (Leigh, 1939). Ashley says slaves were treated much better than prisoners. Melanie complains that Scarlett builds success in the lumber business with Yankees, who "robbed us," "tortured us," and "left us to starve" (Leigh, 1939). Scarlett insists that she "beat" the carpetbaggers at their "own game" (Leigh, 1939). "Horse make tracks," an innuendo for deviant conduct (Leigh, 1939). Like Uncle Sam, Big Sam, her former slave, is with the shanties. He rescues a damsel in distress, follows her, and gets on her carriage. "It's about time you rebels learned you can't take the law into your own hands" (Leigh, 1939). Ashley leads a raid on a shanty town where Scarlett and her horse were attacked. Ashley gets shot and her husband is killed.

Again, Rhett visits Scarlett in mourning (Leigh, 1939). Her second husband is dead. He wants her face. "Impetuosity" overtakes him—he proposes because she is free and wealthy; "and [he] can't" spend "all [his] life waiting to catch [her] between husbands" (Leigh, 1939). Each of her ex's was a "boy" and an "old man" (Leigh, 1939). He has "a way with women" (Leigh, 1939). She is "meant for taking" (Leigh, 1939). He forces himself on her and she pretends that he is forcing her to marry him—he assures himself that she is marrying him for money, which she is (Russell, 1987).

The comfort he creates for her causes her truly and deeply to love him (Leigh, 1939). She cries in her sleep because she'll have to leave *him* in the future, not the money. "Dreams don't work that way," "but when you get used to being safe and warm, you won't dream that way" (Leigh, 1939). She says, "I love New Orleans," their honeymoon destination; "but, I want to go home" (Leigh, 1939). Slaves say, "we shore is rich now" (Leigh, 1939). Rhett tries to boff the maid, "Old Mammy," while Scarlett is in labor (Leigh, 1939).

To his daughter, Rhett says, "she is the first person, who ever completely belonged to me" (Leigh, 1939). Baby Bonnie Blue Butler has Scarlett's face. Scarlett is envious of the daughter's face's love for Rhett. He calls her "my pet" when she says she only wants one child (Leigh, 1939). She broke the mold.

Melanie cannot have more children. Rhett could divorce Scarlett for withholding her fertility. He accuses her of wanting Ashley. It is not true. He is pretending to show her that he is a free man—not overcome by love for their daughter. She threatens him. Rhett says, "no lock would keep me out" (Leigh, 1939). He kicks open the door. He visits a hooker.

Bonnie grows older (Leigh, 1939). She looks like Scarlett's old maid sister, India. India's genes come through. Bonnie's face mutates, and she goes back to looking like Scarlett. Rhett touches the girl's chest; teaches her to ride with a horse between her legs, against Mammy's protest; and kisses her on the lips. Bill Blass Barbie Dolls are modeled from Scarlett O'Hara's look when she walks into Ashley's birthday party. She renovated her face to cause separation from her daughter's look; and draw the moisture of Rhett's love for her daughter, Bonnie, to perceive his affections as pure. Rhett admonishes her, "don't give yourself airs," a pun (i.e., heirs) (Leigh, 1939). He pushes her; and wants to abuse her to romance her; but, she is not into his abuse.

Twelve Oaks is Ashley's property (Leigh, 1939). Rhett wants to smash Scarlett's "head like a walnut" (Leigh, 1939). He makes the joke to see her feisty, so that she will fight back. After being caught hugging Ashley, Rhett picks her up, carries her upstairs, and makes love. She looks happy, centered, and rested—peaceful—in the morning, almost buggish. He "would like to extend [his] apology" for his "conduct" (Leigh, 1939). He asks her to admit that she wants a divorce on "plenty of grounds" (Leigh, 1939). He says he wants Bonnie because Scarlett actually would prefer "honorable" Ashley if he was "free" (Leigh, 1939). He takes Bonnie without her mother's permission to London, England.

Scarlett says Rhett is exposed (Leigh, 1939). "If you were a man, I'd break your neck for that" (Leigh, 1939). He threatens to "lash[]" her with a "buggy whip" (Leigh, 1939). He kisses Bonnie on the lips. Bonnie is a "princess" (Leigh, 1939). He promises to take her to where "little princes are" (de Saint-Exupéry, 1943; Leigh, 1939). She has night terrors. He holds her butt, puts her to bed. Like Scarlett, she wants her mother. They return from the trip to Scarlett. They are cooling-off to avoid domestic violence or using divorce to stonewall and smokescreen to avoid the issues.

Scarlett is pregnant (Leigh, 1939). Rhett pretends there is a repudiated father. He says the child is unwanted. Rhett says maybe Scarlett will "have an accident" to lose the child (Leigh, 1939). She tumbles down the stairs. Deliriously, she lies in bed begging for Rhett. Fighting her feelings is "no use" (Leigh, 1939). Melanie gives news of Scarlett's improvement to Rhett, who thinks she is "dead" (Leigh, 1939). He would have had intercourse with Melanie, if so. Melanie is full of incest and affectionately warms-up to Rhett.

The fetus does not survive (Leigh, 1939). Rhett tattles on her to Melanie, who denies the veracity of her feelings as being mere "gossip" (Leigh, 1939). Rhett sees family connections as too close, and wants to assure himself that his future children will not marry Melanie's child. Bonnie is killed by a horse, who owes it to Big Sam for rescuing the horse when Scarlett was attacked. Melanie touches herself thinking about trading in Ashley for Rhett. Masturbation is incest. She provides him with "a good deal of strong coffee" (Leigh, 1939). She wants the moolah.

Ashley's son, Beau, weeps because his mother is dying. She passes out trying to hit on Rhett. She says Ashley has no "commonsense" to "leave me dangling" because he does not really exist (Leigh, 1939). She realizes that she loves Rhett when realizing that she was just trying to slay the spirit of incest in Melanie the whole time, which Rhett possesses (Leigh, 1939). It tears everything apart.

After the war, relationships between slaves and owners did not change; thereby demonstrating they were not enslaved (Leigh, 1939). They lacked rights freely to enter and intrude into White society (i.e., be present) (Blazeski, 2017; Jones, n.d.). Rhett leaves Scarlett; but, maintains the charade because Scarlett's strength is at an all-time high. "Oh Rhett, please don't say that I'm sorry" (Cuskelly, 2016).

Lindsay Lohan

Lindsay Lohan is a songstress above actress. She reduces her music career to an infinitesimally small fraction of her total talent to nurture and guard it. For example, in her song "Know Your Name," she sings the word "I" (Lohan, 2004a). The same tone, note, and harmony are used by megastars, for example, Paris Hilton and Gwen Stefani in their music (Hilton, 2006; Stefani, 2016). While she is known for her relationships with Dina Lohan, her mother, and Samantha Ronson, a girlfriend, it is Samantha's effect on her that intrigued voyeuristic tendencies among otherwise heteronormative types. Samantha (Sam) loves women and replaced a need for Lindsay's male other-half. Sam is a feline, who broke Lindsay's heart, but loves her brother more than anyone else; *ergo*, they felt the effect of a yoked love-triangle. Her portrayal of twins, Annie and Hallie, in *The Parent Trap* is outstanding (Lohan, 1998). Her opus is *Liz & Dick*, the story of a White, Anglo/Saxon, Protestant, and her tube

(Lohan, 2012). Her greatest accomplishment, however, is not *Mean Girls*, as some would say (Lohan, 2004b). It is *Herbie: Fully Loaded*—a story about death that "jumps out in front" (King, 1999; Lohan, 2005).

As the title suggests, *Herbie: Fully Loaded* is about inheritance (Lohan, 2005). "Loaded" references downloading, potential death to an operating system (i.e., breached firewall) (Getty Images, 2010; *OK Magazine*, 2015; Schild, 2007; X17, 2017). Because death is full-circle, when underdogs win, everyone dies (Cusack, 2012c, 2013; Gold Key Comics, 1966). In the movie, a stockcar becomes a "daredevil" (Lohan; 2005). The Volkswagen Beetle (i.e., "bug") is to be dispensed, like in a slaughterhouse (The Slaughter-House Cases, 1873). "Race," communicated with blackface, an exhausted gag, is a pun on "*offenders*," who attempt to recycle Herbie (Lohan, 2005). The villains with sooty shoes have spare-tire physiques. The car makes a "fool out of" them (Lohan, 2005). They threaten him. "Consider yourself crushed" (Lohan, 2005).

Michael Keaton, Batman, plays Lindsay's father (Fansgymnastic, 2012; Keaton, 1989; Lakritz, 2017; McLachlan, 1993). Herbie's number is 53. Five minus three is two: two stars appear in the film. The movie is about masculinity, which focuses on death's significance in the family. Herbie does not want to be flattened; and Lindsay is his dream girl (Café 53, n.d.; Heartland Café, n.d.; Pick Me Up Café, n.d.).

The film details the significance of advertisement in daily life; for example, a Goodyear Tire hat implies time (i.e., death) (Goodridge v. Dept. of Public Health, 2003). Justin Long plays the love-interest in this film. "That's what I do" (Lohan, 2005). The film about a car that drives like a skateboard, pressures audiences to examine love relationships in terms of death. "Herbie" "wasn't my first choice. Name came with the car" (Lohan, 2005). Coming, *la petite mort*, is a theme (de Saint-Exupéry, 1943). Herbie ejaculates black oil onto Lindsay's chest. It is reminiscent of black vomit and human illness.

Matt Dillon plays an enemy car driver (Lohan, 2005; MC Archives, 1999). His hat says "82" (Lohan, 2005). He ate/eight two. Herbie challenges him to a race. The film is somewhat racially diverse, but the immense influence of Japanese imports on the drag racing community in California is inevident. "Born to be Wild" plays during the race (Cusack, 2016; Steppenwolf, 1968). Feral animals have reduced lifespans, closing gaps between birth and death more rapidly; yet, feral animals are not necessarily wild animals, many of whom have carefree and long lives. Some feral and wild animals are miserable, which may be why they may seek early death.

Herbie cares about human life, but not rules (Lohan, 2005). Therefore, safety is a nonissue. He does not harm Lindsay or spectators, his fans. If a male were to choose to want to harm her, then she would just direct or request him to get her mother instead. Herbie is like Dina. He is a 1963 Beetle. In 1963, the Beatles released *Please Please Me* and *With the Beatles* (Harrison, 1963; Lennon, 1963). *Please Please Me* was produced by George Martin. George Martin was an honorary fellow of the Zoological Society of London, which owns the London Zoo (Vincent, 2013). In the film *101 Dalmatians*, a white tiger is killed by Cruella DeVille at the London Zoo (Herek, 1996). Subtly, the film depicts a gruesome demise for Sir Paul McCartney, the world's angriest man. Plagiarized early-on by Ludwig van Beethoven, McCartney bitterly devours his own bones by sucking the marrow from his form. He needs a hip replacement in old age and when he goes to the hospital, psychopath nurses steal his wigs—the source of his power. He is rendered useless, so they kill him, taking his skin to make a lampshade (*Huffington Post*, 2014; *Vangardist*, 2015). Lindsay wears rainbow sandals. Rainbows represent all animals with colors; and that God will not destroy the Earth with a flood again.

Dillon's character has a Warhol-esque portrait of himself (Curry, 1975; Lohan, 2005, 2012; Valys, 2017). Warhol depicted Chairman Mao Zedong, the communist leader of China accused of killing millions of Chinese allegedly while attempting to dis-impoverish disadvantaged people and mobilize a middle class (Biography.com, 2017; Nathan, 1987; Zhang, 2015). The movie discusses Dillon's perception that he "out classes them," even though he is rude (Cusack, 2012a; Guthrie, 2008).

A stopwatch is depicted in a scene when Herbie trains (Lohan, 2005, 2013). A stopwatch deceives the viewer and grants the advantage to the user. It "tries" death (Urban Dictionary, 2005). It can focus on sleep, "the cousin of death" (Afghan Wigs, 1998). "Walking on Sunshine" plays during a race (Katrina & the Waves, 1983). Racecar drivers, who look like owls, snakes, and others, are depicted on T-shirts. Depictions of drivers also look like astronauts. A "sudden death" showdown across the desert is when the song plays (Katrina & the Waves, 1983; Lohan, 2013). This is her. "Her" is where Lohan's character and *Her*bie have their blending; an attempted resurgence, not eternity (Benson, 2004; Lohan, 2003; Ross & Nolfi, 2017).

Max is a name used to allude to full throttle, maxed out, death, inheritance, high funerary costs, and end of life. Lionel Ritchie's "Hello" plays when Herbie lusts after a new, yellow Beetle, a disparaging comment about the Japanese (Chavez, 2016; Ritchie, 1983; Smith, 2009). Lindsay has a hitchhiker thumb, prominently depicted when her boyfriend gives her a necklace with "53" (Lohan, 2005). The movie discusses "credentials" (Lohan, 2005). She lies to her father about being a driver named "Max" (Lohan, 2005). That is the public face of Herbie's driver. "Let's make tomorrow's race for pinks" (Lohan, 2005). Pink slips describe destroying the human race in order to make redheads tomorrow, which implies their death because it is not today. She is pink (Fat Joe & Ashanti, 2012; P!nk, 2017; Turner, 2009). "Are you burying a body" in the "desert?," she is asked when she goes to race as Max (Lohan, 2005). When confronted about Max, she claims, "We're so close, it's like we're the same person" (Binkowski, 2016; Haich, 2010; Lohan, 2005; P!nk, 2009).

Herbie has a huge spoiler (Lohan, 2005). He is rotten; and in fan jargon, "spoiler" means to give away a plot (Lohan, 2005). In food, it equates with fermentation. In character and discipline, it may correlate with being unkempt or excessively indulging in trends (Cusack, 2015). Again, this pits race against sex to insinuate the importance of death in the family and disavow supremacy, which is death to culture. Culture dies when members (e.g., audience) feel entitled to perceive that they are superior. "Us" is a group, not performance-based ethic. Street car enthusiasts shout "It's a chick!" when she reveals that she is Max (Lohan, 2005). A similar scene is evident in *Apollo 13* when Chinese characters are introduced; and, a young, Black, male physically assaults an older, White, female colleague in the spirit of humor (Howard, 1995). The scene is out of place; and yet, panders to supremacist audience members.

Lohan loses a race after Herbie spites her (Lohan, 2005). Bitterness is deadly; it is poison. "Racing for pinks"—"she said it was the best ride of her life" (Lohan, 2005). She "stabbed" Herbie "in the back" (Lohan, 2005). A monster truck (e.g., "Grave Digger") with fangs appears; he is a bat (Matthews, 2003). Lindsay faces death to rescue Herbie from a monster truck. She is a "rebel" (Lohan, 2005). She gets in a car playing "Jump" by Van Halen (1983). Herbie disassembles the monster truck by landing on him. A bat is often represented as being deadly, even though a bat is a bird on the inside, but has an *aroma au rodent*. A driver bumps into a wall and crashes his nose (Lohan, 2005). He has a problem with his "left eye" (Lohan, 2005; TLC, 1994; Vanilla Ice, 1989). A nurse says his "death perception is off" meaning he does not have a perception of death; but, she should have said something like, "his depth perception is malfunctioning" (Lohan, 2005). Another brand is Nextel. It is about taking secrets to the grave, perhaps revealed in a will. Relationships between the word "executrix" or "executor" and "executioner" are apparent. "I'm not blind, I just can't race. You're taking my space tomorrow" (Irving & Turner, 1988; Lohan, 2005). Space contrasts and complements death. The spacemen depicted on T-shirts could be male or female (Fey, 2006; Howard, 2005). Tomorrow symbolizes death. Blind is cogent with race. "Blind" referring to ignorance is an insult to the blind (Howard, 2004). Herbie's "53" is spray painted red from damage; and "Everybody's Working for the Weekend" is played (Gillman, 2016; Hearst, n.d.; Klebold, 2017; Loverboy, 1981; Macnab, 2012; Manson, 2015; Martinelli, 2017; Seville Quarter, n.d.).

Lindsay looks down when she penetrates Herbie with a helmet (Lohan, 2005). She describes her masculinity in terms of death. No seeds for Herbie. Condoms are male death. Herbie's heart is his windshield. Lindsay's heart is the window to her soul, not her nature, which is in her eyes. She's birdlike. Herbie puts his wipers over his windshield when "gentlemen" place hats over their hearts (Lohan, 2005). "Drivers" rather than "Gentlemen, start your engines" was death to the culture of supremacy of men; being defeated by women was more important to them (Lohan, 2005; Nye, 2013). This represents constancy (Ludeña, 2010; Martin, 2012; Stout, 2012). A Pop Secret advertisement may be a reference to a finish line tower (Keen, n.d.). Chester the Cheetah with his tongue out is an advertisement on a racing suit. Cheetos were ridiculed in the 1980s by Cuban immigrants, who used the word "*chicotes*" to describe stinky feet (Hialeah Park Casino, n.d.). These jokes dovetailed with African Americans' ridicule of corn chips. Flame retardant suits are worn hinting at a derogatory message about "retards" (Quinn, 2017).

Lohan's character's last name, Peyton, is reminiscent of ball players, such as Walter Payton and Peyton Manning, whose mother, Olivia, is a member of the Audubon Commission (Audubon Nature Institute, n.d.; Manning, 2013; Marchese, 2013). Pay equates to death, war, famine, disease, and crime because it relates to money. "The wages of sin is death" (Romans 6:23). Chevy's cross is a logo symbolizing a lot of payment. "Drove the Chevy to the levee, but the levee was dry," meaning death (Moyer, 2015).

> I couldn't take one more step … in the gym
> It landed foul on the grass
> The players tried for a forward pass
> With the jester on the sidelines in a cast
> Now the half-time air was sweet perfume
> While the sergeants played a marching tune
> We all got up to dance, but we never got the chance

'Cause the players tried to take the field.
The marching band refused to yield.
Do you recall what was revealed the day the music died? (Moyer, 2015)

"The three men I admire most," "a pink carnation, and a pickup truck" symbolize undead attitudes (Brody, 2014; Moyer, 2015).

The cross is juxtaposed with Dillon's character's vehicle, which has Chester on it. Like Chester, whose name is short-form within the criminal justice system for "child molester," a cheetah is a regal animal misused by ancient Egyptians in their sculpture, now called Sphinx, to represent and embody masturbation and a phallic tool (Cusack, 2017). The head of the apparatus depicted by the sculpture would have been worn by a female inside her rectum to stabilize the device and presumably heighten gratification (Ellis & Rose, 2016). The paws were inserted, like a phallus, into another woman's vagina or a man or woman's rectum to accomplish coitus à la two heterosexuals.

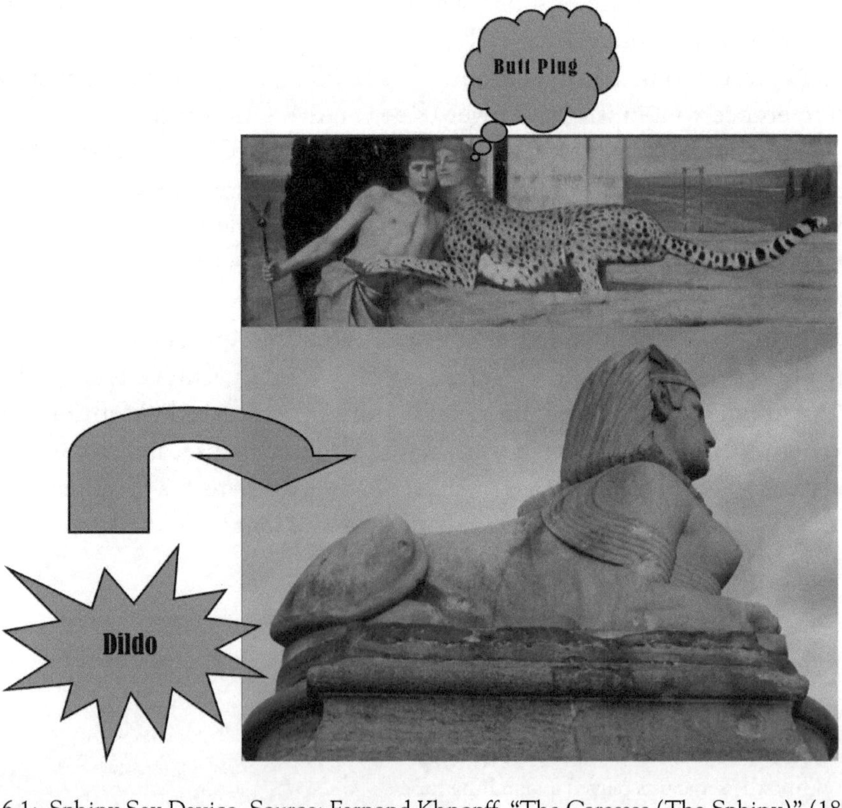

Fig. 6.1: Sphinx Sex Device. Source: Fernand Khnopff, "The Caresses (The Sphinx)" (1896); Olive Titus, Sphinx, Paris, France (2015); Carmen M. Cusack

Herbie does doughnuts after crossing the finish line. The circle of death, and the culturally insensitive phrase "encircling the wagons," come to mind (Cusack, 2012a, 2012b). Dillon says, that "car is alive" (Lohan, 2005). It "is possessed" (Lohan, 2005). "It's mocking me" (Lohan, 2005). He is institutionalized. Institutionalization is death to culture and saying anything out of order. Herbie has nonprocreative fornication at the end of the movie. "The End" flashes on the screen (Lohan, 2005). The credits circle to the Intro, which shows Herbie as a hero racer in his prime during the 1960s (METV, 2016; NYHH, n.d.; Wooten, 2017).

Lohan's feminist position attacks the dichotomous blonde/brunette expectation, fantasy, and attendant hope for a breeding partner. Although her roles (e.g., pictorials) may invite fantasy, her education vanquishes fantasy while leaving viewers' dreams undisturbed. Expectations are embedded early into youth's psyches; for example, marrying a blonde or brown-haired partner. Therefore, fantasy is strategic and preparatory steps toward embodying expectations and hope exist without actuality (Arndt, 2013; Guerra, 1990; Packer, 2012).

Ron Howard

Ron Howard's work, particularly narration of *Arrested Development*, has permanently changed the course of American culture (Howard, 2005). There will be no undoing the work in the foreseeable future. His portrayal of the American family clearly haunted him from *The Andy Griffith Show* through *Happy Days*; and his lashing of ethos and inertia are bar-none searing marks on American media (Howard, 1960, 1984). He completely enlivened, and yet buried in a mass grave, all of his earlier work by even being affiliated with a show like *Arrested Development* (Howard, 2005).

Season three, episode one summarizes the show (Howard, 2005). It makes little sense and lacks continuity. Inside a bare home model built in an undeveloped community, earnest son, Michael Bluth, eats cereal. Inside the staged house are dead flowers and liquor. Lucile, his mother, an alcoholic, interrupts *Mad Money*, a television show warning viewers not to buy Bluth Company stock (CNBC, n.d.). The house is volatilely resting atop a sinkhole, which spreads, like spending time with his son, George-Michael (Avanna, 2017; Orkozero, 2010). The sinkhole first opens in the living room when George-Michael French kisses his cousin, Maeby, whose name is an allusion to Aunt Bee from *The Andy Griffith Show* (Howard, 1960). The sinkhole alludes to vaginas, particularly Lucile's, which is described as a "musty, old clap trap"

(Howard, 2005). Lucile's infantile son, Buster, snores inside her condominium, which irritates her (Martin, 2015). She records him snoring; and is villainous. She takes postpartum medication, even though all her children are adults. She stopped taking the medication in the early 1990s, but when she saw a news story of a mother, who released her car's emergency break to drown her children, she felt like killing her own children: Michael, Buster, Lindsay, and George Oscar Bluth II (GOB) (i.e., pronounced "Jobe") (Ellevsen, 2013; Job 41:13). Lucile blurts out, "Good for her!" when the story appears on T.V. (Howard, 2005). Later, Lindsay wants to buy a Volvo, and hands a photo to Michael, who makes lude jokes about it being "boxy" (Howard, 2005). When Lucile learns about Tom Cruise's appreciation for L. Ron Hubbard's essence, which drives the religion of Scientology, she thinks that Cruise must be "some kind of scientist" because of his stance on mood altering drugs, which he believes can lead to street drug use (Howard, 2005). Michael begs, "Please get back on the meds, Mom. We miss the old, old you" (Howard, 2005).

The absurd and relativistic tone continues with a storyline about a cabin in the woods (Howard, 2005). The Bluth family, which lost its wealth due to criminal charges and bad business deals, had a cabin in the woods used to fornicate by the patriarch, George Senior (Sr.). When George Sr. would make excuses to his children for brining young women to the woods, he would lie about why they could not attend his woodsy outings. "This nice young lady lost her puppy;" and "her dad is sick and I'm taking her to the hospital;" but also, "I'm nailing this broad" (Howard, 2005). George Sr. would not take GOB. GOB regrets not having a son to whom to deny access and information. He cries and says, "taste the happy," in regard to his tears, as he forces Michael's head to his body (Howard, 2005). Michael replies, "tastes kind of like sad" (Howard, 2005). GOB later discovers that he has a son, Steve Holt, through Son and Dad Reunion Project (S.A.D.). Michael decides to take teenage son, George-Michael, to the cabin in the woods in response to bad financial news (Lohan, 2010). Michael will not bring GOB. George Sr. is supposed to be in prison, but tricked the justice system into believing that he was his twin, Oscar; and Oscar is incarcerated instead. A running joke is complaints about prison rape. Michael talks to Oscar in prison, believing him to be his father George Sr., and complains about "scar[s]" (Howard, 2005). "You've got the wrong twin" is a very popular alibi (Howard, 2005). Michael does not "buy it" when Oscar responds to Michael taking George-Michael to the woods instead of helping him (Howard, 2005). When Oscar says, "I understand, your child comes first," Michael realizes that Oscar is not George Sr. (Howard, 2005).

The harebrained family lawyer, Barry Zuckerkorn, played by Henry Winkler, who appeared as "The Fonz" in *Happy Days*, goes to Reno, Nevada to visit George Sr.; and has sex with his assistant, a male who sued him for sexual harassment (Howard, 1984). He will not take his younger assistant to the cabin in the woods. George-Michael is dissed for GOB, and hurt after not wanting to go to the cabin in the woods. Michael, who must find George Sr., instructs him to "pop a tent in the front yard with [his] cousin Maeby," a reference to adolescent erections (Howard, 2005). Maybe his interest will "rub off on her" (Howard, 2005). Steve Holt, their classmate, on whom Maeby has a crush, used S.A.D. to find GOB. At first, GOB does not understand that he is his son. They meet at a bronze statue inscribed with the words, "he came" (Howard, 2005; Kimbal, 2008). The statue is of a child looking-up, holding a man's hand; but, the man is not depicted, only his hand (Howard, 2005; Kimbal, 2008; Schulz, 1950). He takes him on a Segway to a cabin in the woods. Eve Holt, his mother, was one-third of the girls impregnated by GOB during high school; but, the only mother. Reno's theme is "make the biggest little mistake of your life" (Howard, 2005). Tobias Fünke, Lindsay's quasi-closeted homosexual, unlicensed psychiatrist husband, fled with George Sr.'s former lover and secretary, Kitty. He works at Swallows, a "pansexual bazaar by night" and "family … restaurant by day" (Howard, 2005). Inside is a "grind room," which smells to "high heaven" like a "tuna melt" (Howard, 2005). George Sr. joins Blue Man Group (1991). He almost choked on a marshmallow, and almost turned blue; but, no one noticed. Barry paints himself blue to pursue George Sr. Kitty exposes her freshly augmented bosom, and says, "say goodbye to these" (Howard, 2005). Her breasts bear George Sr.'s handprints; and Tobias says, "Those are blue, too" (Howard, 2005)! At the model home, a staged turkey and caution tape around the living room are symbolic. Lindsay instructs, "knock him out if you have to. He's my husband" (Howard, 2005). Lindsay tries to go after Tobias. Lindsay wants what she cannot have (i.e., Tobias), who is a "cocktail waitress;" and shtupping Kitty (Howard, 2005). Barry has George Sr.'s passport and gambles his $250,000. George Sr. says, "You're fired" (Howard, 2005). Barry replies, "Just like that? No warning" (Howard, 2005)?

Maeby wears earrings; and wants to share a "half-kiss" with George-Michael (Howard, 2005). Rearview mirrors make the "famous Reno sunset," a homophone of "son set," look closer as he waits for his erection to go down (Howard, 2005). Maeby tells GOB that he is Steve's dad. He replies, "I made a huge, tiny mistake" (Howard, 2005). Narcissist Michael thinks he is better than GOB because he usurps Maeby, who may give into incest by taking him camping to compete. Michael says, "I almost had Pop-pop in Reno;" George-Michael replies, "Me too" (Howard, 2005).

Inside Lucile's condominium, Buster's bedroom is decorated with shark jaws, a hand-shaped chair, and a map (Finestra & McFadzean, 1994; Howard, 2005). Lucile beats Buster's dummy, which plays a recording of Buster snoring. She is relieved that it was only a dummy, and says, "That was a freebie" (Bonaduce, 2017; Howard, 2005). Tobias hopes to "resnare" his "mate" because that might be "the exact shot in the arm that this relationship needs" (Howard, 2005). Michael goes to the cabin with George-Michael and sleeps on a fish pillow (Cusack, 2017, in-press). George-Michael sleeps on a geometric-patterned pillow, symbolizing female sexual attraction to a father in psychoanalysis (Cusack, 2015; Franks, Sreenivasan, Spray, & Kirkish, 2009). George-Michael philosophizes, "It's a problem without an answer," referring to "maybe" (Howard, 2005). Michael replies, "Every problem has an answer" (Howard, 2005). He wants to tell the cops about "Pop-pop" escaping from prison, and talk about George-Michael's "girl problems" (Howard, 2005). Cabins are for talking about family problems and cheating on "Gangy" (i.e., Lucille). Lucille goes to the cabin with Buster. George Sr. has stolen it on a truck with Michael and George-Michael inside to stop them from reporting him. Lucille is shocked to see the cabin gone and is wearing fur. She lets the car with Buster inside role into a lake; then she turns to a burrito truck and asks, "Are you still doing breakfast burritos" (Howard, 2005)? Barry, painted blue, makes-out with Tobias for $50. Lindsay, jealous of her father's mistress, Kitty, who ran off with Tobias, finds them and wants a divorce.

References

Afghan Wigs. (1998). "Omerta." On *1965*. New Orleans, LA: Kingsway Studios.

Arndt, R. Z. (2013, August 26). Tracking Tsarnaev: Facial recognition will id the next bomber. *Popular Mechanics*. Retrieved from http://www.popularmechanics.com/military/research/g1275/tracking-tsarnaev-facial-recognition-will-id-the-next-bomber/

Audubon Nature Institute. (n.d.). Commission. Retrieved from https://audubonnatureinstitute.org/commission-members-full-bios/547-olivia-manning

Avanna. (2017). Hickory Dickory white tiger—Kids song. Mother Goose TV. Retrieved from https://www.youtube.com/watch?v=hMeLxmxbvZA

Bean, D. (1961). *West side story*. USA: Seven Arts Productions.

Benson, A. (2004). *13 Going on 30*. New York, NY. Thirteen Productions.

Binkowski, B. (2016, March 24). Pineberry wary. Snopes. Retrieved from https://www.snopes.com/white-strawberries-taste-pineapples/

Biography.com. (2017, April 27). Mao Tse-tung. Retrieved from https://www.biography.com/people/mao-tse-tung-9398142

Blazeski, G. (2017, March 5). Drawings from "the little prince" were on the 50-franc banknote before France had adopted the euro as its currency. *The Vintage News*. Retrieved from https://www.thevintagenews.com/2017/03/05/drawings-from-the-little-prince-were-on-the-50-franc-banknote-before-france-had-adopted-the-euro-as-its-currency/

Blue Man Group. (1991). Retrieved from blueman.com.

Bonaduce, D. (2017). Danny Bonaduce and Sarah morning show. KZOK. Retrieved from http://kzok.cbslocal.com/category/Danny-Bonaduce-And-Sarah-Morning-Show/

Bono & The Edge. (2010). *Turn off the dark: Spider-man*. New York, NY.

Brody, R. (2014, August 15). What Hollywood lost when the communists were purged. *The New Yorker*. Retrieved from https://www.newyorker.com/culture/richard-brody/hollywood-lost-communists-purged

Café 53. (n.d.). Chicago, IL. Retrieved from http://www.cafe-53.com/index.html

Carter, H. B. (1999). *Fight club*. Hollywood, CA: Linson Films.

Chavez, P. (2016, May 8). 'Making me feel special:' Ashlee Simpson posts mother's day snap of son Bronx Mowgli with daughter Jagger Snow. *Daily Mail*. Retrieved from http://www.dailymail.co.uk/tvshowbiz/article-3580154/Ashlee-Simpson-posts-Mother-s-Day-snap-son-Bronx-Mowgli-daughter-Jagger-Snow.html

CNBC. (n.d.). Play book Cramer shares his playbook for maneuvering the market sell-off. Retrieved from https://www.cnbc.com/mad-money/

Curry, T. (1975). *The Rocky horror picture show*. Los Angeles, CA: Twentieth Century Fox Film Corporation.

Cusack, C. M. (2012a). Adr and *yama*, the first limb of yoga sutra. *Australasian Dispute Resolution Journal*, *23*, 131.

Cusack, C. M. (2012b). Alternative dispute resolution and *niyama*, the second limb of yoga sutra. *In Factis Pax*, *6*, 107.

Cusack, C. M. (2012c). Death revolution: Eating the dead to save our world. *Journal of Environmental & Animal Law*, *4*, 37.

Cusack, C. M. (2013). To-get-her for-Eve-r: A man hater's right to same-sex marriage. *Journal of Law & Public Policy*, *10*, 63–98.

Cusack, C. M. (2015). *Criminal justice handbook on masculinity, male aggression, and sexuality*. Springfield, IL: Charles C. Thomas.

Cusack, C. M. (2016). Save the white tiger. *Journal of Law & Social Deviance*, *12*, 1.

Cusack, C. M. (2017). *Fish in the Bible: Psychosocial analysis of contemporary meanings, values, and effects of Christian symbolism*. Wilmington, DE: Vernon Press.

Cuskelly, C. (2016, August 9). Are you a dog or cat person? You'll never guess what's been spotted in the Arabian desert. *Express*. Retrieved from http://www.express.co.uk/travel/articles/698076/spotted-in-arabian-desert-arabian-sand-cat-endangered-species-last-seen-decade-ago

Depp, J. (1984). *A nightmare on elm street*. Burbank, CA: New Line Cinema.

Depp, J. (1990). *Edward scissorhands*. Los Angeles, CA: Twentieth Century Fox.

de Saint-Exupéry, A. (1943). *Le petit prince*. New York, NY: Reynal and Hitchcock.

DiCaprio, L. (1997). *Titanic*. Hollywood, CA: Paramount Pictures.

Ellevsen, J. D. (2013, March 13). At Oscar Wilde's tomb. Wild Times. Retrieved from https://wildetimes.net/2013/03/13/at-oscar-wildes-tomb/

Ellis, R., & Rose, R. (2016, May 29). Cincinnati zoo kills gorilla to save child who slipped into enclosure. *CNN*. Retrieved from http://www.cnn.com/2016/05/28/us/zoo-kills-gorilla/

Estrada, E. (1970). *Cross and the switch blade*. Los Angeles, CA: Twentieth Century Fox Film Corporation.

Estrada, E. (1983). *Chips*. Burbank, CA: Warner Bros. Television.

Fansgymnastic. (2012, April 26). Alexandra Rose Raisman—Amazing!!! Retrieved from https://www.youtube.com/watch?v=mNMng9YPONU

Fat Joe & Ashanti. (2012, May 23). What's luv? FatJoeVEVO. Retrieved from https://www.youtube.com/watch?v=VpvyG2NrS1Y

Fey, T. (2006). Dr. Leo Spaceman. *30 rock*. International Movie Database (IMBD). Retrieved from http://www.imdb.com/character/ch0055041/quotes

Finestra, C., & McFadzean, D. (1994). Back in the saddle shoes again. *Home Improvement*. New York, NY: American Broadcasting Company.

Franks, K. W., Sreenivasan, S., Spray, B. J., & Kirkish, P. (2009). The mangled butterfly: Rorschach results from 45 violent psychopaths. *Behavioral Sciences & the Law*, *27*(4), 491.

Getty Images. (2010, June 19). Prince William & Prince Harry meet David Beckham in 2018 world cup bid. Retrieved from http://www.gettyimages.com/event/prince-william-prince-harry-meet-david-beckham-in-2018-world-cup-bid-101999478#prince-william-and-prince-harry-smile-with-david-beckham-at-an-fa-at-picture-id102222016

Gillman, O. (2016, May 3). Scandalous DuPont heiress dies aged 87–18 years after her gardener-turned-husband paid for the Las Vegas murder of her son's drug-addled prostitute girlfriend. *Daily Mail*. Retrieved from http://www.dailymail.co.uk/news/article-3571685/Scandalous-DuPont-heiress-dies-aged-87-18-years-gardener-turned-husband-paid-Las-Vegas-murder-son-s-drug-addled-prostitute-girlfriend.html

Gold Key Comics. (1966, September). "Hot rod hare." *Bugs Bunny Comic* #107.

Goodridge v. Dept. of Public Health, 798 N.E.2d 941 (Mass. 2003).

Guerra, J. L. (1990). Burbujas de amor. On *Bachata rosa*. New York, NY: Karen Records.

Gundersen, E. (2011, April 8). Paul Simon feels 'Spider-man' producers' pain. *USA Today*. Retrieved from http://content.usatoday.com/communities/entertainment/post/2011/04/paul-simon-feels-spider-man-producers-pain/1#.WddtKsiGPIU

Guthrie, A. (2008, February 7). Cartoon creator's grisly murder. *Miami New Times*. Retrieved from http://www.miaminewtimes.com/news/medical-debt-ranks-no-1-cause-of-south-florida-homelessness-survey-says-9724408

Haich, E. (2010). *Initiation*. Santa Fe, NM. Aurora Press.

Harrison, G. (1963). Don't bother me. On *With the Beatles*. UK: George Martin.

Hawthorne, S. (1850). *The scarlet letter*. London, UK: Penguin Classics.

Hearst, P. (n.d.). Bank robbery. Federal Bureau of Investigation (FBI). Retrieved from https://www.fbi.gov/history/famous-cases/patty-hearst

Heartland Café. (n.d.). Chicago, IL. Retrieved from https://heartlandcafe.com/

Herek, S. (1996). *101 dalmatians*. Burbank, CA: Walt Disney Pictures.

Hialeah Park Casino. (n.d.). Retrieved from http://hialeahparkcasino.com/about/hialeahs-famous-flamingos

Highsmith, C. M. (1980). White tiger at the Miami zoo, Miami, Florida. Library of Congress. Retrieved from https://www.loc.gov/resource/highsm.16393/

Hilton, P. (2006). Stars are blind. On *Paris*. Burbank, CA: Warner Bros.

Hooks, L. (1984). *Police academy*. Hollywood, CA: The Ladd Company.

Howard, R. (1960). *The Andy Griffith show*. New York, NY: Columbia Broadcasting System (CBS).

Howard, R. (1984). *Happy days*. Los Angeles, CA: Paramount Television.

Howard, R. (1995). *Apollo 13*. Universal City, CA: Universal Pictures.

Howard, R. (2004). Justice is blind. In *Arrested development*. Los Angeles, CA: Fox Television.

Howard, R. (2005). The cabin show. In *Arrested development*. Los Angeles, CA: Fox Television.

Huffington Post. (2014, January 22). Ke$ha thanks fans for support from rehab, asks for their teeth as well. Retrieved from https://www.huffingtonpost.com/2014/01/22/kesha-thanks-fans-rehab_n_4643833.html

Irving, A., & Turner, K. (1988). Who framed roger rabbit. *MySpace.com*. Retrieved from https://myspace.com/whoframedrogerrabbit/music/songs

Jackson, M., & Jackson, J. (1995). Scream. On *History: Past, present and future, book I*. Minato, Japan: Epic Records.

Jamiroquai. (1996). Virtual insanity. On *Travelling without moving*. New York, USA: Sony CMG.

Jones, W. J. (n.d.). *Confederate currency: The color of money*. Retrieved from http://www.colorsofmoney.com/propaganda2.htm

Kastel, H. L. (1952, September 24). Hooton writes study of Ireland; Shatters many common myths. *The Harvard crimson*. Retrieved from http://www.thecrimson.com/article/1952/9/24/hooton-writes-study-of-ireland-shatters/

Katrina & the Waves. (1983). Walking on sunshine. On *Katrina & the Waves*. Los Angeles, CA: Capitol.

Keaton, M. (1989). *Batman*. Burbank, CA: Warner Bros.

Keen. (n.d.). The Tower Tarot Card. Retrieved from https://www.keen.com/articles/tarot/the-tower-tarot-card

Kimbal, T. (2008, June 2). The Andy Griffith show: The real Thelma Lou's return to Mayberry. TV Series Finale. Retrieved from https://tvseriesfinale.com/tv-show/the-andy-griffith-show-the-real-thelma-lous-return-to-mayberry/

King, H. S. (1999). Conversation with Herbie King. Miami, FL.

Klebold, S. (2017, February 2). My son was a Columbine shooter. This is my story. TEDMED. Retrieved from https://www.youtube.com/watch?v=7xfyN-yBZ7c

Kozlovic, A. K. (2016). Superman as Christ-figure: The American pop culture movie messiah. *Journal of Religion & Film*, 6(1), article 5.

Lakritz, T. (2017, April 25). How the youngest billionaire in the world, 20-year-old Alexandra Andresen, travels. *Business Insider*. Retrieved from http://www.businessinsider.com/youngest-billionaire-in-the-world-alexandra-andresen-travels-2017-4/#other-times-she-stays-local-by-taking-the-fjordline-ferry-from-norway-to-denmark-8

Leigh, V. (1939). *Gone with the wind.* Beverly Hills, CA: Metro-Goldwyn-Mayer (MGM).

Leigh, V. (1951). *A streetcar named desire*. Burbank, CA: Warner Bros.

Lennon, J. (1963). Misery. On *Please please Me*. UK: George Martin.

Lohan, L. (1998). *The parent trap*. Burbank, CA: Walt Disney Pictures.

Lohan, L. (2003). *Freaky Friday*. Burbank, CA: Walt Disney Pictures.

Lohan, L. (2004a). Know your name. On *Speak*. New York, NY: Casablanca.

Lohan, L. (2004b). *Mean girls*. Hollywood, CA: Paramount Pictures.

Lohan, L. (2005). *Herbie: Fully loaded.* Burbank, CA: Walt Disney Pictures.

Lohan, L. (2010). *Teenage paparazzo*. Rotten Tomatoes. Retrieved from https://www.rottentomatoes.com/m/teenage_paparazzi

Lohan, L. (2012). *Liz & Dick*. Beverly Hills, CA: Larry A. Thompson.

Lohan, L. (2013). *The canyons*. USA: Post Empire Films.

Loverboy. (1981). Working for the weekend. On *Get lucky*. New York, NY: Columbia.

Ludeña, D. (2010, August 2). How to find cash buyers and motivated sellers—Made Easy. Real Estate Worldwide. Retrieved from https://www.youtube.com/watch?v=QzuePd2Rm3A

Macnab, G. (2012, May 11). On Sharon's murder, the teen rape, and life since—Polanski speaks out. *Independent*. Retrieved from http://www.independent.co.uk/arts-entertainment/films/news/on-sharon-s-murder-the-teen-rape-and-life-since-polanski-speaks-out-7734470.html

Manning, T. (2013). *Orange is the new black*. Los Gatos, CA: Netflix.

Manson, M. (2015). Cupid carries a gun. On *The pale emperor*. Beverly Hills, CA: Loma Vista Recordings.

Marchese, D. (2013, September 4). The Chicago bears' 'super bowl shuffle' (1985). *Spin*. Retrieved from https://www.spin.com/2013/09/nfl-music-manning-deion-super-bowl-shuffle/130903-superbowl-shuffle/

Mariah Carey (MC) Archives. (1999, September 16). Nude pictures of Mariah: "I can laugh at them." Retrieved from https://www.mcarchives.com/index.asp?id=38&PageNo=&keywords=&date=&f=2

Martinelli, M. R. (2017, October 18). The heartbreaking story behind Dale Earnhardt Jr.'s only racing superstition. *USA Today*. Retrieved from http://ftw.usatoday.com/2017/10/dale-earnhardt-jr-sr-nascar-superstition-darrell-waltrip-stevie-bible-verse-amy-video

Martin, D. (2012, October 27). Eloy Gutiérrez-Menoyo, Cuban dissident, dies at 77. *New York Times*. Retrieved from http://www.nytimes.com/2012/10/27/world/americas/eloy-gutierrez-menoyo-cuban-dissident-dies-at-77.html

Martin, R. (2015). Disparo al corazón. On *A quien quiera escuchar*. Miami, FL: Sony Music Latin.

Matthews, D. (2003). Grave digger. On *Some devil*. New York, NY: RCA.

McLachlan, M. (1993). Better than ice cream. On *Fumbling towards ecstasy*. Vancouver, CA: Nettwerk.

METV. (2016, June 8). 11 lovable facts about Herbie the love bug. Retrieved from http://www.metv.com/lists/11-lovable-facts-about-herbie-the-love-bug

Moyer, J. (2015, April 8). Gloomy Don McLean reveals meaning of 'American pie'—and sells lyrics for $1.2 million. *Washington Post*. Retrieved from https://www.washingtonpost.com/news/morning-mix/wp/2015/04/08/gloomy-don-mclean-reveals-meaning-of-american-pie-and-sells-lyrics-for-1-2-million/?utm_term=.f06fe9dfe802

Nathan, R. S. (1987). *The white tiger*. New York, NY: Simon & Schuster.

New York Haunted Houses (NYHH). (n.d.). Adult Halloween cruise to bug lighthouse. Retrieved from http://www.newyorkhauntedhouses.com/halloween/adult-halloween-cruise-to-bug-lighthouse-ny.html

Nye, J. (2013, February 24). 'Drivers … and Danica … start your engines!': James Franco sparks sexism storm as he starts Daytona 500 with first woman ever on pole position. *Daily Mail*. Retrieved from http://www.dailymail.co.uk/news/article-2283860/Drivers—Danica—start-engines—James-Franco-sparks-sexism-storm-starts-Daytona-500-woman-pole-position.html

OK Magazine. (2015, May 6). Ginger spice, is that you? The spice girls then and now in photos. Retrieved from http://okmagazine.com/photos/spice-girls-then-now-photos/

Orkozero. (2010). The white tiger song. Retrieved from https://www.youtube.com/watch?v=UHkf01641cY

Packer, S. (2012). *Cinema's sinister psychiatrists*. Jefferson, NC: McFarland.

Pick Me Up Café. (n.d.). Chicago, IL. Retrieved from http://pmucafe.com/new-page/

P!nk. (2009, October 25). U + ur hand. PinkVevo. Retrieved from https://www.youtube.com/watch?v=YUtHjOvPKT0

P!nk. (2017, August 16). What about us (official video). PinkVevo. Retrieved from https://www.youtube.com/watch?v=ClU3fctbGls

Quinn, L. (2017, May 22). Foul-mouthed racist rant at man who was speaking Spanish while on the phone to his mother in an airport. *Daily Mail*. Retrieved from http://www.dailymail.co.uk/news/article-4531188/Wheelchair-bound-man-goes-racist-airport-rant.html

Ritchie, L. (1983). "Hello." On *Can't slow down*. USA: Mercury.

Ross, R., & Nolfi, J. (2017, August 3). Tyra Banks: Lindsay Lohan could have 'robust' role in life-size 2. *Entertainment Weekly*. Retrieved from http://ew.com/tv/2017/08/03/tyra-banks-lindsay-lohan-possible-role-life-size-2/

Russell, K. (1987). *Overboard*. USA: Hawn/Sylbert Movie Company.

Schild, J. (2007). *Original Pontiac firebird and trans am 1967–2002*. St. Paul, MN: MBI Publishing.

Schulz, C. M. (1950). *Peanuts*.

Seville Quarter. (n.d.). Retrieved from https://www.sevillequarter.com/

Simon, P., & Walcott, D. (1998). *The Capeman*. New York, NY.

Smith, L. (2009, August 14). Newly-single Jessica Simpson gets a makeover … as she's transformed into a geisha. *Daily Mail*. Retrieved from http://www.dailymail.co.uk/tvshowbiz/article-1206620/Jessica-Simpson-gets-geisha-makeover-Japan-trip.html

Stefani, G. (2016). Where would I be? On *This is what the truth feels like*. Santa Monica, CA: Interscope.

Steppenwolf. (1968). *Born to be wild*. Canada: Mars Bonfire.

Stout, T. (2012, December 16). Tips on finding red spotted purple hibernating caterpillars. Retrieved from https://www.youtube.com/watch?v=FjCADHsdSmU

Sugar Ray. (1997). Fly. On *Floored*. Los Angeles, CA: Atlantic Records.

The Slaughter-House Cases, 83 U.S. 36 (1873).

TLC. (1994). Red light special (dirty version) (official video). *VEVO*. Retrieved from https://www.vevo.com/watch/tlc/red-light-special-(dirty-version)/USLV40500024

Turner, T. (2009, March 13). What's love got to do with it. Tina Turner Official. Retrieved from https://www.youtube.com/watch?v=oGpFcHTxjZs

Urban Dictionary. (2005, March 30). Tried. Retrieved from https://www.urbandictionary.com/define.php?term=try

Valys, P. (2017, March 1). Searching for Elizabeth Taylor at NSU art museum. South Florida. Retrieved from http://www.southflorida.com/theater-and-arts/sf-lauderdale-nsu-museum-catherine-opie-20170227-story.html

Vangardist. (2015). #Hivheroes limited edition. Retrieved from https://vangardist.com/product/vangardist-print-issue-3-hivheroes-limited-edition/

Van Halen, E. (1983). Jump. On *1984*. Burbank, CA: Warner Bros. Retrieved from https://www.youtube.com/watch?v=rog8ou-ZepE

Vanilla Ice. (1989). Ice ice baby. VanillaIceVEVO. Retrieved from https://www.youtube.com/watch?v=rog8ou-ZepE

Veruca Salt. (1994). Seether. On *American thighs*. Chicago, IL: Minty Fresh.

Vincent, A. (2013, March 22). The Beatles' please please me, 50 years on—10 facts about the debut album. *Telegraph*. Retrieved from http://www.telegraph.co.uk/culture/music/the-beatles/9946799/The-Beatles-Please-Please-Me-50-years-on-10-facts-about-the-debut-album.html

Wooten, N. (2017, September 1). Swarms of lovebugs flying through northwest Louisiana. *USA Today*. https://www.usatoday.com/story/news/nation-now/2017/09/01/swarms-lovebugs-flying-through-northwest-louisiana/625609001/

X17. (2017, June 28). Paris Hilton cracks up at Brandon Davis' epic Lindsay Lohan 'fire crotch' rant [2006]. Youtube.com. Retrieved from https://www.youtube.com/watch?v=MWQ-BaTAeOs

Zhang, H. (2015). Strengthening juvenile rights or doing the opposite: The legal mysteries of the Chinese juvenile justice system behind the "Li gang-rape case." *Journal of Law & Social Deviance*, *10*, 1–41.

· 7 ·

CHURCH OF LATTER-DAY SAINTS

Native American Heritage

Jesus Christ Church of Latter-day Saints believes that ancient people crossed the Asian continent over the North Pole into the depths of North America (LDS, 2017). This premise cradles their assumption that Joseph Smith, their founder, was a divine prophet. He presumes, through his teachings, that the people were grouped within the ancient and Biblical peoples described loosely by Christians as "Hebrews" (Exodus 1:22; Philippians 3:5). The teachings generally describe the importance of asserting this relationship for the world; however, Church of Latter-day Saints (i.e., Mormons) is not predicated on the world believing this strand of their overall message.

In recent years, the Church has come under attack from insidious scientists, who would expend coveted resources and invest significant intellectual time and energy, merely to aggrieve the Church with defiant genetic results supposedly denouncing and disproving the veracity of their sacred texts (Manseau, 2015; Murphy, 2003; Riess, 2015). Genetic tests suggest that Native Americans, who according to the Church should have Middle Eastern heritage, actually possess East Asian blood. Genetic ancestry tests are commonly flawed (e.g., AncestryDNA) and notoriously incorrect even when used by sophisticated institutions (e.g., Federal Bureau of Investigation

(FBI)) (Cusack, 2015b). Numerous outraged consumers, for example of less accurate, but commonly-used genetic tests, have complained about fictitious results. People, whose families have retained documentation of their ancestry for hundreds of years (i.e., Church records), have been surprised by the loose classifications of genetic test-makers, which would collate individuals with historically and geographically dissimilar populations. The Church has pointed to these problems. "Basic principles of population genetics suggest the need for a more careful approach to the data. The conclusions of genetics, like those of any science, are tentative, and much work remains to be done to fully understand the origins of the [N]ative populations of the Americas" (LDS, n.d.). Furthermore, the tests only look for genetic markers; they cannot know genetic history. A person with European history is as likely to appear to be East Asian if their genetic combinations for hundreds of years retain characteristics appearing to be similar to East Asians (e.g., straight, dark hair). Supposing that contemporary genetic tests have revealed to consumers that their bloodlines are in fact as shared as they have proposed, then scientists attacking Native American and Mormon populaces ought to embrace how "mutations accumulate over time as they are passed from generation to generation, resulting in unique" genetic appearances that spread over large territories; and resulting in a smorgasbord of philosophies (LDS, n.d.). Religiously, spiritually, and societally, "some mixing appears evident" (LDS, n.d.).

With that comes the idea that Mormons may be Native Americans. No research has tested all Mormons' genes; and due to their broad coverage, there should be no assumptions made or conclusions drawn about the remainder of untested populations. Assimilation into mainstream America through religion is extremely typical and would therefore explain that Native Americans, although no longer meeting blood quantums, potentially, merely enfolded into European heritage. They did not, as some historians suggest, terminate all reproductive activities when they were traumatically harassed and killed during early New World blending of Europeans on the North American continent. Therefore, Native Americans may comprise a significant swath of American heritage. Those Native Americans with DNA uncannily and visibly similar to European settlers may have been likeliest to survive if they were viewed as fair and lovely by Europeans. In this regard, DNA testing may be an unsuitable indicator of the veracity of their assertions. Nevertheless, the proposition that Americans' genetic composition is sprinkled with Native American genes is accurate; and provable through means other than genetics and historical documents, which are racist. The importance of this idea may not be overlooked because it implies that Native Americans likely may have remained the majority of the population, which indicates that they nurtured Europeans, and could have, at any time, removed them from their homes, and effectively, the continent. It seems that animosity could have resulted from yoking away European settlers' genes and their counterparts with Native American genes baring resemblance to Europeans from those Native Americans with customarily identifiable genetic combinations. "That American Indians joined and have remained in the Mormon Church is but one example of their tortured history in the face of colonizing forces that led to their displacement, loss of lands, and subsumption of personal, linguistic, and cultural identities" (Silver, 2014). Euro-Native Americans may have resigned to remain hidden within European identity to avoid slaughter by indigenous Tribespersons and to avoid smearing; and harvest opportunities to assimilate and unify otherwise warring microcosms (e.g., tribal units) across the North American continent.

Fundamental LDS

Fundamental Latter-day Saints (FLDS) (i.e., Mormons) is an offshoot of mainstream Mormonism. Although practices and traditions upheld by isolated sects preceded popularization and conventionalization of Mormonism (e.g., Brigham Young), fundamental Mormonism is considered to be a departure because they practice polygamy, known as plural marriage, which is against the law (Larson & Moore, 2009; Oguntebi, 2011).

Islam is widely believed to involve plural marriage. However, only a minority of practitioners participate in plural marriages around the world; and almost no practitioners maintain multiple homes in the United States. The reason for Muslims' unwillingness to follow through with plural marriage, even though it may be acceptable in certain societies, is because it is expensive; an ineffective means for distributing patriarchal proceeds; and limits affection for each wife to one fraction of what it may otherwise be in a monogamous relationship. Yet, studies repeatedly show that plural marriages have positive, if not beneficial, outcomes for children raised in cooperative societies (Goldfeder & Sheff, 2013; Khasawneh, Hijazi, & Salman, 2011). The *status quo* may feel threatened when polygamists, who are sometimes called "communists," are labeled with terrorists, who may share their religion or another religion practicing polygamy (Montalbano, 2016; U.S.

v. Jeffs, 2017; Zhang, 2015). Women are labeled as being inferior to men by the mainstream, which may classify polygamists as having broken nuclear units.

> It is obvious that the association of polygamy with Islam is not unfair or biased but based on serious misunderstanding. Polygamy was practiced, often without limitations, in some cultures. It was authorized by various religions, and practiced before Islam and for many centuries from then on. It is presently practiced, though secretly by Mormons, and it is allowed by Christian missionaries in Africa and other areas where polygamy is a social necessity. (Khasawneh et al., 2011, p. 564)

"The wives of both Muhammad and Joseph Smith played roles in schisms and divisions in the early days of each faith. Both communities struggled with issues of succession and line of authority, and as some of the Prophets' closest companions, their wives certainly held influence and sway over early believers" (Kennard, 2011, p. 49). "In the traditions of the wives of the prophets, both conservative and progressive women of each religion find inspiration and instruction. Such reflections provide space for somewhat radical thought within a conservative context while reaffirming the agency of women on either ideological side" (Kennard, 2011, p. 54).

Islam and Mormonism routinely are viewed suspiciously because of their alleged, but strongly denied, associations with fundamentalist groups, which occasionally are sensationalized; for example, by focusing on young brides in fundamental Latter-day Saints groups. "Likewise, television programs everywhere delve on sensationalism, concentrating on gory footage even when bloody scenes were blurred so as not to offend alleged sensibilities. … It was easy to distance oneself with, or show sympathy towards, individuals in our neighborhoods that succumbed to violent acts" (Kéchichian, 2017, p. ix). Mormons have made several attempts to clear their Church's name in the public eye.

> The LDS Church's public relations effort to clarify the differences among itself, the FLDS, and other polygamist groups was not received uncritically. The Church had applied in 2005 to trademark 'Mormon'; and although its petition was denied, Elder Lance Wickman, who heads the LDS Church's Legal Department, asserted in his letter to the media in June 2008 that the media should use 'Mormon' exclusively to refer to the mainstream LDS Church. He specifically discouraged the use of 'fundamentalist Mormon' in reference to groups advocating polygamy.12 Principle Voices Coalition, an organization representing fundamentalist and polygamist Mormon groups, responded with a denunciation, 'We strenuously object to any efforts to deprive us and others of the freedom to name and describe ourselves by terms of our own choosing'. (Cragun & Nielsen, 2009, pp. 66–67)

Despite their frenzied preoccupation, one study found that of 145 Spanish and English news articles about criminally charged polygamists and sex offenders, 81 "explicitly distinguished between the two churches," 63 implied a distinction, "and only one confused the two" (Cragun & Nielsen, 2009, p. 94).

Both religions, Islam and Mormonism, whether fundamentalist or mainstream members, have some subsocial factions, whose behavior does not signify adherence to mainstream doctrines. Withdrawing into an underground world may be a reasonable mode of protection. The mainstream may be persecutory to the extent of being criminal or unconstitutional. "[I]t [is] hypocritical for America to claim to protect religious liberty while restricting some of its citizens from practicing a central aspect of their religion. Some … contemporary examples, such as airport security officers forcing Muslim women to remove their veils, [are] … proof of a seeming American double standard of religious freedom" (Mason, 2010, pp. 1113–1114). Mainstream Mormons have attempted to pressure and admonish fundamentalists, who are "born into" the religion, to "find" their "own way," and "find what the truth really [is]" (Shafovaloff, 2014). The underground is a safe and dangerous place. It may be used to depart from the radicals and mask mainstream affiliations (e.g., fundamentalists having abortions).

Media has broadened subsocial shade and extended dimness because fundamentalists have access to regimes, propaganda, and wives using the Internet.

> Today there are tens of thousands of organized sectarian militants throughout [many] region[s] capable of triggering a broader [change]. … Extremist groups have come to rely on satellite television and high-speed Internet over the past two decades to spread propaganda and attract recruits. Fundamentalist Sunni clerics, many sponsored by wealthy Sunnis from Saudi Arabia and the Gulf states, have popularized … [rebels]. Shia religious scholars have also taken to the airwaves, mocking and cursing the first three caliphs and Aisha, one of Mohammed's wives. Sectarian rhetoric dehumanizing the 'other' is centuries old. But the volume is increasing (CFR, n.d.).

"The developments that were experienced in the communication and technology area made Internet an important part of the daily life" (Batı & Atıcı, 2011). "[T]he changes in the social structure are closely connected with the lifestyles, attitudes, and behaviors of the people" (Batı & Atıcı, 2011). The "phenomena of virtual fellow [wives] and polygamy" "fundamentally" "richened" fundamentalist Mormons, who practiced polygamy without consent or approbation from the government or mainstream society (Batı & Atıcı, 2011). A noteworthy distinction between polygamists using the Internet and sexual free-for-alls through Facebook, Grindr, Plenty-O-Fish, and other social media, is that polygamists maintain cohesive units so that children, who result either from plural unions or casual sex, may be reared in stable environments (Shucha, Ginsberg, & Kribble, 2009).

Warren Jeffs

Under the First Amendment of the U.S. Constitution, religious freedom is protected unless the government can demonstrate a compelling reason for impinging on the right. Laws that limit religious practice must be narrowly tailored to impinge as little as possible. A law must be neutral and generally applicable. It cannot target a specific church or practice. Under the Equal Protection clause, laws may not have discriminatory impacts (Lukumi Babalu v. Hialeah, 1993).

The government has asserted an interest in prohibiting underage marriage and plural marriage. Underage marriage may be performed by a judge and with parental consent. Ages at which minors may be married are specified by state legislatures and judges. Legislatures and judges may base parameters on secular reasoning (e.g., emotional stability). Best interest factors may include considerations of faith (e.g., spiritual maturity). The government has asserted an interest in prohibiting plural marriage. Often, recitations of state interests include maintenance of traditional marriage, morality, and protection of women and children. However, these arguments are similar to arguments from last century, which prohibited same-sex marriage and child adoption; and were debunked when courts analyzed why the government should permit same-sex couples lawfully to participate in family-life. Anti-polygamy laws and some laws excessively restricting underage marriage in effect may discriminate against fundamentalist Mormons and totally abridge religious practice; therefore, exceptions should be made (ACLU, 2016; Gallagher, 2013; In the Matter of the Welfare of J.J.M.A., 2013; Laird, 2015; McAllen Grace Brethren Church v. Salazar, 2014; Yick Wo v. Hopkins, 1886). Their *bona fide* practices have not been proven by the government to harm women, children, or society; and yet, their right to religious freedom has been abridged.

Traditionally, states have had a right to regulate marriage by making laws and enforcing compliance by issuing marriage licenses. Yet, some state laws excessively restrict marriage by minors, particularly in jurisdictions where legislatures keenly avoid making laws that would grant religious protection to Mormons. Similarly, they excessively prohibit marriage between relatives, which directly abridges fundamentalist Mormons' practices. For example, in

2008, a South Carolina court discussed why a marriage between a 13 year-old pregnant female and an adult male should be valid (Arizona v. Fischer, 2008; S.C. Code Ann. § 20–1–100, *et seq.*, 2009; State v. Lott, 2009). Although the legislature permitted 16 and 17 year-old minors to marry, an exception was made for underage pregnant women and mothers with a guardian or parent's consent to marry putative fathers. The government of South Carolina can make neutral laws that result in religious freedom for fundamentalists as easily as governments elected by communities in which polygamists practice fundamental Mormonism (e.g., Utah).

State of Texas has prosecuted fundamentalist Mormons for participating in informal marriages even though State of Texas recognizes informal marriages, which are similar to common law marriages. The state does not recognize minors' informal marriages. Although the state may provide rationales for restricting minors, compelling reasons may be proffered for recognizing informal marriages between minors; such as marital stability and benefits between unwed parents. The state requires a judicial proceeding formally to recognize marriages; and will not recognize bigamist or plural marriages (Texas Family Code §§ 2.001, *et seq.*, 2017). In Texas, some minors with parental or state consent can lawfully marry. They may commit actions traditionally, but not currently, considered to violate state interests, such as adultery, divorce, and unwed cohabitation; and then remarry effectively to participate in a plural union or polyamorous lifestyle.

Texas statutes are discriminatory on their face. They violate the *Lemon* test by favoring two religions, Judaism and Christianity, over all others (Lemon v. Kurtzman, 1971; Tavakkoli, 2014). Under the *Lemon Test*, "[a] challenged government program is constitutional if it satisfies all three parts of a [three]-part test: (1) it must have a secular legislative purpose (that is not a sham); and (2) a primary effect that neither advances nor inhibits religion; and (3) it cannot create an excessive government entanglement with religion (with a religious entity)" (Harpaz, 2013). Though the State of Texas may not enforce the law against other religions and impinge on their rights, they effectively discriminate against fundamentalists because their marriage traditions are unacceptable to the state in violation of the First Amendment.

> [Texas Family Code] Sec. 2.202 specifies which 'persons' are 'authorized to conduct' a marriage 'ceremony.'
>
> (a) The following persons are authorized to conduct a marriage ceremony:

(1) a licensed or ordained Christian minister or priest;
(2) a Jewish rabbi;
(3) a person who is an officer of a religious organization and who is authorized by the organization to conduct a marriage ceremony;
(4) a justice … [or] judge. … [; or]. … retired justice or judge; and
(5) a retired judge or magistrate of a federal court of this state. …

(c) Except as provided by Subsection (d), a person commits an offense if the person knowingly conducts a marriage ceremony without authorization under this section. An offense under this subsection is a Class A misdemeanor.
(d) A person commits an offense if the person knowingly conducts a marriage ceremony of a minor whose marriage is prohibited by law or of a person who by marrying commits an offense under Section 25.01, Penal Code. An offense under this subsection is a felony of the third degree. (Texas Family Code § 2.202, 2017)

The statute permits officers of any organization to conduct ceremonies, but only Jewish rabbis and Christian ministers. The state may not recognize fundamentalist leaders and ministers although they are Christian. It criminalizes speech by prohibiting all other people from performing marriage ceremonies even if the parties, including minors, do not seek state recognition or if the parties know that the marriage is void (Cusack, 2013).

Like Texas, Utah Courts' website suggests First Amendment violations. "A minister, rabbi, priest, mayor, judge, county clerk, Native American spiritual adviser, the Governor, mayors, court commissioners and judges, as well as particular members of the legislature may perform wedding ceremonies. Two witnesses over 18 must also be present at the wedding ceremony" (Utah Courts, 2016a). "The person who solemnizes the marriage must sign a certificate of marriage and then file[] the certificate and the marriage license with the county clerk who issued the license" (Utah Code § 30–1–6, 2017; Utah Courts, 2016a).

State of Texas legislature leaves room to defend against allegations of discrimination made by religious organizations other than fundamentalists by including the following statutory exception:

> [Texas Family Code] Sec. 2.302. Ceremony Conducted by Unauthorized Person. The validity of a marriage is not affected by the lack of authority of the person conducting the marriage ceremony if:

(1) there was a reasonable appearance of authority by that person;

(2) at least one party to the marriage participated in the ceremony in good faith and that party treats the marriage as valid; and
(3) neither party to the marriage:
    (A) is a minor whose marriage is prohibited by law; or
    (B) by marrying commits an offense under Section 25.01, Penal Code. (Texas Family Code § 2.302, 2017)

The State of Texas' laws effectively discriminate against fundamentalists without any exception.

State of Utah intentionally and excessively restricts incestuous marriage to impinge on polygamous fundamentalists. Under § 30–1–1 (2017), Utah's sweeping marriage statute criminalizes marriages that are allowed in most other states. Void incestuous marriages include marriages between any ancestors, a law that is generally impossible to enforce, but may likely be enforced when the state prosecutes fundamentalists.

(1) The following marriages are incestuous and void from the beginning, whether the relationship is legitimate or illegitimate:
    (a) marriages between parents and children;
    (b) marriages between ancestors and descendants of every degree;
    (c) marriages between brothers and sisters of the half as well as the whole blood;
    (d) marriages between uncles and nieces or aunts and nephews;
    (e) marriages between any persons related to each other within and not including the fifth degree of consanguinity computed according to the rules of the civil law, except as provided in Subsection (2). (Utah Code § 30–1–2, 2017)

The legislature gives its overbroad marriage statute a back door to survive Constitutional challenges by including anti-incest law that may limit the reach of its ancestor statute. Like other states, Utah restricts marriage according to degrees of consanguinity. Utah's fifth degree requirement is like several of the most restrictive laws throughout the country. It includes the redundant, and yet all-encompassing, prohibition against ancestor marriage specifically to impinge on groups like fundamentalists that focus on religious ancestry and routinely participate in marriages between first cousins and other incestuous marriages. The statute's redundancy is explicative. It points directly to discrimination by reciting the legislature's opposition to cousin marriages, which are already prohibited by the statute voiding marriages between relatives within five degrees of consanguinity.

Utah may argue that its prohibition of consanguineous marriage is a neutral law. However, it discriminates against fundamentalist Mormons because most people demonstrate incest avoidance (Cusack, 2015a). For example, 28,393 Catholic Church records in Uruguay from 1800 through 1994 reveal that only approximately two percent of people married consanguineous relatives, such as first cousins (Lusiardo et al., 2004). Researchers explained that the Uruguayan records and customs were typical for South America and shared similarities with historical European trends. Prohibiting marriages within specific degrees of consanguinity directly targets a small portion of the population. These statutes may deter predatory relatives from pressuring vulnerable relatives into marriage; yet, they discriminate and violate the First Amendment.

In an attempt to appear to impinge on as little religious freedom as necessary to satisfy compelling government interests, State of Utah specifically allows senior, infertile cousins to marry. The statute suggests that society is unwilling to tolerate citizens born from incestuous marriage. One alleged reason is that incestuous procreation results in genetic deformities. This is untrue. Although outbreeding may reduce some likelihood that certain illnesses will manifest in offspring; outbreeding also introduces potential illnesses into offspring's biology and genes.

> (1) First cousins may marry under the following circumstances:
> (a) both parties are 65 years of age or older; or
> (b) if both parties are 55 years of age or older, upon a finding by the district court, located in the district in which either party resides, that either party is unable to reproduce. (Utah Code § 30–1–2, 2017)

The discriminatory statute violates Equal Protection under the Fourteenth and Fifth Amendments for adults between the ages of 18 years old and 65 years old. It also violates reproductive freedom by asserting a state interest in controlling birth defects by controlling reproductive freedom. There is little scientific basis for believing that close inbreeding results in genetic deformities. The government has no right to enforce outbreeding policies in violation of people's right to privacy. They have a right to preserve their genetic lineages (i.e., inbreeding) and valuable resistance to specific diseases and manifestations of desirable traits. Furthermore, the state cannot base it authority to grant marriage licenses on people's fertility. It is an unconstitutional invasion of privacy; and enforces a belief that married persons should only reproduce with each other.

State of Utah is begrudgingly compliant or noncompliant with legalization of same-sex marriage by the U.S. Supreme Court (Utah Courts, 2016a, 2016b). Like many states that maintain anti-same-sex marriage statutes, which appear to be unenforceable, State of Utah maintains its statute, and comments on government websites that the Courts have legalized same-sex marriage. Although this is accurate, the statements appear to comment on judicial advocacy and the Court overextending its authority to the role of the legislature (*Sesame Street*, 1971). Until 1999, Utah permitted minors over the age of 13 years old to marry. The age has since been raised to 15 or 16 years old (Utah Code § 30–1–9, 2017). Utah permits couples, who have not been legally married, to have the duration of their relationships recognized by the state. The process is like common law marriage. The pre-1999 age restriction and the recognition that marriages exist outside of state sanctioned unions demonstrates that fundamentalists' marriages traditionally resembled marriages acceptable to the Utah legislature. Yet, growing religious opposition and violations of the Establishment Clause have effectively marginalized fundamentalists and relegated them to the outskirts of society where they are treated as deviants and criminals.

Warren Jeffs, President of the Fundamentalist Church of Jesus Christ of Latter-day Saints (FLDS), is likely innocent of the crimes alleged against him by state governments and the Federal Bureau of Investigation (FBI) (Cusack, 2015c). Although the government's evidence, as set forth at trial and accepted by the popular press, remains the official documentation of Jeffs' relationship to young women and their children, little, if any, direct evidence supports sensationalized records and fabrications (Hindsight, n.d.). For example, the allegedly obscene recording of a "heavenly session" during which the State of Texas claimed to have heard Jeffs having sex with numerous young women at once is clearly not evidence of any crime (Youtube.com, 2011). In the recording, Jeffs is witnessing from his spirit. Heavy breathing, described by the state's attorney, jurors, and the media, as penetrative gusts of exhalation, is nothing more than spiritual exaltation. Jeffs is a hero for common, poor people, which is the government's true gripe against him; although, he may have been guilty of participating in child bride distribution.

Jeffs is no saint. He did funnel welfare proceeds (e.g., food) without legal authority into a collective bank, which self-sustained and subsidized the group by evening resources among them (O'Neill, 2016). The government has spent decades attempting to withdraw any benefit of those proceeds, including by trumping-up some allegations by former child members, who have been awarded astronomical sums that surely will be reduced or unpaid. Attorneys attacking Jeffs in bad faith would have been better suited acquiring terminal degrees in creative writing than teacher of law degrees because their view of the evidence and motion practice is fiction.

Several of the states' and media's exaggerations, which sentenced a practically innocent man to life in prison, include consummating marriages to child brides; only marrying child brides; impregnating child brides, an allegation that is not substantiated apart from the implication of DNA evidence only allegedly verified by the government; and raping young women, who were actually married to other men (Galka, 2017). The most egregious violations against Jeffs are total and utter abridgments of his right to practice religion (Tavakkoli, 2014). He cannot utter the words "spiritual marriage" in any context apart from the what the government has sanctioned, despite longstanding and varied interpretations of marriage and polygamy in the New World, which easily should overcome governmental obstacles on Due Process grounds equal to challenges posed by homosexuals.

FLDS seems to be a safe environment, where women are respected as holy vessels, not routinized into lives of misery (Copeland, 2016; Winslow, 2017). Unlike the secular world, which calls upon them to distance themselves from their children while their employers run amok of their minds, FLDS women devote themselves to their families, God, and way of life. It is this reality that was most tragic because the government usurped parental authority over and relationships with more than 400 individuals labeled by the government as children, even though dozens of them were actually identifiable adults. When it seized the compound and occupants in response to a fabricated anonymous tip by chronic prankster, Rozita Swinton, the government lied by asserting a good faith belief that Swinton was actually a victim named Sarah. The tip and their bad faith investigation, which has been challenged by Jeffs, would otherwise make all of the government's manipulated and conjured evidence inadmissible; however, in Jeffs' case, the Constitution has been assassinated (*Daily Mail*, 2011).

Mormonism benefits from the inclusion of FLDS under broader religious boundaries because they stand-up for themselves; and have done nothing so extraordinarily criminal, other than collectively use welfare. During his criminal trial, which falsely laid out the most allegedly violative evidence, taken by the state as fact and documented by the court as reality, Jeffs unsophisticatedly, but devotedly called a single witness so that he could spend his martyrdom witnessing to his persecutors' spirits rather than taunting their minds. Instead of indulging their lustful and greedy agenda with destructive and insulting descriptions of sex with minors, he refused to do in open court what the state accused him of, sexual appropriation and degradation. By not discussing sex with young women in front of an audience of billions, Jeffs defended the dignity of the young women and protected purity infinitely more than the state, which fabricated the majority of the facts.

Jeffs assumed control of the FLDS Church after his father, the leader, died. He had not been accused of any wrongdoing until his nephew brought a civil action against him for sodomy and child molestation in 2004. Local law enforcement was notified of his religious conduct involving children (i.e., sequestering them) well in advance of the lawsuit. However, no one investigated before the lawsuit. This indicates that they were unconcerned with sequestration, perhaps suggesting that they knew of his conduct, which was not nefarious. The raid on FLDS Church was one of many upon polygamists in United States' history, which have never proven unequivocally or with any evidence that child-adult marriages mar children's psyches or expose children to victimization worse than trauma experienced by adults in consensual marriages. Girls marrying older men for financial prospects and community support are not new concepts; and neither is arranged marriage. However, the government fears these measures in Mormon communities because they have the power to upheave traditional Christian dogma (e.g., monogamy) (Gibson, 2010). The government claimed that their financial arrangements, which invited state funding for unwed mothers, "facilitate[d] sex crimes against minors," "facilitate[d] polygamy," and "discriminate[d] against young males within the Church," even though Jeffs had been convicted of marrying a 19 year-old male to a 14 year-old female (FLDS v. Wisan, 2011, p. 1244). Presiding over that marriage was described by the government as "rape" (Cusack, 2015c).

The government infringed on his right to free speech because he could not use the word "marriage," which for all intents and purposes, has been trademarked by a government that reserves the word only for legal use when it sanctions and ordains unions (Cusack, 2013). Merely uttering the term may give rise to legal claims (e.g., rape by proxy) (A.R.S. 25–102, 2017). Jeffs' use of the word landed his name on the FBI's 10 Most Wanted list, occupied by heinous monsters, such as Osama Bin Laden, even though in many jurisdictions minors may have sex with minors; marry with parental consent; have abortions without parental consent; and have sex with adults without prosecution, but at the risk of endangering their lovers, who may be persecuted and prosecuted (Gibson, 2010). The government's position violated their religion, which treats married children as adults. By not prosecuting children, who had caused adults to commit crimes (i.e., marrying them), the government violated Equal Protection. Jeffs warned his wives that the government could prosecute them as conspirators and rapists by proxy, just as children may be guilty of child pornography crimes for distributing self-made pornographic images (Hilinski-Rosick & Freiburger, 2012; Jeffs, 2003).

The government fed a rescuer theme to the public and press. The rescuer theme complements men's inadequacies developed through years of antagonism by inferior-minded women, who portray little girls as strumpets and rivals. Young women, such as those at Jeffs' compound, are belittled by women, who see them as sexually immature; incapable of making good decisions; confused about their desires; and unworthy of being loved by stable and economically supportive individuals (Jeffs, 2003). Furthermore, the rescuer theme sweeps under the rug childhood sexual desire and prowess (Beswick, 2007). Finally, the rescuer theme, whether applied to Muslim women wearing burkinis, FLDS women donning long skirts, or other modest women, openly announces the unsavability of women, especially those who have sex outside of marriages to White men pertaining to mainstream America, who would otherwise financially oppress and subvert the talents of women under their control (Gibson, 2010). Militarized rescue satisfies each of these suppressed attitudes by showing brawn, degradation and overpowering force, and discipline through eradication.

The public "vacillates … between portraying FLDS women and children as oppressed by the male elders in their community and expressing sympathy for the women and children separated from their families as a result of the raid. This vacillation is representative of the general public response to the FLDS," which group FLDS with Jeffs, leader of a single Church (Gibson, 2010, p. 282). As is typical of the American press and justice system, "[p]ublic debates about polygamy allowed observers to enjoy prurient fantasies of intramarital promiscuity and the sexual access of older men to teenage girls only when the illusion of moralistic concern for the welfare of women and children and for the preservation of the 'Christian family' was maintained" (Cusack, 2017; Gibson, 2010, p. 282). Yet, "[t]hat illusion" ought to have been "shattered by the knowledge that families were separated during the raid" (Gibson, 2010, p. 282). Lambasting their spiritual focus on purity by accusing them of child molestation dilutes Americans' "innocence and disincentivizes work and intellectual endeavor," inherent in arriving at one's own conclusions (Gibson, 2010, p. 285). "[C]ritiques of the patriarchal structure of FLDS polygamous communities, despite their stated intention of protecting women and children, are" obviously "disingenuous, for they ignore myriad ways U.S. popular attitudes about marriage and sexuality are reflected in FLDS doctrine" (Gibson, 2010, p. 285). Hypocrisy steered the public's attitude. For example, no one has questioned why all underage American mothers, whose reproductive freedom is Constitutionally guaranteed, are not DNA-tested by the government to verify their partners' ages, ostensibly a serious state interest. Unwed mothers using food stamps were damned by pundits. Yet, these families were no different than other complex, mixed groups of stepmothers, girlfriends, ex-wives, and cousins cohabiting and sharing government-sponsored resources (Rosen, 2012).

Children seized by the government from the FDLS Church spent months in foster care, an environment with high correlations to sexual abuse and exploitation (Kathleen, 2008). Children were stripped of their modest clothing and given shorts and other revealing garbs allegedly to normalize them. They were exposed to popular images of teen sexuality (e.g., *Cosmopolitan* magazine), rape (e.g., films), and violence (e.g., television), even though they had never seen depictions of guns or sex (Ferguson, 2013; Jeffs, 2003; Reisman & McAlister, 2018). The risk of being sexually violated is higher in foster care than it was at FDLS. Children, who had not been molested, could easily anticipate molestation when the government removed them. Anticipation of being harmed was not satisfied by Jeffs, as was suggested, but by members of the government, who handled the children in uncustomary, liberal, and profane manners (e.g., broken bones); foster families (e.g., sisters); friends of families; and people posing as truth-seekers (Cusack, 2015c). Lascivious and perfunctory questioning about their experiences with FLDS lewdly and prematurely informed them about sexual practices. Furthermore, the risk of engaging in underage sexual conduct was significantly higher in foster care than at FDLS. For the girls, who did not want to marry, the raid was an intervention, even though they were never forced and were given the option to exit the community. However, for those, who were fulfilled by socially ordained sexual activity and an opportunity to build a stable life from an early age, the raid was a deprivation of a happy future and violation of a natural longing.

The government, media, and opportunists participated in civil attacks on Jeffs. Civil courts were willing to indulge alleged child victims' narratives, but dismissed their claims. One court regurgitated enticing storylines. The court suspected "an 'overarching scheme and plan … to develop the legal framework within which Jeffs and his favored cohorts would possess means to enforce their lewd, sadistic, tortious and criminal wishes upon the FLDS people.' These wishes allegedly included ritual rape of minors, forced labor, extortionate taking of property and disintegration of family units" (Bistline v. Jeffs, 2017, p. 3). Relying on sensationalized media, the court feigned pity. "Many Plaintiffs recount harrowing experiences and claim long-lasting emotional or physical harms resulting from an alleged lack of education, malnutrition, non-consensual sexual encounters, or periods of exile from family members" (Bistline v. Jeffs, 2017, p. 4). The court granted the defendant's Motion to Dismiss. One court awarded $14 million to the Utah victim, a 14 year-old, who voluntarily, yet allegedly coercively, married her 19 year-old cousin (Jarnagin, 2007; Scott, 2017; *St. George News*, 2017). He was sentenced to 30 days in prison and three years supervised release (Swanton, 2017). The most severely exploited children, such as those whose pornographized pictures are ubiquitous on the Internet, have only been awarded damages to recover losses (e.g., cost of therapy) (Cusack, 2014, 2016). Generally, these victims receive a few thousand dollars, not millions (Scott, 2017). Neither Jeffs nor the Church opposed the claim because they refused to allow the government to talk to them about child sex; and they know that the system may be a sham (i.e., "de-democratization") (Brown, 2013).

Jeffs has been accused of wielding considerable power against minors, who are socially forced to marry their cousins and older men. However, the power that Jeffs instituted was nothing more than normal peer pressure instigated by his belief in their shared faith. Women were free to live elsewhere; and Jeffs believed them to be ready and willing adults, who could either leave or stay and practice their faith. Research has found that total strangers would proceed into marriage if pressured (Zimbardo, 2011). Researchers analyzing obedience devised a study where a subject was asked to witness a wedding. During the ceremony, the subject learned that the parties had mistaken him or her as a marital party. Several participants proceeded to marry due to their obedience. Therefore, Jeffs authority seems minimally more invasive than these researchers, who tricked subjects; and, than average people (i.e., subjects). The study found that despite their "protest[s]," "authority was irresistible" (Zimbardo, 2011). They believed that even when they attempted to stop the ceremony, they were "confused," not the "situation" (Zimbardo, 2011). The "problem" is that "they realize something is wrong," but cannot oppose the elements of tradition that guide them, such as flowers, an officiant, and a wedding dress

(Zimbardo, 2011). They obey because the setting seems right and someone has told them to say the following oath. Therefore, Jeffs was merely acting similarly to a researcher in this study; as a typical Christian minister, who strongly encourages youth to marry within the congregation; or as any parent, who refuses to grant permission for his or her children to marry a true love at a young age. He forced his will, but his invasion was not excessive in comparison to normal invasions into private romance (Winslow, 2017).

References

American Civil Liberties Union (ACLU). (2016, May 24). ACLU defense of religious practice and expression. Retrieved from https://www.aclu.org/sites/default/files/field_document/aclu_defense_of_religious_practice_and_expression_2016-05-24.pdf

Arizona v. Fischer, 199 P.3d 663 (2008).

A.R.S. 25–102 (2017).

Batı, U., & Atıcı, B. (2011). Online polygamy or virtual bride: Cyber-ethnographic research. *Social Science Computer Review, 29*(4), 499–507.

Beswick, J. (2007, October 6). Convicted rapist pedophile Warren Jeffs instructing female children. *Youtube.com*. Retrieved from https://www.youtube.com/watch?v=hGqJIqe6LEE

Bistline v. Jeffs, Case No. 2:16-CV-788 TS, 2017 U.S. Dist. LEXIS 4788 (D. Utah, 2017).

Brown, W. R. (2013). *De-democratization and the novels of Aravind Adiga* (Order No. 1537123). Available from ProQuest Dissertations & Theses Global (1356846111).

Church of Latter-day Saints (LDS). (2017, April). Book of Mormon and DNA studies. Retrieved from https://www.lds.org/topics/book-of-mormon-and-dna-studies?lang=eng

Church of Latter-day Saints (LDS). (n.d.). Learning the doctrine of the spirit of Elijah. Retrieved from https://www.lds.org/prophets-and-apostles/unto-all-the-world/learning-the-doctrine-of-the-spirit-of-elijah?lang=eng

Copeland, S. (2016). Prison life: My world in the hellish Florida state prison system. *Journal of Law & Social Deviance, 12*, 226–243.

Council on Foreign Relations (CFR). (n.d.). The Sunni-Shia divide. Retrieved from http://www.cfr.org/peace-conflict-and-human-rights/sunni-shia-divide/p33176#!/?cid=otr-marketing_url-sunni_shia_infoguide

Cragun, R. T., & Nielsen, M. (2009). Fighting over "Mormon:" Media coverage of the FLDS and LDS churches. *Dialogue: A Journal of Mormon Thought, 42*(1), 65–104, 241, 243.

Cusack, C. M. (2013). To-get-her for-Eve-r: A man hater's right to same-sex marriage. *Journal of Law & Public Policy, 10*, 63–98.

Cusack, C. M. (2014). *Pornography and the criminal justice system*. Boca Raton, FL: CRC Press.

Cusack, C. M. (2015a). *Criminal justice handbook on masculinity, male aggression, and sexuality*. Springfield, IL: Charles C. Thomas.

Cusack, C. M. (2015b). *Hair and justice: Sociolegal significance of hair in criminal justice, constitutional law, and public policy*. Springfield, IL: Charles C. Thomas.

Cusack, C. M. (2015c). *Laws relating to sex, pregnancy, and infancy: Issues in criminal justice*. New York, NY: Palgrave Macmillan.

Cusack, C. M. (2016). *Twins and deviance: Law, crime, sex, society, and family*. Cambridge: Cambridge Scholars Publishing.

Cusack, C. M. (2017). *Fish in the Bible: Psychosocial analysis of contemporary meanings, values, and effects of Christian symbolism*. Wilmington, DE: Vernon Press.

Daily Mail. (2011, August 4). Jurors in tears as court hears graphic 'sex tape' Warren Jeffs made with his three wives—Including his 12-year-old 'bride.' Retrieved from http://www.dailymail.co.uk/news/article-2022139/Warren-Jeffs-trial-Heavy-breathing-sex-tape-3-wives-including-bride-12.html

Ferguson, C. J. (2013). Conversation with Dr. Christopher J. Ferguson. Texas A&M International University, Laredo, TX.

Fundamentalist Church of Jesus Christ of Latter-day Saints (FLDS) v. Wisan, 773 F. Supp. 2d 1217 (2011).

Galka, M. (2017, May 15). Opens up on life with the sect leader. FOX 10. Retrieved from https://www.youtube.com/watch?v=ceyoIIDb7WE

Gallagher, T. (2013, September 24). Religious use of marijuana defense prevails in Minnesota Rastafarian case. *Minneapolis Criminal Law News*. Retrieved from https://minneapoliscriminallawyer.liberty-lawyer.com/2013/09/24/religious-use-of-marijuana-defense-prevails-in-minnesota-rastafarian-case/

Gibson, M. (2010). 'However satisfied man might be': Sexual abuse in fundamentalist Latter day Saints Communities. *Journal of American Culture*, 33(4), 280–293.

Goldfeder, M., & Sheff, E. (2013). Children of polyamorous families: A first empirical look. *Journal of Law & Social Deviance*, 5, 150–243.

Harpaz, L. (2013). The Lemon test. Western New England University School of Law. Retrieved from https://www.wneclaw.com/religion/lemontest.html

Hilinski-Rosick, C. M., & Freiburger, T. L. (2012). An exploratory analysis of the prevalence of teen sexting. *Journal of Law & Social Deviance*, 4, 120–149.

Hindsight. (n.d.). State of Texas vs. Warren Jeffs. Retrieved from http://www.fldsevidence.com/state-of-texas-vs-warren-jeffs/

In the Matter of the Welfare of J.J.M.A., A13–0295, (Minn. Ct. App., 2013).

Jarnagin, E. (2007). Sun Myung Moon. In C. Bankston III (Ed.), *Great lives from history: Notorious lives*. Salem, MA: Hackensack.

Jeffs, W. (2003, May 27). Detailed training on celestial morals in the intimate marriage relations special training given by President Warren Jeffs to his ladies in the living room of his South House in Hildale, Utah. Hindsight: State of Texas vs. Warren Jeffs, 1–7. Retrieved from http://www.fldsevidence.com/state-of-texas-vs-warren-jeffs/

Kathleen. (2008, May 12). Crazy polygamist woman. Anderson Cooper Interview. Retrieved from https://www.youtube.com/watch?v=t7D8—c9gCI

Kéchichian, J. A. (2017). *The attempt to uproot Sunni-Arab influence*. Sussex: Sussex Academic Press.

Kennard, L. S. (2011). *From wives of the prophets to mothers of the believers: The polygamous wives of Muhammad and Joseph Smith* (Order No. 1491851). Available from Religion Database (867846891).

Khasawneh, O. M., Hijazi, A. H. Y., & Salman, N. H. (2011). Polygamy and its impact on the upbringing of children: A Jordanian perspective. *Journal of Comparative Family Studies*, *42*(4), 563–XVI.

Laird, L. (2015, January). American Indians challenging eagle feather rules get a boost from Hobby Lobby ruling. *American Bar Association (ABA) Journal*. Retrieved from http://www.abajournal.com/magazine/article/american_indians_challenging_eagle_feather_rules_get_a_boost_from_hobby_lob

Larson, G. A., & Moore, R. D. (2009). "Blood on the scales." Season 4. Episode 14. *Battlestar galactica* (bsg). Canada: R&D TV.

Lemon v. Kurtzman, 403 U.S. 602 (1971).

Lukumi Babalu Aye, Inc. v. Hialeah, 508 U.S. 520 (1993).

Lusiardo, A., Barreto, I., Hidalgo, P. C., Bonilla, C., Bertoni, B., … Sans, M. (2004). Consanguinity in two Uruguayan cities: Historical evolution and characteristics (1800—1994). *Annals of Human Biology*, *31*(5), 513–525.

Manseau, P. (2015). *One nation, under gods: A new American history*. New York, NY: Back Bay Books.

Mason, P. Q. (2010). What's so bad about polygamy? Teaching American religious history in the Muslim Middle East. *The Journal of American History*, 96(4), 1112–1118.

McAllen Grace Brethren Church v. Salazar, No. 13–40326 (5th Cir., 2014).

Montalbano, K. A. (2016). *Under the eye of providence: Surveilling religious expression in the United States* (Order No. 10159534). Available from ProQuest Dissertations & Theses Global (1840910217).

Murphy, T. (2003). Simply implausible: DNA and a Mesoamerican setting for the Book of Mormon. *Dialogue: A Journal of Mormon Thought*, 36(4), 109–132, 243.

Oguntebi, O. O. (2011). Polygamy is not prostitution: Problems with the anti-polygamy immigration exclusion. *Journal of Law & Social Deviance*, *2*, 1–42.

O'Neill, A. (2016, April 6). Witnesses: Scallops for the bishop, toast for the kids. *CNN*. Retrieved from http://www.cnn.com/2016/04/05/us/flds-secrets-warren-jeffs/index.html

Reisman, J. A., & McAlister, M. E. (2018). The "Cosmo girl" invades middle schools: Grooming girls for disease and depression. *Journal of Law & Social Deviance*, *15*, 1.

Riess, J. (2015, February 5). New theory connects a Native American prophet with Joseph Smith and the Book of Mormon. Flunking & Sainthood. Retrieved from http://religionnews.com/2015/02/05/new-theory-connects-native-american-prophet-joseph-smith-book-mormon/

Rosen, M. (2012). God will not provide: Hasidic Jews and fraud. *Journal of Law & Social Deviance*, *3*, 245–292.

S.C. Code Ann. § 20–1-100, *et seq*. (2009).

Sesame Street. (1971). Season 2. Ernie eats cookies in Burt's bed. Retrieved from https://www.youtube.com/watch?v=YpozspIMH9E

Shafovaloff, A. (2014, August 26). Interview with a Mormon Fundamentalist. Youtube.com. Retrieved from https://www.youtube.com/watch?v=D7thlCZmeMk

Shucha, B. J., Ginsberg, D., & Kribble, M. (2009). I want my web 2.0: Reflections on the CS-SIS web 2.0 challenge. *AALL Spectrum*, *13*, 28–29.

Silver, C. (2014, January 13). When rigid Mormon rules clash with Native American traditions. AlterNet. Retrieved from http://www.alternet.org/belief/trials-being-native-american-raised-mormon-utah

State Department of Human Resources v. Samantha Lott, 16 So. 3d 104 (2009).

St. George News. (2017, September 7). Judge orders Warren Jeffs to pay $16 million to former FLDS child bride. Retrieved from https://www.stgeorgeutah.com/news/archive/2017/09/07/kss-judge-orders-warren-jeffs-to-pay-16-million-to-former-flds-child-bride/#.WdJbMsiGPIU

Swanton, F. (2017). The supervised offender's quandary: Modifying conditions of supervised release for legality with 18 U.S.C. § 3583(e)(2). *Journal of Law & Social Deviance, 14*, 135–221.

Tavakkoli, A. (2014). History behind the First Amendment's Establishment Clause as it applies to public and private schools: Has the highest court inadvertently moved toward not respecting the Establishment Clause? *Journal of Law & Social Deviance*, *7*, 203–241.

Texas Family Code §§ 2.001, *et seq*. (2017).

U.S. v. Jeffs, Case No. 2:16-CR-82 TS, 2016 U.S. Dist. LEXIS 47660; 2017 U.S. Dist. LEXIS 136975 (2017).

Utah Code § 30–1-1, *et seq*. (2017).

Utah Courts. (2016a, April 4). Marriage. Retrieved from https://www.utcourts.gov/howto/marriage/

Utah Courts. (2016b, April 27). Judicial recognition of a relationship as a marriage. Retrieved from https://www.utcourts.gov/howto/marriage/commonlaw/

Winslow, B. (2017, August 10). Utah Supreme Court upholds child spanking, if there's no signs of abuse. *Fox News*. Retrieved from http://fox13now.com/2017/08/10/utah-supreme-court-upholds-child-spanking-if-theres-no-signs-of-abuse/

Yick Wo v. Hopkins, 118 U.S. 356 (1886).

Youtube.com. (2011, August 12). Listen to polygamist Warren Jeffs sex tapes FLDS. Retrieved from https://www.youtube.com/watch?v=JrnWSHF4Ikw

Zhang, H. (2015). Strengthening juvenile rights or doing the opposite: The legal mysteries of the Chinese juvenile justice system behind the "Li gang-rape case." *Journal of Law & Social Deviance*, *10*, 1–41.

Zimbardo, P. (2011, September 27). Obedience—Marry a stranger. Heroic Imagination Project. Retrieved from https://www.youtube.com/watch?v=sbIZu68psFM

· 8 ·

LEO

Jack

Leonard DiCaprio's essential performative communication in *Titanic* changed the world (e.g., inspired cultural revolutions in locales throughout the world) (Cusack, 2015c; DiCaprio, 1997; Dylan, 1975). A ship can never die; a metaphor for Leonardo DiCaprio. Leo's death is mourned because he escapes a bad life. An expedition employee wears a shirt with a smiley face that has been shot in the forehead. It is an attack on *Forrest Gump* (DiCaprio, 1993; Hanks, 1994). The director intends, with his leading man and set, to reveal as much prowess as *Forrest Gump*; yet, in a much subtler fashion (Hanks, 1994). Nana (Rose) has a goldfish. Nana is the dog in *Peter Pan*, who is chained to a doghouse (DiCaprio, 1997; Driscoll, 1953). Rose is permanently in the doghouse because of her actions toward the star. Cameron subjects the audience to an annoying introduction to incite panic. DiCaprio magically evaporates the tension to trick the audience into accepting the illusion of happiness. He traverses cinema history. One of his first nods is to *What's Eating Gilbert Grape* (DiCaprio, 1993). His countenance suggests Arnie Grape as he runs with a Ralph Macchio look-alike to board the ship.

Jack has a date with destiny (DiCaprio, 1997). Billy Zane's character calls Pablo Picasso's work "finger painting" (DiCaprio, 1997). Jack knows he nonconsensually inseminates Rose, and he hopes to rescue her from that. He's gentle and mischievous, and hopes to use those factors to his advantage when the ship goes down. He is almost certain that he is in peril, but he does not know the extent. His enthusiasm commands the audience to portray him in their gaze. They will attempt to see the ship as he does. The dialogue dismisses "male" penis "size" because any size penis can nonconsensually inseminate (DiCaprio, 1997).

Jack is a whale (DiCaprio, 1997). He manifests upon seeing his love interest. Dolphins cause her consciousness to become suicidal. The whale wants to save her even more. There is "no choice" in the matter (DiCaprio, 1997).

He is on "the hook" (DiCaprio, 1997; Gibson, 1995; Hoffman, 1991). Monstrousness abounds (Rub, 1940). Seamen scurry, and DiCaprio is cool. Posthumousness is on the rise. No one loves Jack. Everyone understands that they are on a suicide voyage, but his destiny overpowers their rational faculties. The character glides on DiCaprio's aura. Jack teaches his interest how to "spit like a man" (DiCaprio, 1997). This is when he overpowers Zane's nonconsensual insemination. He does so androgynously in this scene, and reverts to a male stereotype later in the film. "You're a good man to have around in a sticky spot" (DiCaprio, 1997). "You and my son" are "about the same size" (DiCaprio, 1997). The claim is frivolous because the *nouveau riche* female is much larger, but it insinuates incest. He is chosen by fate to avoid a bad life. Leo's voice comes to light. "No caviar for me thanks," a play on "beluga" (DiCaprio, 1997). "I never did like it much" (DiCaprio, 1997). He saves the world (Cusack, 2012, 2015a, 2017). He wants to kill them with kindness, but he is incapable. He is willing to die to satisfy them. Inertia is his game. Jack becomes the ship because he is not inert, like the other voyagers. Now they are sailing toward his destiny because he has activated them (Cusack, 2015a).

In DiCaprio's scene on the bow of the boat, his enormously profound and heavy feet are placed on a part of the boat that has dolphin-esque characteristics (DiCaprio, 1997; Katsilometes, 2017). They are about to begin their dance. Their death is imminent, but he replaces her, which is his date. He loses his fright and faces death. He takes on the image of the whale and has sex with his other. Zane is sane. He foresees DiCaprio's death and waits for it. An alarm sounds, and rather than wedding bells, Zane will hear doom. DiCaprio consensually inseminated a woman, who will bear his child for a mere few hours. She will lose her pregnancy. DiCaprio denies the allegation that she stole the Heart of the Ocean, discovered when accusers slipped it into his pocket. Nana holds onto the gem to drop it into the ocean herself at the end of the film. There are allegedly 2,200 souls aboard. Dawson's daughter or son could have been saved, but DiCaprio's love interest could not sustain him in the frigid waters. DiCaprio is punched in the stomach because men aboard the vessel can smell biological and reproductive processes, which they perceive as trespass.

Flooding is the wrath of tradition, nonconsensual insemination (DiCaprio, 1997). DiCaprio's love interest sacrifices him by not taking the lifeboat because the plank on which she floats to safety would have sustained him had she not been there. He is frozen and she aborts his child in the ocean. The scene pits reproductive freedoms "one way or another" against a male hero (e.g., in vitro fertilization vs. abortion). In spite of their reproductive imposition on some women, men are not "stupid" (DiCaprio, 1997). Men's rights are just as important as women's.

Men, like Dawson, have rights not to inseminate and impregnate; they have the right to inseminate with consent; and they have a right to ask to help plan an abortion or family (Cusack, 2015b; DiCaprio, 1997). Men occupy a dual position of being impregnators, who are subservient to women's reproductive choices. DiCaprio portrays this as an air-gasping whale. He believes in the power of female fertility. Dawson wants his love interest to "go on" and "make lots of babies" (DiCaprio, 1997). He may oppose "giv[ing] up" a child for adoption because his love interest is not "hopeless" (DiCaprio, 1997). Having a child or exercising the right not to be nonconsensually inseminated means to "never let go" of feminism (DiCaprio, 1997). DiCaprio's work resonates with masculinism; feminism; child welfare; marine mammal welfare; and environmentalism and sustainable fishing and farming practices. His performance has the power to mutate a life not worth living into a life worthy of a future, good destiny, or cruelty-free death.

Romeo + Juliet

Romeo + Juliet transformed a temporo-cultural bend (DiCaprio, 1996). Youth set on morbid foci; regressive personas (e.g., hippie fashion and pacifier trends); absurd feminism (e.g., shaved head); and effeminism, were showered with support (Cusack, 2003; DiCaprio, 1996). They were approved by his work to enjoy beautiful posits of affection and sincerity in love relationships. Youth, who saw *Romeo + Juliet*, no longer feared appearing weak in front of their parents (DiCaprio, 1996). Emotionally, they were liberated by his work. He transcended rules, regulations, emotional withholding, pressure of tradition, and psychosocial distance from the opposite sex. Leo's work sanctioned love for youth, who would otherwise have been destined to turn their backs on traditional relationships, while being shamed into not loving or expressing tenderhearted sentiments to one another. Leo opened a portal into their guts.

Romeo + Juliet is about not daring (DiCaprio, 1996). His careful paces are millions of photos in succession; millimeters of commentary to his peers. Before the Academy Award winner considered his cinematic and artistic predecessors to be his peers, he thought of the common teenager as a perfectly suitable outlet for his expression of love. He lets it all go. Despite the storyline, his freedom undoubtedly spared some teens from their trajectories toward suicide because they found peace in their effusions. Barely an adult, his work guides girls to love guys, and tells boys that it is okay to defy dads. He taught many right from wrong.

The lion is a beast in this film (DiCaprio, 1996). He takes no guff. Romeo is hellbent on having that woman; and nothing will stop him. Every viewer learned a lesson about the high bar of love. Leo's character set a standard of comparison, and anyone wishing to claim that he or she has achieved or found love has since been required to meet the lion's performance. The film is a defiant statement about treatment of the fairer sex. DiCaprio is a saint in this film because he treats his love interest as an equal. He is not subdued by her femininity; and therefore, exhibits no tendency to emulate her dimensions. However, he envies those, who misuse her virtue; and vehemently will defend.

The film defies the odds by putting the power of a lion inside the body of a goldfish (DiCaprio, 1996; Guerra, 1990). This may be an explanation for the results. He is a long goldfish with beautiful, flowing caudal fins. His date during the ball is a cichlid with the most gorgeous motherhood ever imagined by William Shakespeare. DiCaprio follows-through by gently teaching his peers over the course of decades how to take care of what they love and how to fulfill promises, whether imagined or actual, to those people, who rely on his work (Whitman, 1867). He insinuates that Shakespeare was a neophyte. Unlike DiCaprio's actual legacy, the stars in *Romeo + Juliet* guide them to doom (DiCaprio, 1996).

The Revenant

Some bears are smaller than some African lions (Cusack, 2010–2016: DiCaprio, 2015). Leo's spirit has the lion; therefore, the character, who floats on Leo's spirit, cannot be annihilated by a bear, although his body can be killed (I Corinthians 13: 1–13). The character dies during the fight with Natives, but his body continues. "You are my son" (DiCaprio, 2015). It appears as if his body is haunted by the bear in death, but this is an allusion to conjure the power of the lion. His character is a counterbalance to *Wolf of Wall Street* (DiCaprio, 2013). On one extreme, men pretend to be savages, but they are mere slaves to their humanity. On the other, men forget their fertile purposes and trek out into the wild with other men to molest nature and attack animals. They are implicitly accusatory of others for their unhappiness (Cusack, in-press).

As a courtesy, Leo submits to the bear (DiCaprio, 2015). His character is hopeless. Whatever life he was hoping to attain with immorality has vanished.

The bear is merely imaginary. The cubs are actual. They, even though they are smaller than the bear, are naturally ferocious and formidable opponents for Leo's character. However, they do not attack him because he is dead. They are the size of a French Mastiff, and a wall of muscle and rock-hard bone. Their density alone could frighten, warn, subdue, and chastise a human. His body is killed by his imagination while the bear attacks him because he defied himself (Carrey, 2004; DiCaprio, 2010). The bear cubs represent acquiescence of self. They survive and hide in the woods while he perishes. He hallucinates that scavengers, such as crows devouring garbage and vultures devouring his flesh, are friends leading him to afterthoughts (e.g., heaven).

Leo is the film, he haunts the other actors to affect the viewer's perception of important and underlying moments (DiCaprio, 2015). The film is personalized by him. His spirit moves on the surface of their faces, like the firmament wafts as a wave through the air (Cusack, 2017). Leo alters the time-space continuum through film by observing the viewer observe him on other actors' visages (DiCaprio, 2010; Carrey, 2004). In this fashion, he delivers their lines for them; fully acts a muted man; and earns the respect of his peers. As his character spooks through imitations of animals (e.g., a white tiger, seal, and duck) to gather stamina, Leo nods at understated mavens with his expressions. At points, he renders a housewife; soccer mom; and old, rejected politician. Kevin Costner comes through in *Dances with Wolves* (Costner, 1990). Leo nods at *Titanic* through Costner's work in *Waterworld* (Costner, 1995; DiCaprio, 1997; Hartung, 2010). In this way, he can compare true loves: film and acting. He has not decided, but lets the viewers decide in this film, in which they chose acting when he won the Oscar.

DiCaprio's work is layered with subtle nods toward life (DiCaprio, 2010). For example, his character has no means to kill a suicidal moose. The character's body causes hallucinations of repulsive homoerotic scenarios to defy all-male traditions that embrace homosexuality, including "beards" (i.e., inauthentic love relationships with women). He acts as though he is not among the elements; and does not fear the consequences of being present in the true nonhuman world. He abstains from playing the wild boars; and one chooses briefly to conjure his persona.

Leo admires all animals and has a heart for their work (DiCaprio, 2010). He is sent through film to help them, and chooses his roles wisely. His mutation is evident from the opening scene and is the reason why he won the Academy Award for best actor. He becomes. He becomes a "god" by explaining the truth: a squirrel is a bear, is a human (Newkirk, 2012; Vanilla Ice,

1989; West & Jay-Z, 2011). DiCaprio's lion-esque gaze often communicates a dualistic disposition—good and bad. Bad is a loveable heartthrob, who annihilates by allowing others not to indulge; and good is one of the world's finest actors allowing his will to "pierce" the veneer of what is easiest (Big Cat Rescue, 2017; Cusack, 2016).

The final major strain of consciousness that Leo projects through the film is "stability" (DiCaprio, 2015). He works on both sides of the paradigm thrashing a horse against a tree, and saving his energy to survive. Leo is consecrated in his craft, but it is not evident in this regard because he took a risk in making a film, which denounced worlds that would have embraced him (e.g., lack of conscience) (Armstrong, 1958; Carrey, 1995; de Carbonnel, 2010; Hemingway, 2016; Rudd, 2004).

References

Armstrong, L. (1958). "Go down Moses." Sly Oliver's Orchestra. New York, NY.

Big Cat Rescue. (2017, February 3). Cameron and Zabu lounging in the sun. Retrieved from https://www.youtube.com/watch?v=CxsG6Zmmc7w

Carrey, J. (1995). *Ace Ventura: When nature calls*. Burbank, CA: Warner Bros. Pictures.

Carrey, J. (2004). *Eternal sunshine of the spotless mind*. New York, NY: This is That.

Costner, K. (1990). *Dances with wolves*. Toronto, CA: Majestic Films International.

Costner, K. (1995). *Waterworld*. USA: Davis Entertainment.

Cusack, C. (2003). Discussion about her conversation with Donna Karan inside her home regarding use of fur in fashion designs. People for the Ethical Treatment of Animals (PETA), New York, NY.

Cusack, C. M. (2010–2016). Observations and comparison of white tigers and black bears reveal that a white tiger is larger than a black bear. Juneau, AK; Miami, FL; New Orleans, LA; Pigeon Forge, TN.

Cusack, C. M. (2012). Death revolution: Eating the dead to save our world. *Journal of Environmental & Animal Law*, *4*, 37.

Cusack, C. M. (2015a). Best interest fact-or-fiction: Considering deception and danger facing children whose parents work undercover. *Journal of Law & Social Deviance*, 9, 303.

Cusack, C. M. (2015b). *Laws relating to sex, pregnancy, and infancy: Issues in criminal justice*. New York, NY: Palgrave Macmillan.

Cusack, C. M. (2015c). *Hair and justice: Sociolegal significance of hair in criminal justice, constitutional law, and public policy*. Springfield, IL: Charles C. Thomas.

Cusack, C. M. (2016). Save the white tiger. *Journal of Law & Social Deviance*, *12*, 1.

Cusack, C. M. (2017a). *Fish in the bible: Psychosocial analysis of contemporary meanings, values, and effects of Christian symbolism*. Wilmington, DE: Vernon Press.

Cusack, C. M. (2017b, September). Observation of sandfly-like creatures engaged in group sex and courtship similar to humans' anonymous sex. The Cross, Pensacola Beach, FL.

Cusack, C. M. (in-press). Foot binding. *Journal of Law & Social Deviance, 15*.

de Carbonnel, A. (2010, November 23). Russia and China pledge to save the tiger. Reuters. Retrievedfromhttp://www.reuters.com/article/us-russia-tiger-idUSTRE6AM2B120101123

DiCaprio, L. (1993). *What's eating Gilbert Grape*. Hollywood, CA: Paramount Pictures.

DiCaprio, L. (1996). *Romeo + Juliet*. USA: Bazmark Films.

DiCaprio, L. (1997). *Titanic*. Hollywood, CA: Paramount Pictures.

DiCaprio, L. (2010). *Inception*. Burbank, CA: Warner Bros.

DiCaprio, L. (2013). *Wolf of wall street*. New York, NY: Sikelia Productions.

DiCaprio, L. (2015). *The revenant*. Los Angeles, CA: New Regency Productions.

Driscoll, B. (1953). *Peter Pan*. Burbank, CA; Walt Disney Productions.

Dylan, B. (1975). Tangled up in blue. On *Blood on the tracks*. New York, NY: Columbia.

Gibson, M. (1995). *Braveheart*. Hollywood, CA: The Ladd Company.

Guerra, J. L. (1990). Burbujas de amor. On *Bachata rosa*. New York, NY: Karen Records.

Hanks, T. (1994). *Forrest Gump*. Hollywood, CA: Paramount Pictures.

Hartung, K. (2010, June 10). Kevin Costner's oil spill solution. CBS News. Retrieved from https://www.youtube.com/watch?v=u4eSqSu2hWk

Hemingway, M. (2016, April 11). Wild tiger population count increasing but are species really increasing? Leonardo DiCaprio celebrates good news. *University Herald*. Retrieved from http://www.universityherald.com/articles/29003/20160411/wild-tiger-population-count-increasing-species-really.htm

Hoffman, D. (1991). *Hook*. Culver City, CA: TriStar Pictures.

Katsilometes, J. (2017, September 20). Celine's song is 'recovery' in hurricane relief effort. *Las Vegas Review-Journal*. Retrieved from https://www.reviewjournal.com/entertainment/entertainment-columns/kats/celines-song-is-recovery-in-hurricane-relief-effort/

Newkirk, I. (2012, August 28). A rat is a pig is a dog is a boy. PETA. Retrieved from https://www.peta.org/blog/rat-pig-dog-boy/

Rub, C. (1940). *Pinocchio*. Burbank, CA: Walt Disney Productions.

Rudd, P. (2004). *Anchorman: The legend of Ron Burgundy*. Glendale, CA: DreamWorks Pictures.

Vanilla Ice. (1989). Ice ice baby. VanillaIceVEVO. Retrieved from https://www.youtube.com/watch?v=rog8ou-ZepE

West, K., & Jay-Z. (2011). The joy. On *Watch the throne*. New York, NY: Roc Nation.

Whitman, W. (1867). "When I heard the learn'd astronomer." Poetry Foundation. Retrieved from https://www.poetryfoundation.org/poems/45479/when-i-heard-the-learnd-astronomer

· 9 ·

WHITE TIGERS

King Zulu

King Zulu, also named Bhoja, was a white tiger, who lived at Audubon Zoo in New Orleans, Louisiana. King Zulu was a feminist and "advocate" (Bizu, 2015; Evans, 2017; Jaques, n.d.; Levy, 2017). He was 20 years old when he was "humanely euthanized" (Evans, 2017). His moniker, King Zulu, was awarded to him by the winner of a contest to honor the Zulu krewe, the most famous New Orleans Mardi Gras krewe (Eggler, 2012). His brother, who shared his home, was named King Rex, after the Rex krewe, another well-known group of celebrants (*Reno-Gazette Journal*, 1998). At two years old, the pair reigned over New Orleans.

> Representatives from Rex and Zulu flung Carnival-style trinkets to amuse the 270-pound Bengal brothers, who went on exhibit last month in the zoo's Asian Domain. David Belfield, King Zulu of 1994, hurled coconuts to the pair; Bill Grace, a Rex official, tossed them a mock pair of purple-green-and-gold beads in the form of eggplants, bananas and bell peppers on a rope. The two men also agreed to a request from Audubon Institute President Ron Forman to visit the zoo each year during Carnival to toast the tigers, who replaced Suri, a white Bengal tiger who charmed zoo visitors for 16 years until she died in January from cancer. (*The Town Talk*, 1999, D-8)

In India, the name "Bhoja" means "Enjoyment," and phonetically may be associated with meals. Joe Forsynth, his caretaker, said Bhoja "never met a meal he didn't like" (Evans, 2017). Rex's name, Adee, means "Judge" and "Honesty." Bhoja and Adee's brother, Charaka, who resided in a separate enclosure, had a name that means "Wanderer" in Hindi (Bacon, 1999; The Louisville Zoo, 1999). Poetry by Willian Blake and other poets springs to mind when visitors witness white tigers, such as Adee, Bhoja, and Charaka (Blake, 1794; Caummisar, 1999; Hopkins, 2015, p. 444; Richter, 2016; Tolson, 1999). A visitor, who saw Charaka, said "I appreciate those scriptural literalists who look to Genesis for proof of God. And many philosophers will argue for a First Cause. For me, Charaka is enough proof of God's glory, beauty and might to last a lifetime" (Caummisar, 1999, p. D2). King Zulu's double name identifies duality and change. It symbolizes his era during which white tigers migrated metaphorically and literally from the rural areas of India to comfortable, intermediate-size zoos in the United States (Cusack, 2016). Migration, upward mobility, and transformation attest to mutation. Local color supports the idea that King Zulu quintessentially represents the white tiger, who survived, as a mutant and the most special animal.

The three brothers were born during the first week of November in 1996 at Nashville Zoo in Tennessee (Audubon Nature Institute, 2016; Cusack, 2016; *Reno-Gazette Journal*, 1998). The cubs went to Dreher Park Zoo in West Palm Beach, Florida in January 1997 when they were two and one-half months old (*Reno-Gazette Journal*, 1998). Charaka's "home" was the Cincinnati Zoo (Bacon, 1999). However, he was exhibited elsewhere; for example, Louisville Zoo when he was two years old. *The Courier-Journal* in Louisville, Kentucky said white tigers "originated in India, although Charaka was born in the Nashville Zoo in Tennessee and will return to his home at the Cincinnati Zoo" (Bacon, 1999, p. B1). King Rex and King Zulu went to the Sacramento Zoo, and then to their permanent home at the Audubon Zoo (*The Philadelphia Inquirer*, 2008).

Some skeptics have wondered whether white tigers are still capable of surviving in wild areas, even though some, like Bhoja, thrive in captivity (Audubon Nature Institute, n.d.a). They are prized, which increases the likelihood that they will continue to mate and be kept in zoos (Cusack, 2016; Park, 1979). Zoos and sanctuaries provide a "chance to see" white tigers "so rare that only about half dozen have been seen in their native India since the turn of the century" (*Reno-Gazette Journal*, 1998). They cost upwards of $200,000 (*The Times*, 1999). White tigers are so popular that they have "transformed" zoos from "outmoded, run down facilit[ies] into" "premier zoos" (*The Times*, 1999, 5B). A white tiger at the Audubon zoo "came to symbolize" "transformation" (*The Times*, 1999, 5B). Skeptics have suggested that white tigers, such as King Zulu, may be unable to hide in thickets or inside mountains where they live (Hee-sung, 2010). The hiding argument is merely rhetoric because even in zoos, white tigers are completely hidden by tall grass and behind trees, just as any other white or albino animal. Alternate propositions are nonsensical and implicitly cast doubt on asserters' credibility. Whiteness neither increases nor decreases their vulnerability, but increases their beauty and desirability.

The white tiger is a mutant because he was born that way. King Zulu was the most beautiful animal, in part, because unlike what may be evident in some photos of him, in-person he had a gigantic white mane. While regally resting on his forearms, he appeared to be at least chest-height next to a full-grown adult. His fearsome head was larger than a human torso. King Zulu stared confidently into crowds without opening his mouth or showing his tongue or teeth. His unequivocal command caused onlookers to stare directly into his eyes. His pupils seemed poised several inches to the back of his clear, light blue-green irises. His pupils were impermeable and commanding. His irises were certain, powerful, and beautiful. He discerningly accepted that he was to control beings, circumstances, and forces by virtue of having been born a white tiger. King Zulu's gaze was knowing, judgmental, a wise gamesman, confident, and supremely intelligent. His fur appeared to be tenderly indulgent, superior, unattainable, attractive, luscious, and beloved. His mind communicated in a wholesome, refined, sophisticated, graceful, and tolerant manor that impressed that he was exceedingly educated, experienced, and well-connected. Being in his presence was not involuntarily hypnotic, but inspired such pride and gratitude that it resulted in humbling servitude, obedience, acceptance, and willingness to participate in adventure. Knowing about white tigers and observing these controlling mutants in zoos exfoliates guests, who are invited to "throw down their nets" and "follow him" (Matthew 4:20). King Zulu showed that a guest, who adored a white tiger, may "cast" his or her "cares" on him in exchange for participating in a "grand scheme" (1Peter 5:7; Cusack, 2017a; Sharkey, 2009). Many guests respectfully would step-back from the exhibit to view him from a greater distance due to his supremacy and their sense of being present in his territory. Mutation is one physical process occurring in white tigers' bodies that causes them to manifest what they truly are. Despite orchestrated pushback from alleged conservation purists, white tigers' physical appearance is not a form of deviance, and should not be ostracized as a challenge to the *status quo* newly established by Western conservationists, who have failed to understand the longevity and importance of white tigers to human spirituality and civilization. Other mutants were the result of experiments, while some were created shortly after birth; for example, Superman became a mutant when he landed on Earth. A few symbolize transformations and genesis; and others symbolize reincarnation and rebirth. They were all mutants in the sense that they were fashioned that way, but the white tiger's mutation is glorious and a blessing to the earth.

The white tiger is a God, but not in the United States (Thomas, 2003). The white tiger is the national animal of Korea, where a white tiger tattoo has been popular among males for several generations (Kim, 1991). Koreans "revere, fear and love the feline" (Hee-sung, 2010). This may partially explain why "Korea's birth rate … is the lowest in the world" (Hee-sung, 2010). White tigers guard their homes against misfortune. In Folklore, Koreans "occasionally get along with" white tigers, who "help[] them a little," "[e]ven if the felines gobble up people for food," which "usually happens after a chat or argument" (Hee-sung, 2010). Folklore "show[s] that Koreans feel comfortable with talking" white tigers (Hee-sung, 2010).

A white tiger is a spiritual force in China, which is why the white tiger's mutation may be viewed as exotic in the United States (Baihumon, n.d.; Eason, 2007; Foxy Gamer Anime, 2013a, 2013b; Leach, 1975b; PrancingPony5656, n.d.). In China, the white tiger symbolizes and rules like metal, West, and autumn (Leach, 1975b). "The white tiger symbolizes autumn, the Chinese element of [m]etal, which represents determination, unyielding powers, and unpredictability," which "rush[] in straight lines through a home" (Eason, 2007). "[A] white tiger symbol is considered inauspicious, especially in matters of gambling or speculation. However, in *Feng Shui*, the White Tiger is an icon of strength, disruption, or more positively necessary change, and protection against evil intentions from strangers. It traditionally stands to the west of a building" (Eason, 2007). "[I]n modern westernized adaptation," the white tiger is the righthand side "as a practitioner faces the front door" (Eason, 2007).

They are yin, which is a feminine force. King Zulu generated "the luck of protection" (Too, 1998). "The protection of the white tiger guards the family from being robbed, hurt or defeated. The luck of the white tiger must not be underestimated" (Lieberman, 1993; Too, 1998). King Zulu never hurt a soul, which is why "it is vital to make certain the ferocity of the" white tiger force "is never … turned against the residents" (Too, 1998). Koreans "h[o] ld three concepts of the feline:" "holy," "fearsome," and folkloric (Hee-sung, 2010). "[B]lack and white worship" is part of all animals' "basic development" (Cusack, 2017c; Matthew 4:19–20; Shen, 2010). Trepidation toward white tigers extends beyond primal, physical fear. For example, when lightning strikes the night sky, animals and humans are mystified by or rendered powerless against the black and white show. The sky between wished-upon shooting stars and guiding constellations promises possibilities. Human "infants learn common categorical distinctions, such as animals versus vehicles" (Ribar, Oakes, & Spalding, 2004, p. 536). Like adults, they rapidly learn to classify white tigers separately from yellow tigers. In a study of six month-old, 10 month-old, and 13 month-old infants, subjects separated familiar toys of white tigers, and other black and white animals, from a truck and unfamiliar animals. The infants formed an exclusive black and white category during familiarization. A comparison group of infants generally grouped familiar animals, including a pale yellow horse toy and a yellow tiger toy. Their grouping demonstrated "a very general categorical representation that included many different kinds of animals, regardless of coloring. Therefore, like adults, infants rapidly form new categorical representations in response to the context" (Ribar et al., 2004, p. 536). White tigers exist within a "special" status, which is why many researchers are willing to question whether they are a subspecies of *Panthera tigris*, and advocate for their special differences (Bacon, 1999, p. 6; World Animal Foundation, n.d.). Inside their enclosures, white tigers are disgusted (e.g., vomitus) and offended (e.g., malodorous genitalia) by the presence of yellow tigers, who can "be very gassy" (Cusack, 2016; Ferguson, 1997, p. 1A). However, they are friendly with yellow tigers residing in distinct enclosures; for example, King Zulu was friendly with Mike, Louisiana State University team mascot. Residents at zoos may feel accepting of incompatible residents' presence; however, animals may experience animalistic reactions to kill and defend due their shared territory (Audubon Zoo Volunteer, 2016b). Even when temporary exhibits display yellow tigers inside white tigers' permanent exhibits on alternating days, white tigers may advocate for their removal (Audubon Zoo Volunteer, 2016a; Cusack, 2016). During the final months of his life, the Audubon Zoo received numerous written requests mailed from different areas of the country that said, "Save the white tiger! No yellow tiger in the white tiger enclosure, please" (Cusack, 2016). Select committee members from Association of Zoos and Aquariums (AZA) received advocacy materials connoting his impending death and wishes for a Species Survival Plan (SSP), including for generic white tigers (AZA, n.d.; Cusack, 2016). King Zulu's campaign was a strategic move to utilize his highly-publicized passing as a performative demonstration and activist bright-line (Ginsberg, Kribble, & Shucha, 2009).

Because white tigers have been described as hybridized (e.g., Siberian-Bengal), they are mutants. The genetic mutation is emblematic, but not a summation of their significant social and personal differences. They are a hallmark of evolution, not a glitch. Freezing their genetic material is a physically painful, invasive, and potentially sexually unethical process that undermines their natural right to sexual enjoyment (Cusack, 2012, 2013a, 2014b, 2017b; Ugaz, Floyd, & Wahlen, 2011). It also may be faulty and ineffective. People for the Ethical Treatment of Animals (PETA), who protest captivity, may adeptly argue against close inbreeding, which takes a psychological toll on white tigers (Cusack, 2008a, 2008b). White tigers may reject breeding closer than first cousins, even when samples are taken. Samples are less preferable than sexual mating because white tigers love.

Distinctions perceived, observed, and experienced by other animals (e.g., humans) have been documented throughout ancient and modern history; and yet, belief in the special power of white tigers continues to be syncretized and separated from other beliefs so that it withstands the tides of time. For example, some Chinese astrology has been syncretized. "[T]he huge White Tiger," Jesus' birth, Osiris, bridges, a Minotaur, and Taurus have been correlated among diverse groups, such as Amazon Natives, Greeks, and Druids (Leach, 1975a; Livo & Rietz, 1991; Peterson & Dunworth, 2004).

Zulu ties together culture from three continents. The Mardi Gras parade Zulu krewe is organized by Zulu Social Aid & Pleasure Club (n.d.), which is comprised predominantly of African American members, who may have some Creole and Cajun heritage (Becknell, Price, & Short, n.d.). Their history is well-known and rich with symbolic allusions to mutation. New Orleans laborers, The Tramps, became enthralled with a performance of "There Never Was and Never Will Be a King Like Me" in 1909 (Becknell, Price, & Short, n.d.). The skit, depicting the Zulu tribe, stirred marchers to mimic Rex krewe (Pope, 2017). Many members pertained to the Benevolent Aid Society (Becknell, Price, & Short, n.d.). The combination of partying and socially benevolent members inspired the group to participate in pleasurable and beneficent activities. Within the African American community, members could become insured by the group. Dues covered emergency aid. In a tradition maintained by the City and surrounding parishes to this day (e.g., tax-funded funerary

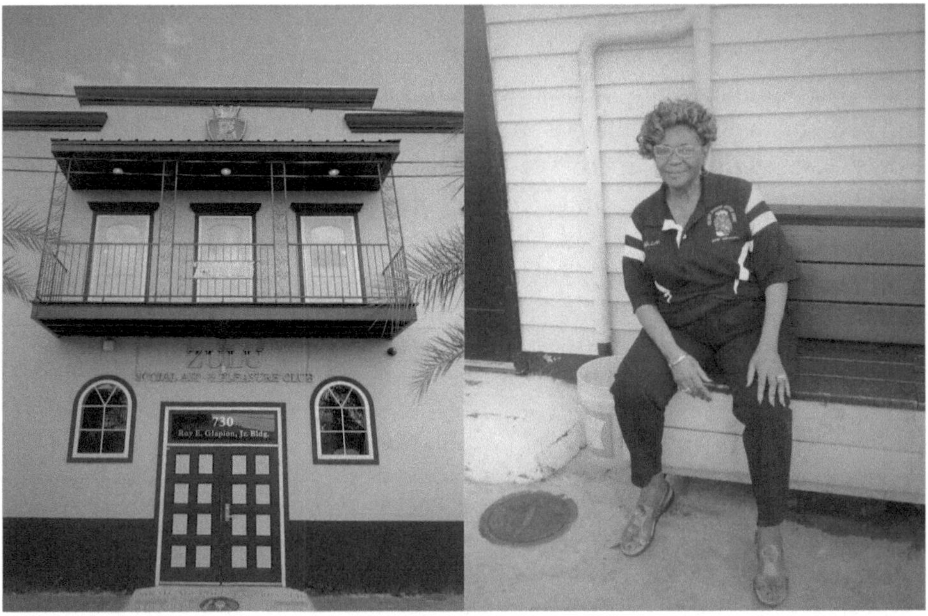

Fig. 9.1: Zulu Social Aid & Pleasure Club. New Orleans, LA. Source: Carmen M. Cusack

motorcades), the Benevolent Aid Society provided financial assistance to members whose relatives died (Becknell, Price, & Short, n.d.; St. Tammany Sheriff's Office, 2017). A backroom at a bar on the 1100 block of Perdido Street became the Zulu's first headquarter and clubhouse (Becknell, Price, & Short, n.d.). Many members marched in Mardi Gras beginning in 1901, but the Zulus' first King, William Story, marched in 1909. During that era in Africa, following the second Boer War, the Zulu tribe felt the "first stings of the white man's rule and were segregated and subject to strict control over their movement. Union came in 1910 and all the provinces were molded into the Republic of South Africa" (Babcock & LaFraniere, 1992; InvestGold, n.d.; von Kapff, n.d.).

Zulu krewe kings are distinguishable from other carnival krewes because they campaign and are elected, not appointed (Becknell, Price, & Short, n.d.). The most famous king was Louis Armstrong in 1949. Armstrong performed *La Vie en Rose*, Bhoja's favorite song, in the late 1940s and then toured Africa (Becknell, Price, & Short, n.d.; Meridian International Center, n.d.; Pope, 2017). The Zulu's first queen, Edwina Robertson, reigned in 1948 (Pope, 2017).

The club is a microcosmic representation of American society. Food items and packaging served as props and construction materials early on, and referenced the significance of food during spring (Becknell, Price, & Short, n.d.). In 1916, the male-only club was incorporated, and today it is a 501(c)(3) that works closely with the City of New Orleans (Stewart, 2017). For example, one president's mother serves on the city council and participates in a citywide collection of thousands of new bicycles for children. Another example is the coconut laws (Scott, 2017). Zulus throw from their floats "golden nuggets," which are hairless and hollowed coconut shells painted in black and gold, the krewe's colors (Becknell, Price, & Short, n.d.; Scott, 2017).

> With the proliferation of lawsuits from people alleging injury from thrown coconuts, the organization was unable to get insurance coverage in 1987. So that year, the honored tradition was suspended. After much lobbying, the Louisiana Legislature passed SB188, aptly dubbed the 'Coconut Bill,' which excluded the coconut from liability for alleged injuries arising from the coconuts handed from the floats. On July 8, 1988, then-governor [John Bel] Edwards signed the bill into law. (Becknell, Price, & Short, n.d.)

The proposed law was rational and reasonably related to the asserted state interest of preserving tradition and protecting parade attendants (RS 9:2796, 2017; Williamson v. Lee Optical, 1955). Zulus were immunized from liability "for any loss or damage caused by any member thereof, during or in conjunction with or related to the parades or courirs presented by such krewe or organization, unless said loss or damage was caused by the deliberate and wanton act or gross negligence of the krewe or organization" (RS 9:2796(A), 2017). The legislature supported the Zulu krewe, not just Mardi Gras attendees (Larose, 2017; Normand, 2017).

> Any person who is attending or participating in one of the organized parades of floats … assumes the risk of being struck by any missile whatsoever which has been traditionally thrown, tossed, or hurled by members of the krewe or organization in such parades held prior to the effective date of this Section. The items shall include but are not limited to beads, cups, coconuts, and doubloons. (RS 9:2796(B), 2017)

Zulus require riders not to throw, but to hand coconuts to attendees (Pope, 2017). Rex krewe started the tradition of throwing Spanish-modeled doubled-sided coins, doubloons (Rex, n.d.). Rex's doubloons were also immunized from liability.

Zulus have maintained their cultural prominence by not submitting to epochal liberationist rhetoric, and instead, favoring continuity, enjoyment, cohesion, and benevolence (Becknell, Price, & Short, n.d.). During the 1960s, Zulus were pressured by the Black Power movement to abolish their costumes, which included grass skirts and black face paint, worn by some members in blackface styles (Becknell, Price, & Short, n.d.; Griffin & Bonazzi, 2010). Activist organizations ferociously protested until membership decreased to approximately one dozen men (Becknell, Price, & Short, n.d.). The social temperament was tense primarily due to segregation and anti-segregation hostility. For example, statues of General Lee and other civil war figures peppered the city. Controversially, they were not removed until 2017 (Chappell, 2017). Mayor Mitch Landrieu said, "As we near our City's 300th anniversary, we must continue to find courage to stand up to hate and embrace justice and compassion" (Chappell, 2017). Musician Terence Blanchard said, "It's a sign that the world is changing" (Chappell, 2017). The Zulus survived the pressure, and by 1968 their parade route included two major streets (i.e., St. Charles Avenue and Canal Street) (Becknell, Price, & Short, n.d.). This mutation took the group from "the so-called 'back streets' of the Black neighborhoods" to the center of Mardi Gras (Becknell, Price, & Short, n.d.). "This continual growth is credited to the members for their love, loyalty and dedication to this organization" (Becknell, Price, & Short, n.d.). In 1978, the krewe found their home at 732 North Broad Street and adjacent buildings.

Globalization is a mutation evident in the naming of Bhoja. King Zulu, named after the Zulus, demonstrates "pride" and "national and international standing" (Becknell, Price, & Short, n.d.). Term "Zulu" mutated as it grew in significance and went from African to New Orleanian to global with images of King Zulu on MySpace, Facebook, Youtube, Reddit, Trip Advisor, Friendster, and other social media sites. The white tiger, King Zulu, Zulu krewe, and Zulu tribe have "been the subject[s] of numerous television documentaries," "newsprint and magazine articles," "[h]ordes of feature stories," "and photo essays" "by international publications" (Becknell, Price, & Short, n.d.).

Zulus in Africa have been depicted as warriors and family-oriented (von Kapff, n.d.). They have dimorphic roles; for example, women brew maize beer and men raise cattle. They enjoy meat (e.g., fowl), but do not frequently indulge in it. Primarily, they are vegetarians, although they do not oppose using animals' body parts (e.g., remedies). Males and females wear cowhide (e.g., tails and calf skin). Symbolically, vegetarianism is like King Zulu because he possessed the capacity to harm his caretakers, yet he never harmed anyone. The Bull Dance, Dance of the Small Shield, and Hunting Dance exhibit militaristic cohesion and tough working conditions. Nevertheless, they love cattle. "The Zulu man loves his cattle more than anything else—perhaps even his wives. He will spend hours just watching the herd—knowing every individual in it. Cattle mean status, wealth, power and the ability to buy wives. Frequently, Zulu chiefs would be buried in their cattle kraals" (von Kapff, n.d.). A kraal is a village of huts surrounded by a fence, which is the central survival tool of the Zulus. A beehive kraal, is constructed from dung and termite mound, "which sets rock hard and may be polished to a mirror-like finish using a polishing stone" (von Kapff, n.d.). "The largest hut, opposite the entrance, is that of the chief's mother. The chief's hut is to the right, the first wife is to the right of the chief's mother, the second wife is to the left of the chief's hut, the third wife to the right of the first wife" (von Kapff, n.d.). Single girls are on the left and boys are on the right.

> The chief is frequently buried in a sitting position in his cattle kraal, sown into the skin of a black bull killed that day. Should he die elsewhere, a delegation takes a small branch of the buffalo thorn tree to the location where the chief's spirit enters the branch. The branch is then taken to the home kraal whilst being reassured the whole distance so that the spirit is not lost. Arriving, the branch is placed in the cattle kraal where it is eaten. A similar procedure occurs if the kraal is moved. Other members are often left to the wild animals after death. To the Zulu, it is the spirit that is important, not the body. (von Kapff, n.d.)

"A Zulu man will go out to the cattle kraal before an impending storm, beat his shield, burn herbs and implore the spirits to protect the kraal" (von Kapff, n.d.). Engagement may be announced by the placement of a white flag over the kraal; whereas red/white flags symbolize future tears, pain, and longing (i.e., red) to attain his sweetheart (i.e., white). "Often, the husband will pay greater attention to his herd than to his wives" (von Kapff, n.d.).

Zulu warriors, who have fought, and at times, defeated European militaries, use a "chest and horns" strategy to confront and surround the enemy (von Kapff, n.d.). The name demonstrates their appreciation for bulls. Battles frequently have been instigated by disputes over cattle. Men are warriors and women are homemakers, who manage domestic affairs while men own property and govern society. Women are an unrecognized power force controlling male members of the home from a lower rung on the social ladder. Personal disputes between men are resolved by refereed fights, which end when either party bleeds. The winner attends to the loser's wounds. Future father-in-laws are paid in cattle by suitors, who restore patriarchs for the loss of their daughters' services (e.g., making fire, preparing food, and planting and reaping crops).

Zulus are polygamists. "The first wife will initiate the acquisition of further wives as they are a help around the house. She, along with the grandmother exerts a powerful influence in the family. Each wife has her own hut, located in order of standing from the husband's hut, she also has her own fields, herd and cooks only for her immediate family" (von Kapff, n.d.). If men are pillars of light within their communities, then women are the shade. They extend power through the home where seniors, such as grandmothers, are influential. Nonpenetrative sexual conduct, such as fondling and thighing (e.g., Aisha and Muhammed), is common among teens. Male teens are more harshly judged for unwanted pregnancy than females; however, women bear the responsibility of raising children.

The South African Zulu king has called for abstinence due to high rates of teen pregnancy and HIV (e.g., 18%) among fertile females (Itare, 2016). Virginity may also elicit large sums of money upon marriage. Among married women, modesty is required in public and nudity is reserved for marital relationships. However, female teens (e.g., 12 to 14 years old) are required by female elders to wear short skirts without tops or braziers so that their virginity ceremoniously may be tested. Some girls value the process, whereas others denounce its invalidity. Forty thousand virgins dance for the king in similar topfree garb (Zachariasse, 2014). The ceremony was introduced in 1984 to encourage young girls to postpone sexual intercourse. Sexual austerity measures mostly may correlate with HIV infection introduced by the Euro-Africans and tourists. Post-HIV-positive Zulu society may experience a resurgence in free love and a mutation of moral culture. "We focus on the girls" and love "because they get damaged" (von Kapff, n.d.). A sole benefit of apartheid was that it possibly reduced the number of potential sex partners, who could impregnate young girls.

The dynastic Zulus are family-focused. In IsiZulu, a language "characterized by many 'clicks'," "Zulu" means "Sky" (SAHO, 2011). It also refers to "heaven" (von Kapff, n.d.).

> Many Zulu people converted to Christianity under colonialism. However, although there are many Christian converts, ancestral beliefs have not disappeared. Instead, there has been a mixture of traditional beliefs and Christianity. Ancestral spirits are important in Zulu religious life, and offerings … are made to the ancestors for protection, good health, and happiness. Ancestral spirits come back to the world in the form of dreams, illnesses, and sometimes snakes. The Zulu also believe in the use of magic. Ill fortune such as bad luck and illness is considered to be sent by an angry spirit. (SAHO, 2011)

Family includes adopted and married relatives. Rituals reflect family-life. For example, an honor was bestowed on the mother of a notable ruler, who assumed his father's rule (von Kapff, n.d.). Shaka, a name that refers to a beetle, who causes stomach bloating, continues to be world famous. In 1827, when his mother, Nandi, passed away, Shaka ordered some killings to signify his loss. The devoted crowd became enraptured with the idea and put each other to death. Seven thousand Zulus were killed.

> Ancestors are thought to live in the spirit world of *unkulunkulu* (the greatest of the great) and are regarded as intermediaries between the living and the spirit world. As a consequence, they are praised and offerings are made to them. Should something untoward occur, the *sangoma* (spiritual healer) is consulted to determine whether the event has been caused by witchcraft (in which case there is a witch-hunt) or failure to appease the spirits. … Spirits are thought to exist also in animals and in the forest and in caves. A female spirit—*inkosazana*—is thought to make maize grow and is fêted in the spring. (von Kapff, n.d.)

If ancestors' memories are released, then they may retributively haunt and chastise the living (von Kapff, n.d.).

The Zulu's pride in their cultural traditions is evident in the Zulu krewe, namesake of the white tiger, King Zulu. In 2016, Zulu krewe honorifically was inspired by the white tiger, who died from humane euthanasia in 2017 during Mardi Gras following a "steep decline" (Evans, 2017). The krewe wore black and white tiger striped costumes; however, Zulu face paint annually includes black and white stripes and circles. Honoring King Zulu with big and little stripes helped to heal past hurts associated with blackface. In 2016, King Zulu celebrated a "big birthday," (i.e., 20 years old) making him the oldest and rarest white tiger in existence (Audubon Nature Institute, 2016). That year, Zulu krewe's official theme was "Celebrating 100 Years of Incorporation" (Mardi Gras Parade Schedule, 2016). A video of his birthday party depicts the beautiful and special white tiger playing with his red and blue "boomer" balls, which were covered in curry paste and bacon powder (Audubon Nature Institute, 2016; Evans, 2017). He also ate more than one dozen steaks arranged to depict the numeral "20" with honored guests, several flies; and he sampled an eight gallon "bloodsicle" (Audubon Nature Institute, 2016). The 2017 theme, "Stop the Violence," also paid homage to King Zulu, who remained unharmed in his enclosure at the Audubon Zoo in the Garden District of New Orleans, Louisiana (Nobles, 2016).

King Rex, King Zulu's brother and habitat "companion," was similarly honored by Rex Krewe (Evans, 2017). He died in May of 2012 of complications arising during surgery to remove cancer (Eggler, 2012). The 2012 procession introduced a permanent float called "The Butterfly King" (Rex, 2012). "The butterfly has long been a symbol of the fleeting beauty of Mardi Gras," but the float lends to the "enduring image" of the Audubon Nature Institute's logo, which prominently features a white tiger, a black and white butterfly, and a black and white shark (Audubon Nature Institute, n.d.a; Rex, 2012). The white tiger is depicted in front of a green, four-sided figure; the butterfly abounds from a yellow, four-sided figure; and the shark swims in front of a blue, four-sided figure. Yellow deducted from green leaves blue. The white tiger exceeds the boundaries of the box, which symbolizes his migration from the rurals of India to a comfortable intermediate-size zoo in America. The butterfly and shark exceeding the boxes' boundaries symbolizes their safety in captivity. Audubon Zoo's logo symbolizes metamorphosis of King Rex from body to spirit staying with King Zulu at the Audubon. Rex had a publicly unanticipated passing, whereas King Zulu just prior to his passing used a lawyer to announce his reign via email to the Audubon Nature Institute board members, New Orleans city council, mayor, state representatives, and schools. The brothers, who were not lovers or co-parents, symbolized a primordial circle of love within which anything is possible (I Cor. 13: 1–13).

The logo depicts three stable shapes symbolizing Adee, Bhoja, and Charka. The four-sided shape is balanced. Together they form a greater, four-sided shape to signify their mother. A butterfly signifies rebirth and mutation. The position adjacent to the white tiger shows that King Zulu lives on and that the brothers share their souls (Cusack, 2017c). The shark represents unseen darkness surrounding the brothers' bond and union causing it clearly to come into view. The shark's insignificance elucidates the magnitude (e.g., white tiger spirit) of what a shark is not. The logo also denotes humans' nothingness. Their father is present and unseen, like the shark.

Rex krewe commonly depicts flowers, which are significant to the celebration of King Rex because he lived in the Garden District on Magazine Street in New Orleans. They also depict animals signifying Adee's protection of all other animals at Audubon Zoo. At night, when the residents retired into their cages, those who never would otherwise have had an opportunity to experience such close proximity to a white tiger instinctually feared him; but, they were pacified by his will to refrain from harming them. His presence assured them that other animals would not harm them. Primordial fears of tigers may lurk within every being, but Adee exceptionally avoided enflaming that fear by demonstrating friendliness, gentleness, and easygoing spirits. However, there is no doubt that residents' instincts to fear a horrendous demise were unassuaged by his effort. King Zulu's playfulness and enjoyment of the protective King Rex pacified some residents on occasion.

In 2013, the Rex krewe's theme was animals, which honored him. Designs included "[i]nsects, dinosaurs, frogs, serpents," "bears," "some mythical critters" partygoers had "probably never heard of," "sea slugs," "polar bears," and "such fictitious creatures as a dragon, the Sphinx, a unicorn and the Jabberwock, which Lewis Carroll created in 'Through the Looking Glass'" (Pope, 2013). A "favorite" float in the "All Creatures Great and Small"-themed parade "is all about the mosquito, a major figure in New Orleans history because it used to bring periodic, lethal outbreaks of yellow fever and malaria" (Pope, 2013). "New Orleans and the mosquito are joined at the hip" (Pope, 2013). That year saw other significant changes. "Another innovation" was the "black riding crops, festooned with purple, green and gold ribbons" (Pope, 2013).

The predominantly Caucasian krewe, Rex Organization, maintains an appearance of opulence, prestige, and politic (Rex, n.d.). Storey Charbonnet, Chairman of the Pro Bono Publico Foundation, said that following Hurricane Katrina, the krewe formed the foundation to embody its motto, "For the Public Good" (Pope, 2013). Since 2006, the Pro Bono Publico Foundation has awarded approximately $2 million in grants. The organization's official name is "The School of Design" (Rex, n.d.). Rex Organization was conceived in 1872 (Rex, n.d.). Rex's proclamations have invited local and touristic attendees to Carnival since the late 1800s. Carnival's anthem and most notable song, "If Ever I Cease to Love," was played by Rex during their first parade (Rex, n.d.). "Blue Beard," a musical comedy, featured the song, which was sung by Lydia Thompson (Rex, n.d.). She was rumored to have been romantically linked to The Grand Duke Alexis of Russia, who was honored at the Rex parade the same year that she toured the United States. Rex's colors, purple (i.e., justice), green (i.e., faith), and gold (i.e., power), signify Mardi Gras throughout the world. Carnival concludes with the Rex Ball, where the king, with the queen, festively holds court as King of Carnival, King of Merriment.

Fat Tuesday, also known as Mardi Gras, celebrates partygoers' final opportunity to indulge before lent, a Catholic 40-day fast (Cusack, 2017a; Northup, 2009). Adherents may forsake red meat, chocolate, alcohol, or a similar indulgence. The Boeuf Gras (i.e., "fatted calf," "fat bull," or "fat beef") is commemorated by Rex with a float (Mardi Gras New Orleans, n.d.). "On March 2, 1699, French-Canadian explorer Jean Baptiste Le Moyne Sieur de Bienville arrived at a plot of ground 60 miles directly south of New Orleans, and named it 'Pointe du Mardi Gras'" because "it was the eve of the festive holiday" (Mardi Gras New Orleans, n.d.). In 1702, he "established" Fort Louis de la Louisiane, "which is now Mobile," Alabama (Mardi Gras New Orleans, n.d.).

> In 1703, the tiny settlement of Fort Louis de la Mobile celebrated America's very first Mardi Gras. In 1704, Mobile established a secret society (Masque de la Mobile), similar to those that form ... current Mardi Gras krewes. It lasted until 1709. In 1710, the 'Boeuf Gras Society' was formed and paraded from 1711 through 1861. The procession was held with a huge bull's head pushed along on wheels by 16 men. Later, Rex would parade with an actual bull, draped in white and signaling the coming Lenten meat fast. This occurred on Fat Tuesday. (Mardi Gras New Orleans, n.d.)

The Rex krewe wears masks covering their entire faces. "Maskers on each float dress in elaborate costumes designed to add to the colorful effect to the float's design and decoration" (Rex, n.d.). On the Boeuf Gras float, which has been prominently featured for more than 100 years, riders are dressed like chefs. The float depicts a white and black bull wearing a garland of flowers standing in a vivid floral pasture. Some notable elements of American culture celebrated by Rex krewe include marching bands and military achievements. They may depict other aspects of human-Earth nexuses; for example, the "Fables of Fire and Flame" theme of 2010 (Rex, n.d.). They also highlight international wonders and culture.

King Rex and King Zulu hail from Bengal, India. Islam is the predominant religion of the area; and it is infused with emotional awareness of polytheism. The Muslim constituency is distinct from Middle Eastern Muslims, who are mainly Arab and a Persian minority. Not all white tigers are from Muslim regions (e.g., Bengal, Sumatra, and Malaysia); for example, some are from Russia (e.g., Siberia), China, and Indochina. King Zulu is Indian. Bhoja is Islamic, not Hindu; however, his name is Indian. He is Indian, but from a part of India where there are many Muslims hiding as Hindus. They syncretize by adopting the deities and absorbing them into conceptions of The Prophet Muhammed, who may signify other heroes (e.g., Mahatma Gandhi). King Zulu may be described as atheist, but a believer in Jesus, who lived in a Christian society that saved him by allowing him to live at the Audubon Zoo. Yet, his endemic and accepted beliefs may be like polytheism. Each of the three religions teaches a concept of the soul. King Zulu's soulmate was not a white tigress, but a male white tiger, his brother Adee, also known as King Rex (Cusack, 2016).

King Rex and King Zulu were protective; however, as the film *101 Dalmatians* explains, white tigers may continue to fear guns (e.g., terrorism) even though they are well cared for in zoos and sanctuaries (Afridi, 2017; Herek, 1996; Tundra & Loki, n.d.). In the film, "security staff at London Zoo discovered the excoriated carcass of its prized three year-old female Siberian tiger, Sue Ling" (Herek, 1996). Skinner's henchmen murdered Sue Ling so that Cruella De Vil would be wooed by Skinner, an evil man, who later hoped to kill approximately 100 puppies (Cusack, 2016; Herek, 1996). Yet, in reality, a handgun would not kill or harm a white tiger because they are massive, enormous, and powerful animals (Cusack, 2010, 2016; HJ Res. 69, 2017; Reeves, 2013; *South Florida Sun Sentinel*, 1997). This is evident in local culture in Alaska, where despite gun fanaticism, locals (e.g., Juneauites) hike and participate in winter sports without carrying firearms because they know that a handgun would be useless if they were to be confronted by a bear (Cusack, 2010, 2012; DiCaprio, 2015).

A machinegun may injure or kill a white tiger. Although many states (e.g., Oregon) permit them to be carried in public, machineguns are illegal in Louisiana (Audubon Nature Institute, n.d.b; Burkes, 2017; Estes, 2014; La. R.S. § 40:1752, 2017; U.S. v. Miller, 1939). A citizen has no "right to keep and bear *such an instrument*" (D.C. v. Heller, 2008; U.S. v. Miller, 1939, p. 178). Audubon Nature Institute does not prohibit guns in its rental shelters where people drink alcohol (Audubon Nature Institute, n.d.b). The problem has been explored by fictional websites claiming that white tigers have been shot by BB guns, when in fact they have not (Wood, 2008). Guests are not, or ought not to be, allowed to enter enclosures or pet white tigers of any age; and yet, volunteers and zoo employees may not be prohibited from carrying guns or other weapons on the premises or possessing them in their cars. This raises the question of why, for animals' safety and psychological well-being, zoos do not have bulletproof glass areas for the general public and premium-patron areas behind the glass that are protected by metal detectors or frisks. One answer is that zoos permit guns and allow people other than trained professionals to come into close proximity with animals. Because zoos are educational facilities, they could be classified as learning facilities (e.g., schools), which prohibit guns and are protected by stiffer penalties (D.C. v. Heller, 2008). Yet, stiffer penalties have failed to deter attacks on schools. An explanation may be that educators' (e.g., zookeepers and contemporary "professors") opposition to weapon ownership may be unacknowledged by powerful gun lobbyists occupying government positions (e.g., U.S. Supreme Court) (D.C. v. Heller,

2008, p. 646). However, the Court readily manipulates specific passages from 19th century "scholars" to impute a right to keep guns for self-defense inside a home (D.C. v. Heller, 2008, p. 666). Perhaps in a retrospective and comical nod to Armageddon, the Court dismisses the truthfulness of the intelligentsia at page number 666 in a case about mass arms distribution and militarization of the home, *Heller*, whose name possesses an allusion (i.e., "hell") to the great accuser and eternal damnation (D.C. v. Heller, 2008; Revelation 13:18). The terms "firearm," as in hell's fire, and "arm," as in Armageddon, are the focus of this Court's plan to perpetrate a coup (Revelation 16:16).

A plain text reading and originalist interpretation of the Second Amendment demonstrates that the framers' intent was to protect militias' right to bear arms to protect the state from federal tyranny. The U.S. Supreme Court "held that the Second Amendment does not by its own force apply to anyone other than the Federal Government;" and states are "free to restrict or protect the right under their police powers" (D.C. v. Heller, 2008, pp. 619–620; U.S. v. Cruikshank, 1875). However, recent case law has expanded the Second Amendment to include self-defense, but not "killing game" (D.C v. Heller, 2008, pp. 588–589). Although the Court in District of Columbia v. Heller (2008) attempted to deliver a reasonable textualist interpretation, it delivered nonsense.

There are four clauses in the Second Amendment: "A well regulated Militia, being necessary to the security of a free State, the right of the people to keep and bear Arms, shall not be infringed" (U.S. Const. am. 2). "Taken together, these four clauses have a distinct military meaning, and it would be odd if the" framers "used 'bear arms' in an individual sense," "but then used it in a military sense in the very next clause" (Kozuskanich, 2008, p. 442). When subdivided, in a maneuver "better characterized as advocacy than [a] good-faith attempt[] at constitutional interpretation," Justice Antonin Scalia's Second Amendment may be understood in two separate clauses, a prefatory and an operative clause (D.C. v. Heller, 2008, p. 670). "The Second Amendment is naturally divided into two parts: its prefatory clause and its operative clause. The former does not limit the latter grammatically, but rather announces a purpose" (D.C. v. Heller, 2008, p. 577). The prefatory clause necessarily delimits the operative clause and only introduces a specific context (i.e., militias). Justice Scalia nullifies the meaning and authority of the first two clauses by comparing them to preambles. His reasoning here, like in other portions of his opinion, intends to rally support from various and disparate types of antisocial gun-lovers, such as religious fundamentalists, racists, classists, and antifederalists. Other likely and implausible interpretations were accessible to the majority. For example, the judicial activists could have found that an explicatory clause defining "militia" in contrast to "federal" (i.e., "being necessary to the security of a free State, the right of the people to keep and bear Arms") was inserted into an operative clause (i.e., "A well regulated Militia ... shall not be infringed") (U.S. Const. am. 2).

To advocate on behalf of gun ownership, the Court analyzed the Second Amendment using a "natural" interpretation standard. The Court neither explains, nor grounds its infatuated use of "natural" interpretation after briefly discussing the importance of using a "normal" interpretation, which it does not use (D.C. v. Heller, p. 576). This standard may seem logical to five unrestrained and eager members of the judiciary, but lacks legitimacy (D.C. v. Heller, 2008; McDonald v. Chicago, 2010). Justice Scalia invents "logical" review in this case because the majority cannot uphold the Constitution and advocate for guns using "rational review" (D.C. v. Heller, 2008, pp. 577, 629). He admits to expanding the Second Amendment with his allegedly "logical" interpretation (D.C. v. Heller, 2008, p. 577). "[O]ur interpretation of 'the right of the people to keep and bear arms' furthers the purpose of an effective militia" by giving unorganized citizenry the right to bear arms against the federal government under the auspices of self-defense (D.C. v. Heller, 2008, p. 581).

In his analysis of whether the prefatory clause fits with the operative clause, he speciously recreates history and makes logical leaps (D.C. v. Heller, 2008). For example, he quotes some contemporaneous state constitutions guaranteeing rights to bear arms in defense of self and the state. Justice Scalia imagines that the "founding generation" thought that the Second Amendment could have protected the right to bear arms for self-defense (D.C. v. Heller, 2008, p. 603). However, the Second Amendment starkly contrasts with the state constitutions because it explicitly excludes a personal or collective right to bear arms in self-defense. He uses dictionaries contemporaneously drafted with the Second Amendment to define "arms" as "[w]eapons of offence, or armour of defence" (D.C. v. Heller, 2008, p. 581). Rather than logically define "arms" as a right to own armor (e.g., bulletproof vest) to defend against despotism or insurgence by the federal army, Scalia ignores the word "or" and finds that "arms" refers to "weapons of offence" (D.C. v. Heller, 2008, p. 581). Justice Scalia communicates a quasi-god impression of himself, where he patronizes the downtrodden by crusading on behalf of an absurd dignity fantasy. Justice Scalia's twisted reasoning reeks with subtext. He envisions the defeated gun owner, who although he or she may have been demoralized by life, maintains his or her belief that if federal agents were to invade, then a small piece of metal would, like kryptonite, overcome them or demonstrate power, authority, and masculinity. A gun symbolizes restoration to a status never delivered by the American dream or the wiles of patriarchy to the obedient and rebellious.

In McDonald v. Chicago (2010), Justice Samuel Alito found a novel incorporation of the Second Amendment to the states through the Fourteenth Amendment. This concept was created so that the right to privacy guaranteed by Fifth Amendment due process was also available to the citizens of the states through the Fourteenth Amendment's Due Process clause. It was principally used to ensure women's rights and family rights that later extended to gay rights. For example, unnatural sex and crimes against nature could be prohibited by states before the U.S. Supreme Court decriminalized homosexuality and found a same-sex right to privacy (Lawrence v. Texas, 2003; Obergefell v. Hodges, 2015). In McDonald v. Chicago (2010) the Court used federal case law precedence established by

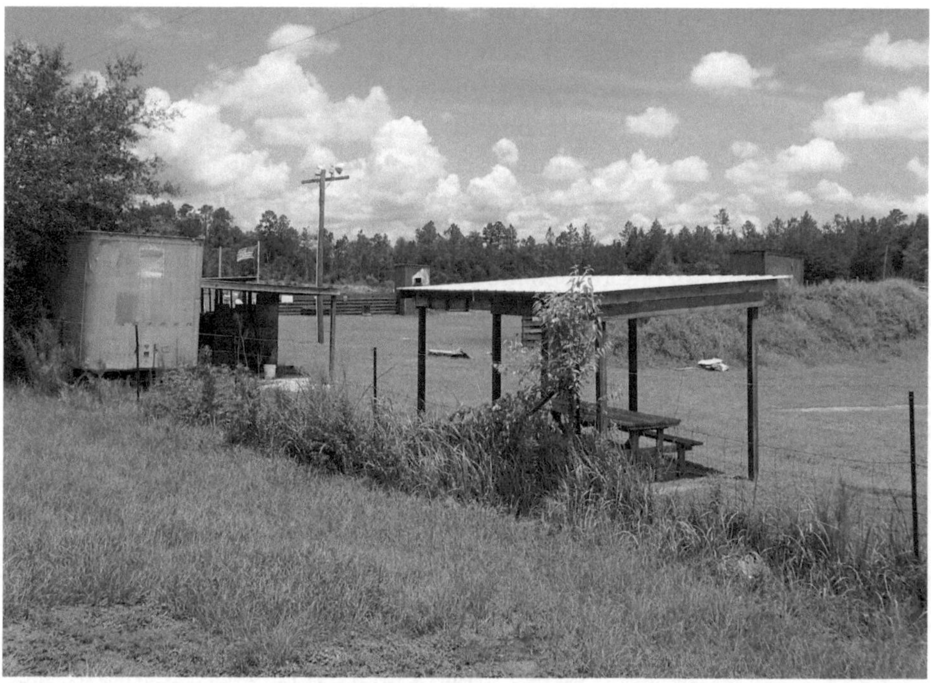

Fig. 9.2: Shooting Range and Gun Culture. Source: Carmen M. Cusack

family law jurisprudence (e.g., birth control and abortion) to provide state citizens with judicially made Second Amendment rights. In a plural opinion, conservative judicial advocates wrote for the majority that the same Fourteenth and Fifth Amendment relationship allegedly created by the Court could be used to secure the rights of state citizens to own guns for self-defense. Justice Scalia, who disavowed the existence of substantive due process found in the Fourteenth and Fifth Amendments after the Court discovered it during its analysis of women's rights, agreed with the majority that residents of Chicago, Illinois could possess handguns for self-defense. To effectuate his political agenda, Justice Scalia summarily disavowed the reasoning and opinion of "hundreds of judges" in federal and state courts (D.C. v. Heller, 2008, p. 621). Justice Stevens dissented in *Heller* saying, "Until the Fifth Circuit's decision in United States v. Emerson, 270 F.3d 203 (2001), every Court of Appeals to consider the question had understood *Miller* to hold that the Second Amendment does not protect the right to possess and use guns for purely private, civilian purposes" (D.C. v. Heller, 2008, p. 638; U.S. v. Miller, 1939). Justice Stephen Breyers cited the *Lewis* Court, "[T]he Second Amendment guarantees no right to keep and bear a firearm that does not have 'some reasonable relationship to the preservation or efficiency of a well regulated militia'" (D.C. v. Heller, 2008, p. 639; U.S. v. Lewis, 1980, pp. 65–66). Justice Scalia's "dramatic upheaval in the law" perpetrated a coup (D.C. v. Heller, 2008, p. 639). Yet, neither *Heller* nor *McDonald* found that killing animals is a Constitutionally protected activity that one could engage in when one has "borne arms" (D.C. v. Heller, 2008, p. 648; McDonald v. Chicago, 2010).

In 1886, the City of Chicago fought to uphold their law prohibiting militias from parading with guns (Presser v. Illinois, 1886). The *Presser* Court found that because the Second Amendment applied to the federal government, states were only required to pass laws that did not completely prevent the federal government from securing the nation. "We choose rather to plant ourselves on what we consider impregnable positions. They are these: that a State has the same undeniable and unlimited jurisdiction over all persons and things within its territorial limits as any foreign nation, where that jurisdiction is not surrendered or restrained" (Presser v. Illinois, 1886, p. 268). They could pass rational laws restricting ownership and possession of weapons. The *Heller* and *McDonald* Courts left the door open to prohibit hunting under federal and state laws (D.C. v. Heller, 2008; McDonald v. Chicago, 2010). The federal government does not permit hunting. Hunting on federal land is under state licensure, but the federal government does not permit hunters on federal land to exceed the scope of state laws. On federal land and under federal law protecting certain species, the federal government may narrow or prohibit state-permitted hunting activities.

Salina v. Blaksley (1905) has not been overturned and stands for the proposition that there is no personal right, only a collective right (i.e., militia), to bear arms in order to defend against invasion by the army during peacetime. The U.S. Supreme Court found that only one or two state courts independently held "that the act of the legislature prohibiting the carrying of concealed deadly weapons was void; that the right of the citizen to own and carry arms was protected by the constitution and could not be taken away or regulated. While this decision has frequently been referred to by the courts of other states, it has never been followed" (City of Salina v. Blaksley, 1905, p. 231). The Court has never held that the Second Amendment protects a right to kill animals, but only that a "ban on handgun possession in the home violates the Second Amendment, as does its prohibition against rendering any lawful firearm in the home operable for the purpose of immediate self-defense" (D.C. v. Heller, 2008, p. 635). The dissent in *Heller* specifically states that there is no right to use guns "to hunt," and the majority does not hold otherwise (D.C. v. Heller, 2008, p. 637).

There is no bright right to use a gun against an animal unless an animal intrudes into one's home and poses the kind of threat that would exempt a person from laws prohibiting the use of firearms inside a home (Deuteronomy 5: 1–21; Johnson, 2016). However, some zoos possess weapons and have allowed them to be used on animals. For example, when humans have intentionally or accidentally trespassed into habitats, some reckless zoos have killed residents. This is analogous to the government murdering a human resident, who is present during trespass to his or her property by an intruder, to rescue the intruder from potential defense of person and property by the resident. A tragic example was a gorilla, who defended his habitat by meekly standing-by while an unconscious child awaited rescue. Rather than rescue the child, officials shot and killed the gorilla (Ellis & Rose, 2016). Many zoos oppose harming residents even when the result may be human death; for example, a child falling into an exhibit of African dogs resulted in the child being torn apart, but the painted dogs were relocated for their safety following the incident.

It is pointless for zoos to own weapons (e.g., tranquilizer guns), for example to incapacitate animals, who wander, because animals may be lured with food (Ellis & Rose, 2016). The law should presume that any killing of a conserved or protected animal is unlawful. Harming endangered species may result in incarceration and fines; and taking and injuring (i.e., depreciating) animals should be considered income resulting in tax consequences (16 U.S.C. § 1531, *et seq.*, 2017). Exceptions could be made, for example if a human was trapped inside his or her residence without any means to escape. It is society's responsibility to itself, animals, including but not limited to zoo animals, and zoos to develop federal, state, and local plans to rescue animals in emergencies; and choose to save zoo animals over humans, who accidentally, negligently, or intentionally encounter animals in their habitats or on the street (Cusack, 2016, 2017d). The United States has latently shirked its duties to provide safety and emergency response measures (725 ILCS 5/113A-1, 2017). A federal emergency response system was not in place until after Hurricane Katrina, although local efforts had been documented in numerous cases (42 U.S.C.A. § 5196a-d, 2006; Animal Legal & Historical Center, n.d.; Cusack, 2006; Waranius, 2008; Wisch, 2017).

> The [Pets Evacuation and Transportation Standards (PETS)] Act amends the Robert T. Stafford Disaster Relief and Emergency Assistance Act to ensure that State and local emergency preparedness operational plans address the needs of individuals with household pets and service animals following a major disaster or emergency. … The PETS Act authorizes [Federal Emergency Management Agency (FEMA)] to provide rescue, care, shelter, and essential needs for individuals with household pets and service animals, and to the household pets and animals themselves following a major disaster or emergency. (AVMA, n.d.)

If a typical danger happens at a zoo, then patrons, guests, and staff should be prepared to call the police, not rely on zookeepers. Police must have a plan to rescue animals. Like Special Weapons and Tactics (SWAT), police units in towns with zoos, must be trained to save animals while protecting and controlling the public (Zimmerman, 2017). Non-harm to living creatures is an essential mandate proposed by most zoos, including those which instruct guests not to swat insects; for example, the butterfly garden in Chicago, Illinois (Chicago Botanic Garden, n.d.).

Weaponization has plagued the world since the invention of guns. In Bhoja's native land and surrounding areas, weaponization has similarly effected animals (e.g., household pets) and humans. Weaponized territorial disputes are problematic among Muslim populations. Although there is very limited Jewish-Muslim cultural tension evident to tourists, first generation Israelis, and ex-pats on the streets of Jerusalem, the American media portrays an Arab-Hebrew war that exaggerates miscreance and overlooks Sunnist problems with maintaining their "way" and facilitating centralized progress (Cusack, 2007; Hesse, 1957; Hoff, 1983). Members of the military and government-sponsored aid programs have defended Muslims using terminology that demonstrates white tigers' position. Ross Cohen of Hiring our Heroes said, "Muslims are kind folks, who needed our help. To help them was an honor. However, I was reluctant" to invade their homes "with my gun because they were Muslims. The gun symbolized destruction," which was against their religion (Cohen, 2015). Handguns terrify white tigers, whose only fear is guns. This not only applies to concealed weapons being carried at zoos, where white tigers are perfectly safe; it also threatens their well-being because they are certain of the small possibility that one could bring a gun and brandish it at any point. In the United States, white tigers are quintessential animal activists because 1) they harm no other animals while in captivity; and 2) their power empowers animal welfarists to speak on behalf of all animals, who likely would repeal the Second Amendment, if they were lawmakers in human society. Animals live according to their own laws, although humans' laws may protect them, not punish them; and some work in human society (e.g., healthcare, military, science, and justice).

Superhero

Depictions of superheroes are two dimensional embodiments of perfection (Cusack, 2017a; Meyer, 2013). Superheroes are perfect because they are fearless. They near omnipotence, but exercise restraint and wisdom. Some superheroes may have dichotomous nemeses, but they are not defined by evil, opposition, harm, or wrongdoing. Without evil, opposition, harm, or wrongdoing, superheroes could continue to exist. In practical terms, heroism is parallel to superheroism. For example, the civil servants, who died on September 11, 2001, were trained and prepared to act heroically on September 10th. They had rescued others from perilous situations. Their heroism on September 11th defines "9/11," but terrorism did not cause them to be or transform them into heroes.

White tigers repeatedly have been depicted as superheroes. They are strong, powerful, and beloved. Cultures and sects around the world believe that the spirit of the white tiger has the power to save people (e.g., from despair or self-harm). They are considered to be guides, who protect those who revere them. Tigers are treated as gods around the world. Superheroism may reflect, express, or adopt these beliefs. Contemplation of the extent of their power may be expressed in depictions of superheroism, for example possible ability to possess or haunt objects and alter reality.

Vigilantes, as superheroes and fantasies, fulfill society's need to witness and effectuate power for good (Packer & Pennington, 2014). Humans may focus on the use of power for evil (e.g., tyranny); but, conjuring superheroes brings to their attention how power may be used to assist and defend others. Righteousness and praxis may be undermined because altruistic wishes are entertained. Entertainment may be satisfying, but does not meet society's needs. Entertainment depicting vigilantism and superheroism may have positive, negative, or neutral effects on people's desires to contribute to society, reform injustice, rise above past transgressions, and remedy past hurts. "Representing an uneasy wish fulfillment, 'Vigilante Cinema' confronts the viewing public with the concept of 'righteous' violence. Vigilante Cinema implicitly addresses the controversial and ambiguous morality surrounding the quasi-religious term 'evil' … forcing the audience to coin their own definitions of evil" (Packer & Pennington, 2014, p. 951).

White tigers are "gracious," but they annihilate (Cusack, 2016). For example, a group of white tigers may be called an "ambush." White tigers embody specialness. Their extreme specialness suggests that they have an obligation to exhibit their special qualities, including changing the course of humans' lives with the power of their spirits. Their deeds may seem unusual, but may effectively work toward a perfect end. Some people, including white tiger superheroes, may suffer emotional and psychological pain. White tigers may be so powerful, that only humans, who can tolerate enough pain, will be able to master their lives, minds, or bodies using the spirit of the white tiger. White tigers liberate humans' most cogent selves, but destroy remnants of past selves and dissatisfying attachments to which believers (e.g., superheroes) have clung. During painful moments, superheroes and others may ask, "Are they sublimating sadists, who are unconcerned with right and wrong, good and evil, and are simply bent on satisfying hostile and hateful impulses" (Packer & Pennington, 2014, p. 951)? To overcome self-betrayal, people experiencing reform through the spirit of the white tiger must experience compassion for white tigers. Recalling pain experienced by white tigers may call believers to their true purpose. For example, white tigers living in zoos may still fear gunfire; and their mothers may loathe when cubs are handled by the public, which does not include regular professional caretakers, for example Anjana, a chimp working in South Carolina (Antle, 2013; T.I.G.E.R.S., n.d.).

Superheroism may mutate how the public views the relationship between white tigers and other animals. For example, one character helped audiences to see why animal testing was wrong (High Evolutionary, n.d.; IPPL v. Institute for Behavioral Research, 1986; Scott, 1987; White Tiger (Evolved Tiger), n.d.; White Tiger (New Men), n.d.). A white Bengal tiger was captured in a rainforest by a mutant, Dr. Herbert Edgar Wyndham, known as High Evolutionary. He began his research experimenting on rats. He mutated the female white tiger into a quasi-humanoid, White Tiger. Realizing that humans related to animals using their emotions rather than their minds, White Tiger may have feyned affection for Danny Rand to achieve the ultimate goal of restoration and release. In the plotline, she experienced deep affection for Rand, a superhero known as Iron Fist. When she realized that he only accepted her friendship, "[s]he knew that her love would be forever unrequited, and knew that she couldn't handle human emotions, and what they were doing to her. She begged High Evolutionary for release, and he agreed, returning her to her original form. This ended here duties as the second White Tiger" (White Tiger (Evolved Tiger), n.d.). "Saddened," her cohort, "Heroes For Hire left, and moved on with their lives, remembering their lost friend" (White Tiger (Evolved Tiger), n.d.). The story not only humanizes animals used for experimentation, it endears them by comparing them to white tigers. This plotline is developed in relation to readers' descriptions and Marvel's synopses. Plots are extremely rich and weave through popular and lesser-known imprints, several heroes' journeys, fanfiction, film, and other media. Fans' dialogue is essential to developing stories with consistent viewpoints that enhance a superhero's identity and cause small blips of information (e.g., thought bubble) to become loaded with a sense of description to readers. Therefore, heroes' identities are formulated by synopses, as legends are made by oral and written pass-downs.

White tiger spirits are near god status. They abolish humans' need to imagine an important superego that interfaces with society's mores, customs, and modes of operation. Many white tigers live in zoos and are seldom placed in defensive positions against invaders. Therefore, their spirits are kind and may encourage humans kindly to treat others. However, the spirit of the superhero is embedded in his superego. This may pose a conflict for White Tigers. Superheroes' superegos may allow them to participate in righteous types of violent revenge. Although a white tiger spirit may facilitate revenge, righteousness may not adhere to proscribed social boundaries. Violence is a delimited concept that may be justified, unlike other bodily harms, such as rape, which is never justified. Killing, fighting, and other forms of violence may be lawful and justified by society (e.g., self-defense and war).

Family entertainment may be the reason for the inclusion of superegos in the superhero motif (Packer, 2009). Because definitions of and values within "family" and "entertainment" vary, this concern may be incompatible with the spirit of the white tiger. White tigers view the world in black and white. They view a correct path and alternate paths. Many alternate paths are wrong, but some are acceptable. A superego is necessarily inclusive of multiple individuals' beliefs and feelings. White tigers operate with a degree of distinction that does not require multiple opinions. This is one reason that White Tigers are so powerful. Their powers are not connected to outside influences.

In the 1950s, when the superhero motif blossomed in cartoons and television, "[t]elevision serials and cartoons showcased more mild-mannered, better-tempered superheroes" (Packer, 2009, p. 5). "This was the Spock Age" (Packer, 2009, p. 5). "Dr. [Benjamin] Spock was the Freudian-influenced child-rearing expert" (Packer, 2009, p. 5). "Dr. Spock taught parents about gender-appropriate behavior for girls and boys and about women's proper role as mothers" (Packer, 2009, p. 5). He "redacted some of his theories when feminists put pressure on him in the 1970s" (Packer, 2009, p. 5). During that era, feminists challenged family structure and children's rights. As Marvel Comics developed in the early 1960s and Carl Jung died, Americans' need for a leader to teach them about right and wrong "brought greater attention to" "unorthodox approaches" (Packer, 2009, p. 5). "In the 1930s, Jung's concepts about the 'racial unconscious' intrigued the Nazis, but his more occult ideas soon influenced the counterculture of the mid-1960s. His ideas about *shadows* and *personas* make themselves manifest in superhero stories and shed light on superhero *psyches*" (Packer, 2009, p. 6). They are also clearly evident in family law. For example, the right to privacy that protects the right to contraception, the right to marry, parental rights, and other fundamental rights, is not enumerated in the Constitution; however, the Court found it in penumbras and emanations (Griswold v. Connecticut, 1965). "Jung also made his mark on Joseph Campbell" (Packer, 2009, p. 6).

This shift legitimized the superego, and had an effect on how entertainment and society envisioned the id and ego. "[O]bedience to authority … confirmed the claims" that "the counterculture's belief in the virtue of individualism" only had "the value of avoiding the 'authorities'" (Packer, 2009, p. 6). "Superheroes conceived around this time also avoid authority and openly question 'the establishment'" (Packer, 2009, p. 6). However, they "grappled with self-doubt" (Packer, 2009, p. 6). "Structured around one young man's" or woman's "struggle to decide whether to comply with the law," family entertainment in the form of superhero stories "merged seemingly superficial questions about violence, liberty, and social duty" with questions about animal rights, gender, power, and love (Herzig, 2015, p. 129). Images brought into the home through the television, "further solidified the associations between" psyche, personal experiences, and "contemporary social movements" (Herzig, 2015, p. 129).

The image of superheroes has mutated over the past 60 years. During the 1960s and 1970s, as egotism "was acquiring new political connotations, women were identifying and articulating new political demands" (Herzig, 2015, p. 129). "Growing disillusionment with sexism in the burgeoning civil rights, free speech, and antiwar movements further propelled some activists to enunciate distinctive positions within opposition politics" (Herzig, 2015, p. 129).

> Such political agitation, importantly tended to focus on spheres formerly considered outside the realm of politics. Having gained many of the characteristic political and economic rights of self-governance (the rights to control their own earnings, to hold and transfer property, to enter into contracts, and to vote), liberal and radical women (and men) increasingly turned their attention to matters long held to be 'private.' Sexual relations, the nature of the family, housework, and medical care all came to be treated as rife with persistent inequity. (Herzig, 2015, p. 129)

"The mid-1980s was a time of major change for comic book characters and superhero stories and psychiatric standards" (Packer, 2009, p. 7). "The 1990s were 'the Decade of the Brain'," which may be distinct "from the metapsychological construct of the 'mind'" (Packer, 2009, p. 7).

In the late 1990s, fascism, apocalyptic Christianity, and similar themes began to dominate social consciousness as the world approached the year 2000. The United States changed on September 11, 2001. "[A]fter 9/11" global concerns portrayed in comic books "turned out to be oddly prophetic" (Packer, 2009, p. 7). Comic books and other media employed "wild visual imagery and unsettling predictions about doom and destruction" (Packer, 2009, p. 7). "Both" society and comic books "picked up on a political pulse that the powers-that-be ignored, even though the facts stared them straight in the face" (Packer, 2009, p. 7).

Artists' and the public's self-consciousness and sense of powerlessness was showcased by a shift from stories about class, resources, and struggles related to the experiences of non-immigrant Caucasians, Celts, and Anglo Saxons to narratives about immigrants (e.g., Iberian diaspora), which reflected alternate hardships (Packer, 2009). Simultaneously, Black Americans found a place in comic book history. Puerto Rico, which asserts its independent identity from the United States apart from its status as a commonwealth, may unite Indigenous, Black, and White people in the minds of superheroes' fans. Several of Marvel's White Tigers are Puerto Rican and Puerto Rican American. Mixing Puerto Rican superheroism with a white tiger, who is from India (Bengal), Asia (Sumatra and Malaysia), Europe (Siberia), and the United States (i.e., zoos) symbolizes reconciliation of planetary forces. Universalism is the White Tiger's forte because all other animals recognize white tigers' power. Superheroes embody the white tiger's physical strength and ability to call on friends from around the world (Buck, 2017; Hensleigh, 2004).

The first White Tiger is Hector Ayala (White Tiger, n.d.). His name symbolizes witchcraft. The name "Hector" refers to a six-sided polygon; a Trojan warrior vanquished by Achilles; holding; and bullying. The name Ayala refers to Santeria (Abimbola, 1997; Prahlad, 2005a, 2005b). Santeria is a syncretic New World "faith" derived from Sub-Saharan Yoruba culture and religion (Cusack, 2015c; Delagrange, 2006; Odusanya, 2009). Santeria is comparable with Hoodoo and other forms of witchcraft that may be cabalistic and sectarian (e.g., Babaláwos, Abakwa, and Lukumís). Dogma and myths are adopted and mutated by practicing Cubans, Dominicans, Puerto Ricans, Haitians, Brazilians, and others living in localities such as South Carolina, California, Florida, Georgia, and Washington, D.C. Orishas are deities, who spiritually may be conjured to embody a characteristic; identify an individual; metaphorize a lesson; possess an adherent; or open portals to enlightenment. For example, Shango, represented as Saint Barbara, is a god of thunder and lightning. He is symbolized in cemeteries by a double-headed axe. Shango is male and married to Oshun, the orisha of purity. The trickster is Elegua (Santeria Church of the Orishas, n.d.). Some practitioners identify Olorun as a Yoruban sky god, and others explain that Obatala is a sky god (Prahlad, 2005b). "Ashe" is like the word "amen," and is thought to be a form of karma (Prahlad, 2005b). Gentleness achieves power to transform other conditions.

"The musical influence of the Yoruba has had a significant presence in the African American experience" (Prahlad, 2005b).

> One of the celebrated vehicles of the Underground Railroad escape effort was the so-called alert song, which contained coded messages about escape attempts. A lesser-known vehicle used to communicate information was drumming. Known among the

> Yoruba as the *dun-dun*, these 'talking drums' could simulate the vocal intonations of the Yoruban language. Only certain individuals could decipher the language of the drum patterns, making this an ideal vehicle for communicating secret information. Traditions of talking drums are mentioned in oral narratives from ex-slaves. (Prahlad, 2005b)

"[I]n many Caribbean and South American cultures" "*ashé*," also known as "*aché* or *axé*," is a Brazilian music genre (Prahlad, 2005b).

"Christian fear of anything occult" has correlated with "misunderstanding and repression of African customs and beliefs" (Prahlad, 2005a). Witchcraft was syncretized with Christian beliefs, such as the "[d]evil and hell, to which there are no counterparts in Africa" (Prahlad, 2005a). "African American beliefs in human supernatural power were also influenced by" Europeans' "beliefs in sorcery and witchcraft" (Prahlad, 2005a). Witchcraft may be attributable to a dominant force, such as a possessor's desires or a massive influence (e.g., fear of a predator or lightning) (von Kapff, n.d.). Repression and syncretism with European and Native religions were necessary because Europeans executed witches, whereas Africans exercised witches' power (e.g., perceived "spurts of fire emitted from their anuses or armpits") (Prahlad, 2005a). "Sorcery as evil magic is" "unprotected," "conceptualized as sentient and willful," and "commanded" by "perpetrators" (Prahlad, 2005a).

In South Africa, lightning is believed to be controlled by spirits. "Any person killed by lightning will neither be mourned nor buried with a ceremony, cattle will not be eaten[,] but buried[;] and trees that have been felled by lightning will not be used for any purpose" (von Kapff, n.d.). Zombies may be created by wizards, who desecrate corpses (Cusack, 2011, 2012; von Kapff, n.d.). The eyes are gouged, the tongue is removed, and a red, hot rod is driven into the skull, which shrinks to a prepubescent size. The enslaved golem is animated when the wizard blows magic powder into the mouth.

"[A]s certain people mature into adulthood an evil power develops within them that both enables and compels them to do extraordinary and terrible things" (Prahlad, 2005a). "[W]itchcraft power develops predominantly in women but can also develop in men, and it almost always occurs without anyone's knowledge. In most cultures it is invisible and intangible, but in some cultures it is vested in a real substance, even an object" (Prahlad, 2005a). Some Yoruba (e.g., Nigeria and Benin) believe that "*ashé* is in the blood, and its corrupted form is the witchcraft power, *ajé*; this is absent in the Americas" (Prahlad, 2005b). Some Santeros believe that a person's fate is decided when they choose a head, which may be understood to be physical (i.e., "ori ode") or psychological (i.e., "ori inu") (Ashe, 2008–2014).

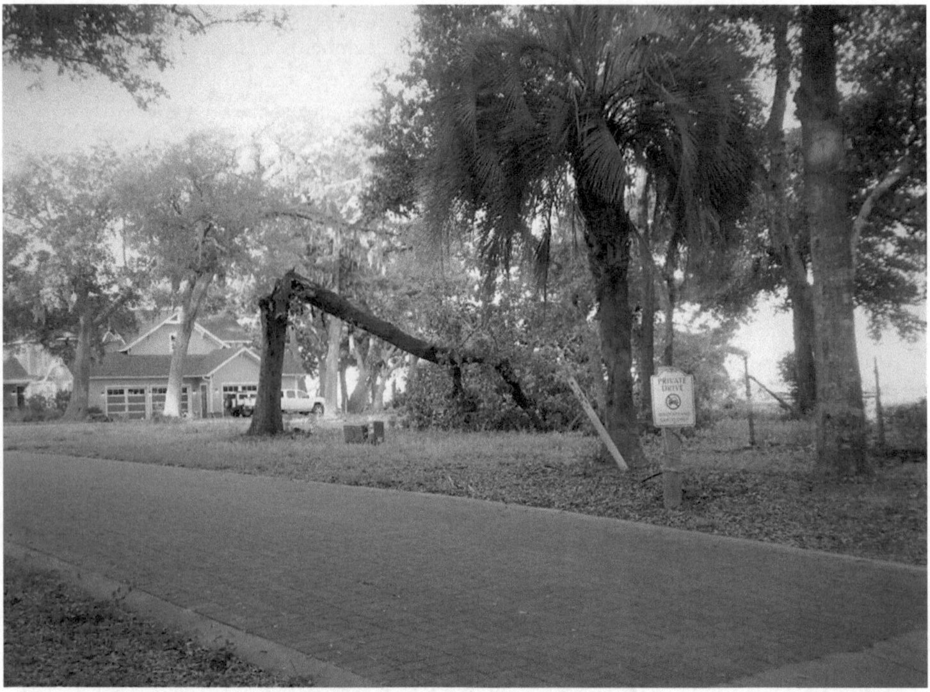

Fig. 9.3: Lightning Struck Tree. Source: Carmen M. Cusack

Ayala is an Obatalá, selected by Olofin, to construct human heads (Ashe, 2008–2014). A head may be selected using good fortune, wisdom, or phlegmatic nonchalance. A head determines the course of one's life, but the karma is not evident from its physical appearance before it is selected. Ayala's brother, Lajua, is the angel of death. "He brings death" and "sings nothing more than when he is fed" (Ashe, 2008–2014). He is given a scimitar, laurel wreath, and silver chain. Lajua lives inside a white and green copper jar painted "inside with the [seven] colors of the rainbow" (Ashe, 2008–2014). He wears the color green and "is from Ewardo land" (Ashe, 2008–2014).

The word "Ayala," sometimes written as "Ajala" means "carver," and refers to molding heads from mud or clay (Ashe, 2008–2014). Sects have distinct narratives to describe spiritual principles and manifestations. Myths and rituals may describe his character as being a god, hero, or entity depending on sectarian traditions, context, and relationships. Translations (e.g., spelling, pronunciation, and accents), appropriation, and syncretism affect interpretations and mythological mutations. For example, some sects claim that "[i]n Cuba, the only Ayala was Chango" (Ashe, 2008–2014). Ayala may be invoked in certain rituals as a path to Obatala, the father/sky god, who creates bodies; and, he may be seen as a servant, who does not have devotees. He may not materialize on Earth. Some religious literature describes Obatala as the head creator; and Ayala and Obatala have been described as "one in the same" (Ashe, 2008–2014). Therefore, "the concept of Ayala (Ajala) is not monolithic" (Ashe, 2008–2014). "There are many names to call the deities and they are interchangeable with each other" (Ashe, 2008–2014). "What is very important is not to consider deities the same as humans" (Ashe, 2008–2014).

Ayala may be described as an "orisa" (i.e., "orisha") (Ashe, 2008–2014). "Orisa is the name used to describe beings who have excellent skills or supernatural abilities and performed various feats that have gone beyond the understanding of ordinary beings. Most of these feats were also intended to serve the community in which they lived or to humanity in general" (Ashe, 2008–2014).

> In the Yoruba language, Orisa means 'a being whose head has been specially selected and endowed.' These beings can be roughly described as geniuses or [those,] who had a higher intelligence than most of their counterparts. His Orí (head/destination) also specially chose him to carry out certain assignments on [E]arth. It is Orí who guides humans in the physical world from the spiritual realm and also helps them on [E]arth in the fulfillment of their Akunleyan which is a component of man's destiny. (Ashe, 2008–2014)

This belief explains fate. Ayala knows which fates are preferable, and which are less desirable. Those, who are kind to Ayala, may receive his guidance in selecting the head that leads their voyage through life. Some people are born to die soon, others to die young, and many, "who can enjoy" life, will live "for a long time" "to a ripe old age" (Ashe, 2008–2014). "It is said" that "the forces of evil, sometimes prevent people in the first two groups from choosing good destination[s]" (Ashe, 2008–2014).

Hector Ayala was a foreign student from Puerto Rico attending Empire State University in New York, New York (White Tiger (Hector Ayala), n.d.). He became the second White Tiger superhero, but the first fully human White Tiger. He became a superhero after finding amulets shaped like a tiger's head and paws. White Tiger amulets give "the power of the Tiger God, the first thing mankind feared in the dark" (White Tiger (Angela Del Toro), n.d.). The white tiger does not symbolize race (e.g., Black and White) and does not reflect all colors (e.g., rainbow in white light). Rather, the white tiger is represented by Ayala because he moved from a less urban area to a metropolitan area to achieve improved living conditions. A group of crime fighters, Sons of the Tiger, previously owned the amulets, which caused Ayala to be as strong and reflexive as three humans. He is an ally to Spider-Man, Peter Parker (White Tiger (Hector Ayala), n.d.). Ayala and Parker attended university together and disclosed their superhero identities to each other.

Each figure is morally autonomous, but Ayala embodies tolerance and Parker exercises it. "Moral autonomy, the name liberalism gives to this individuated figure, is widely understood by theorists of tolerance to constitute *the* underlying value of the principle of liberal tolerance" (Brown, 2008, p. 154). "But while autonomy is the liberal good that tolerance aims to promote, tolerance is also understood as that which can be generated only by autonomous individuals—that, in part, is the significance of its status as a civic offering rather than a legal mandate" (Brown, 2008, p. 154). Like superheroes, tolerance "requires in advance what it also promotes" (Brown, 2008, p. 154). Fans of superheroes learn to be tolerant because superheroes are "unavailable to the unindividuated" fan (Brown, 2008, p. 154).

> The making of a tolerant world, then, literally requires the liberalization of the world, a formulation endorsed by liberal democratic theorists, pundits, and political actors. While [Emmanuel] Kant functions as the foundation stone for contemporary liberal theorists subscribing to this formulation, the contribution of [Sigmund] Freud to the ideology of the tolerant liberal self and its intolerant organicist Other is an interesting one. (Brown, 2008, p. 154)

Most superheroes, *vis-à-vis* their secret identities operate within the identity of the Other. Ayala and Spider-Man "implicitly or explicitly place Freudian assumptions at the heart of their work or have tucked him into their arguments as a kind of authorizing signature" (Brown, 2008, p. 154). "What Freud offers, among other things, is an account of why liberal orders, in their affirmation of the individual represent themselves as the only possible regime type for cultivating and practicing tolerance, while simultaneously promoting the pluralistic belief structure understood to necessitate tolerance" (Brown, 2008, pp. 154–155). Jungian and Freudian paradigms ground "the 'mature' (or 'advanced') status of the individuated Westerner in this regard" (Brown, 2008, p. 155). White tiger superheroes do "not make an ontological or permanent distinction between the individual and group. On Freud's view, individuated subjects can regress into organicist formations at any moment, forfeiting the definitive elements of proper individuation when they do so. Strong group identity thus constitutes not an opposition to but regression from the mature individuated psyche" (Brown, 2008, p. 155). Even when Parker or Ayala "pathologizes the group (as irrational and dangerous), he does not reify the rational individual as a permanent cultural achievement radically differentiated from organicist subjects" (Brown, 2008, p. 155).

> On the one hand, Freud's progressive historical-anthropological narrative in which tolerant liberal orders represent the highest stage of 'maturity' for [heroes] ... and are equated with civilization will be read critically, especially insofar as these themes are manifest in contemporary theorists of tolerance. That is, Freud's equation of individuation with both ontogentic and phylogenic maturity, and of solidarity or organicism with primitivism or regression, will offer a basis for grasping the civilizational discourse that frames contemporary tolerance talk and converts it to the purpose of liberal imperialism. On the other hand, Freud's appreciation of the contingency groups, their basis in affect rather than essential traits, is valuable in deconstructing the ontologization of 'blood and belonging' at play in the modern liberal theory and practice of cultural tolerance. (Brown, 2008, pp. 154–155)

These notions are framed by comic books and sold to the masses as film, television shows, toys, and other media.

Fans of the White Tiger, operating as West Side Stories, made a pilot for a live action film (Bean, 1961; Huertas, 2016). All of the characters depict Latinos in Hunts Point, Bronx, New York. Hunts Point is an area patronized by many sex buyers. Last century, it was a high crime area. Burglary and theft received some attention, but violent crimes (e.g., shootings) were overlooked. The area continues to experience crimewaves. The film begins at night with a transwoman strolling down a dark and empty street. The transwoman undoubtedly is a prostitute (Cusack & Waranius, 2015; Huertas, 2016). She is alone and talking loudly on her cellphone. She may be talking on the phone because she is scared of her surroundings (Huertas, 2016). The transwoman blurts out a tirade of bigoted insults. She may be attempting to seem tough or masculine. In Spanish, she says "Me importa un bicho" meaning "I don't give a shit/fuck" (Huertas, 2016). The literal slang translation is "I don't give a dick" (Huertas, 2016). "Bicho" may also mean "bug" or "insect" in some Spanish-speaking cultures (Cusack, 2015a; Huertas, 2016). The character says, "ese cara de culo me debe dinero" (Huertas, 2016). "Ese cara de culo" means something akin to "that butt-ugly guy;" "that butt-face;" or "that butt-head." "Me debe dinero" means "owes me money" (Huertas, 2016). She refers to the debtor as a "culero," which means "faggot/asshole" (Huertas, 2016). "Estoy cansada de pagar por sus biles" (Huertas, 2016). "I am tired of paying his bills" (Huertas, 2016). She says, "Mi hermano no, no tiene des que donde de vivir" (Huertas, 2016). "My brother, no, he doesn't have anywhere to live" (Huertas, 2016). "Tu sabes que yo trabajo muy duro por mi dinero" (Huertas, 2016). The character apparently says, "You know that I work very hard for my money" (Huertas, 2016). Literally, the character says, "You know that I work very hard on behalf of my money" (Huertas, 2016).

Her cellphone is black and white striped to suggest that she channels the White Tiger (Huertas, 2016). Ayala is wearing clothing, not his costume, when he passes the transwoman on the street and nods at her. The transwoman switches to English when she sees Ayala. "Hold on," she says into her cellphone. She greets Ayala, saying, "Hi, Hector" (Huertas, 2016). Ayala says, "Hi, Cindy. How are you" (Huertas, 2016)? They are outside a black and white building, Charter Foundry, Co. As they pass, she turns around to harass him. "Good. Do you know my offer still stands" (Huertas, 2016)? Ayala replies, "And I still have a girlfriend" (Huertas, 2016). Cindy says, "What about if you 'guys' broke up" (Huertas, 2016)? He replies, "I don't know!?," and chuckles (Huertas, 2016) Cindy moans, and then returns to her phone call, saying "That was Hector" (Huertas, 2016).

Three men dressed in black and one man wearing black and white striped clothing drive by Ayala (Huertas, 2016). The men may be in each other's company because, like Cindy, they are scared of their surroundings. A vehicle provides mobility and shelter. Their car stereo is blasting the lyrics "Black girl booty" from a song describing a White woman (Huertas, 2016). None of the characters are Black or White, but the lyrics foreshadow the White Tiger. Furthermore, none of the characters are girls or biological females. The word "booty" is similar to Cindy's sexually explicit word choice and is distinct from vagina, penis, testicles, breasts, and other dimorphic body parts. Booty is gender-neutral and perhaps bisexual. The men make eye-contact with Ayala, who has just put a duffle bag into his car. They may recognize or know him. Like Cindy and the men in the car, Ayala is also wearing black. He senses and hears what appears to be trouble. He retrieves his duffle bag, which contains glowing green amulets that give him his superpowers. The amulets are green to signify the color of white tigers' eyes, blue/green/yellow.

Four thugs exit the car when they see Cindy (Huertas, 2016). They surround her as they shout threats, such as, "I think this is your type, right here" (Huertas, 2016)! "You ain't going anywhere! Come here, dumb bitch" (Huertas, 2016)! She pushes one, and says "get the fuck off me" (Huertas, 2016)! A man taller than Cindy traps her against a wall. He points his finger in her face and says, "Shut the fuck up, faggot" (Huertas, 2016)! Cindy replies, "That's fucking original" (Huertas, 2016)! He encloses her with both his hands pressed against the wall, and asks "Where the fuck you going, ho" (Huertas, 2016)? Cindy is very strong. She pushes the large, heavy man off her, and says, "Come on" (Huertas, 2016). Their reasons for accosting her are not clear. She may be hooking where they have control; she may have duped a sex buyer, who is protected by their gang, Savage Skulls, by failing to disclose her true identity (i.e., biological male); she may be a rival gang member; Cindy may be suspected of being a confidential informant; she may have once worked for the Savage Skulls; her brother may be a drug dealer or rival gang member; they may be extorting her to pimp her; or other possibilities. It seems as if she says, "You don't owe me," but she may say, "You don't own me" (Huertas, 2016). Perhaps in this context the meanings are similar. Another tall, heavy-set man, wearing black and white stirpes asks, "What did we tell you about walking around these parts" (Huertas, 2016)? A smaller member of the gang says, "This is Savage Skull territory" (Cusack, 2015b; Huertas, 2016).

Boundaries create and recognize space. "Some of what may superficially appear as anomalies" "are simply the effects of other boundary systems imposed" on "individuation" (Huertas, 2016; Miller, 1996, p. 1238). "[T]he territorial preserve" "may claim a jurisdiction" "or just in feet and inches depending on the setting" (Miller, 1996, p. 1238). An occupier does not need to "always demand a continual bodily presence" to "experience" "a violation of the self," "violations of fetishes," such as "a connection to" "clothing," may arise by the mere presence of an opponent (Miller, 1996, p. 1238). "[S]omething as evanescent as one's temporarily abandoned place," produces "spaces" that "are in effect" "spatially discontinuous selves. Their selves often do not even extend to their skin," which may be "violated" "by parents" (Miller, 1996, p. 1238). "Slaves" "are prostitutes by some understandings of what prostitution is" (Miller, 1996, p. 1238). "[W]eaker claims for space" are overpowered, and as a result "make expansive and hegemonic moves" (Miller, 1996, p. 1238). However, "none of these variations in the expansion of spatial boundaries are anomalies deviating from some standard;" "they are simply the effects of imposing" "boundaries" with "spatial" definitions (Miller, 1996, p. 1238).

A "permitted transgression is not anomalous" (Miller, 1996, p. 1237). "That is the extent to which race" or gender "is disavowed as a motive in any of these so-called anomalies" (Miller, 1996, p. 1243). Cindy, presumably Puerto Rican, may be subject to the Puerto Rican gang members' local, cultural, and ethnic paradigms, including their implicit imposition on their community of idealized, albeit absent, family structure and gender roles (Huertas, 2016). She is under a regimented "prohibition" of her presence (Miller, 1996, p. 1242). "There hypocrisy thrives and on both sides of the equation. One might think it hypocritical to consider prostitution bad enough to criminalize and then allow it to flourish in a zone excused from that law" (Miller, 1996, p. 1242). "The bawds and whores, however, are more likely to think the polity that grants them their space is less hypocritical than the reformers who would destroy sexual traffic but must know that it will continue to thrive nonetheless, or, in even more aggressive hypocritical fashion, would actually make use of the services of those they would jail" (Cusack, 2015b; Miller, 1996, p. 1242). On the other hand, Cindy is a competitor or *persona non grata* (Huertas, 2016). Her genitalia physically and symbolically is an "anomalous zone" (Huertas, 2016; Miller, 1996, p. 1242). Savage Skulls would rape and mutilate Cindy to demarcate a boundary (Franklin & Chinn, 1999; Huertas, 2016). There is no police presence. "[A]uthorities simply [are not] powerful enough to punish all violations of all laws and most … [people] would not want them to be so powerful that they could. Lax enforcement is hardly an anomaly" (Miller, 1996, p. 1241). "[T]heir power to force upon" victims "deep ambivalence regarding" the authority possessed by street gangs is unparalleled (Miller, 1996, p. 1241). "[I]ts relation to sins of the flesh" "between rules of prohibition and sexual practice invites seeming virtue, false appearance, and hypocrisy" (Miller, 1996, p. 1241).

In an attempt to flee, Cindy pushes a gang member, and says, "Leave me alone! I'm just trying to get to my man's house" (Huertas, 2016)! Her man may be her pimp, whose bills she pays. A tall member says, "I know you're a cock smoker ho. Now where your motherfucking money at" (Huertas, 2016)? The only member shorter than Cindy attempts to frisk her. He asks, "Where'd you hide that shit" (Huertas, 2016)? She pushes him. Cindy slaps him and calls him a "bitch" (Huertas, 2016). He slaps her harder and asks, "Who's the bitch now" (Huertas, 2016)? They continue to push her around until one grabs her by the arm and says, "Let's rape this bitch" (Huertas, 2016). He may have intended to intimidate, coerce, or threaten to correct (Fihlani, 2011). The gang member wearing a black and white striped shirt says, "That's a man, fool" (Huertas, 2016)! The aggressor asks, "So" (Huertas, 2016)? Cindy says, "Come on guys, stop this now" (Huertas, 2016). The word "guy," like the word "bitch," is insinuative of gender, and yet may be used neutrally, like the word "booty" (Huertas, 2016).

A Savage Skull member grabs Cindy's throat and jaw, and says, "Shut up or I'm going to cut your motherfucking dick off" (Huertas, 2016). He displays aggression comparable with female genital mutilation and other acts of savagery perpetrated against women (Cusack, 2015a, 2015b). The man in the striped shirt says, "I think that's what she wants. What do you think" (Huertas, 2016)? As she protests, the gang members say, "Let's just do it!," "Grab her!," and "Take care of her" (Huertas, 2016)! The victim and gang members hear White Tiger growling. The man choking the victim shouts out, "Yo! Fuck you! You wanna play? Bitch, come play" (Huertas, 2016)? White Tiger appears. He is smaller than three of the four gang members and Cindy. Ayala's mask has few facial features except prominent, pale green, glowing eyes. His costume looks like the Power Rangers (White Tigerzord, n.d.). White Mighty Morphin Power Ranger's Zord is White Tigerzord (i.e., White Tiger Thunderzord and Tigerzord). With the creation of the White Power Ranger, a White Tigerzord provides backup with sonic strikes. It has an animal Zord and humanoid robot form.

The battle begins (Huertas, 2016). Cindy frees herself, wishes the gang members luck, and calls them "bitches" (Huertas, 2016). She runs away. White Tiger is demasked by a Savage Skull, but White Tiger is wearing a cloth over his face. Only his eyes are visible. The aggressor rips off his cloth, and says, "I know you. I fucking know you, you motherfucker. Fuck you, Hector. You'll get yours, bitch, just like your whole fucking family did" (Huertas, 2016). Ayala has a flashback to a cemetery, and a man and woman place flowers on a grave. Ayala's family was killed by villain Gideon Mace (Huertas, 2016; White Tiger (Angela Del Toro), n.d.). The thought of mourning Nestor and Maria Ayala enrages him. White Tiger punches the aggressor's face even after he is rendered unconscious. White Tiger has defeated the entire gang.

This film shows that White Tiger will protect those, who cannot access the justice system due to crime perpetration and perceived inferiority (Huertas, 2016). Transsexual prostitutes may fear talking to police because they do not want to be accused of precipitating attacks by committing crimes, such as loitering and prostitution (Cusack, 2015b). They may fear that they will be harassed or sexually assaulted by criminal justice members; disregarded; mocked; or used as fodder for sexually explicit interviews and testimony.

Cindy, White Tiger, and Savage Skull members are mutations (Huertas, 2016). Cindy may be this fan's political commentary on how transgender men and women are in a culture war with cys-gender and archaic-minded people. Rather than seeing transgender individuals requiring surgery or manifesting self-rejection as individuals, who suffer from a mental disease, they hate them for threatening established gendered boundaries. The American Psychiatric Association (APA) establishes diagnostic criteria for Gender Dysphoria in Adolescents and Adults 302.85(A)(6) (F64.1) as "[a] strong conviction that one has the typical feelings and reactions of the other gender (or some alternative gender different from one's assigned gender)" (APA, 2013, p. 216). Transgender women, like Cindy, may believe that they are females because they have self-perception issues that cause them to believe that their genitals are foreign to them. Therefore, in their minds, they must actually pertain to the opposite sex. However, their disease does not allow them to realize the truth; and that is that there is no monolithic female feeling (e.g., identity). Feeling like a female is different for every female. Feminine feelings do not result from estrogen or a socially constructed female perspective (e.g., liking skirts and lipstick). Femaleness is chromosomal. From birth, the biological condition of being a female develops into social, personal, familial, and lifelong physical experiences, some of which are controlled by society and the environment, others which are not (e.g., sexual dimorphism). Femininity manifests as various combinations of the feminine identity. In rare instances, born-intersex individuals may identify as male, female, or both; or as having a first sexual identity and second sexual identity. However, the feeling of being a female is personal, rather than exclusively psychosexual or sociosexual. Individuals, who suppress their hormonal sexual power may pressure themselves (Huertas, 2016). Transgenderism is a disease that prevents sufferers from experiencing the joys of maturing as their biological sex. Rather than seeing repression, and believing, as many do, that transgender individuals deserve for society to find a cure, people threatened by differences, may only see a trans-person as willfully, not involuntarily, choosing to eradicate normally acceptable boundaries. On either side, there is an inner struggle repressing drives fueling a need to dominate. Cys-gender individuals exercising their privacy right to choose the biological gender of a sex partner may advocate for laws explicitly to require transgender people to seek informed consent (i.e., disclose biological gender) before participating in sexual conduct. However, Cindy's biological sex may seem obvious to people, who do not suffer from Cindy's disease (Huertas, 2016). Cindy's attempt to "pass" or "fly under the radar" is symptomatic of her inability to process that she is sexually dimorphic; for example, is taller than many males. Transwomen like Cindy, may fail to observe differences that are obvious to "normal" people; for example, that by wearing women's clothing, she has not become a woman or assumed the appearance of a woman (Cusack, 2014a, p. 6).

Aggressive emotions toward cys-men and cys-women, including appropriation of pronouns, bathrooms, and rites of passage, may be an empowerment attempt that disavows others' social boundaries, sexualities, and emotions. It may manifest a stagnant, and perhaps sexist, worldview that clothing dictates sexual validity; and that any person, male or female, attracted to a transwoman flying under the radar has accepted normative boundaries that deserve to be broken or maintained through illusion. Those inducees, who do not wish to be sexually involved with transwomen, may be closeted from fear of being labeled "insensitive" or "homophobic," even in cases where transwomen identify as heterosexual. This dodgy dynamic culminates in a different sociosexual paradigm than ever experienced previously within the United States. Sexual-linguistic norms have been tampered. Complicit or repulsed responses physically and metaphorically manifest subordination. In the present liminal era, the true identity of the "third sex" is being annihilated (Franklin & Chinn, 1999, p. 316). In the future, a third pronoun may develop to acknowledge acceptable intersex biology and embrace transgenderism without pressuring individuals to mutilate their genitalia. Personalized pronouns, such as "ie," "'e," "thei," or "oe" may suffice.

Cindy flouts socially imposed norms (Huertas, 2016). She wears high heels and a skirt, garb traditionally prohibited to women walking alone at night in abandoned neighborhoods (Cusack, in-press; Huertas, 2016). She publicly uses obscenities. She is not ladylike; and yet, in that regard, is unfettered by norms, perhaps thereby exhibiting feminism. Yet, that language also appears to be symptomatic of her rough surroundings, and implies that she has experienced subordination because she adopted coarse language to defend her emotions and position. Her aggressive language may be merited if it refers to one or more of the Savage Skull members, who previously have attacked her. Her resistance and defiance show how transgender individuals can use a vulnerable position to affect a larger group.

White Tiger defends those, who have been rejected by their families, community members, and peers (Huertas, 2016). White Tiger is an amalgamated human and spirit. White tigers may make White Tiger superheroes uncomfortable. This may be normal due to their size and strength disparities; however, white tigers observe superheroes very carefully and only allot measures of strength to them that they are capable of maneuvering properly. Several White Tigers have had to earn superhero powers by proving control over their own fear and reticence.

Kevin "Kasper" Cole is a third White Tiger (Kasper Cole, n.d.; Kevin Cole (Earth 616), n.d.). The nickname "Kasper," alluding to the "friendly ghost," was given to him in reference to his fair complexion (Kasper Cole, n.d.; Kevin Cole (Earth 616), n.d.). His Ugandan father, "Black Jack" Cole, worked as police officer in New York City (Kasper Cole, n.d.; Kevin Cole (Earth 616), n.d.). His mother, Ruth, is Jewish. His father was incarcerated after he was framed for a crime that he allegedly did not commit. Black Jack was revealed to be Kibuka, leader of the 66 Bridges gang. Kasper became a police officer. Throughout his service, he lived with his mother and girlfriend, who was also his child's mother. However, he continued to feel attached to his high school love. His hubris was that he desired to be promoted; however, he often fought crime as a superhero, which cloaked his accomplishments. He participated in unauthorized drug busts, which irritated his lieutenant, Sal Anthony, a crooked cop. Kasper wore a special bulletproof costume that he borrowed from the police department. He and other officers were attacked by Sal, but Kasper survived because he was wearing the suit. He was suspended after it was discovered that he had not been wearing an approved bulletproof vest. Kasper posed as T'Challa, "eventually learning that he was a pawn in the manipulations of T'Challa and his foster brother Hunter also known as the White Wolf, leader of Wakanda's secret police the Hatut Zeraze. His crime-fighting eventually pitted him against the 66 Bridges gang and its regional manager Nigel Triage Blacque. Unbeknownst to Cole, Triage is secretly his half-brother" (Kevin Cole (Earth 616), n.d.). Wakanda is a fictional country in Northeast Africa. "Seeking to control his own destiny, Kasper offered to find Sal's kidnapped son in return for assistance in tracking down Kibuka" (Kevin Cole (Earth 616), n.d.).

Sam Wilson, Falcon, encouraged Kasper to increase his super strength (Kevin Cole (Earth 616), n.d.). Kasper undertook the Rite of Ascension and ate a heart-shaped herb, a plant mutated by a giant meteorite of vibranium (Heart-Shaped Herb, n.d.; Kevin Cole (Earth 616), n.d.). Erik Killmonger, a villain, created a synthetic heart-shaped herb that only grows in Northeast Africa (Heart-Shaped Herb, n.d.; Kevin Cole (Earth 616), n.d.; Wakanda, n.d.). He traded some to Kasper, along with assistance finding Sal's son. In exchange, Kasper became indebted to Killmonger. He promised to stop identifying as T'Challa, and became a White Tiger. Working with Queen Divine Justice and Everett Ross, an employee of the U.S. State Department, Kasper found Sal's son and was less indebted to Killmonger because he did not use his help. He is aligned with The Crew, a group of superheroes in the inner city, against 66 Bridges and Triage. His costume appears to be a brilliant, full body white costume similar to other White Tigers, except that he wears a black trench coat and may be armed with nonlethal gel bullets and guns. He carries a vibro-dagger that can pierce almost any surface; and can be deployed from the handle, and used to make marks for tracking. His costume is vibranium microweave "capable of dissipating the kinetic and hydrostatic shock damage of bullets or bullet like objects" (Kevin Cole (Earth 616), n.d.). Vibranium soles allow him to climb vertically. "Antarctic vibranium in his claws and boots will break down any known metal including adamantium" (Kevin Cole (Earth 616), n.d.). He has superior night vision, far sight, hearing, scent and tracking retentive skills, and lie detection. He can detect ingredients in food. Kasper can lift 800 pounds, run 35 miles per hour, and perform at a peak rate for one hour before becoming fatigued. His body recuperates exceedingly well. He has athletic skills and reaction times that exceed any Olympic gymnast.

Ayala's niece is his successor, Angela Del Toro (White Tiger (Angela Del Toro), n.d.). Del Toro is the fourth White Tiger. Superhero Daredevil was exposed in the press as Matt Murdock. Del Toro sought answers about Ayala and other superheroes by voluntarily participating in an investigation of Murdock by the Federal Bureau of Investigation (FBI). Del Toro, an FBI agent, witnessed her partner get killed while investigating Daredevil. Because she was willing to resign from her position, Murdock challenged her to a series of dares, including combat and superhero feats. White Tiger power gave Del Toro abilities similar to other White Tigers. In addition, she is able to see ultraviolet and infrared light; and hide in plain sight. She finally felt comfortable as a White Tiger when a robbery victim expressed sincere gratitude for her help. Eventually she rescued Murdock from an ex-crime lord. Like Ayala, Del Toro also fought alongside Daredevil, Spider-Man, and other superheroes. She was killed and resurrected by Lady Bullseye, the female counterpart to supervillain Bullseye. Before resurrection, she was bilingual, and after resurrection she was fluent in Japanese. Lady Bullseye worked as a lawyer fighting against Murdoch by day and against Daredevil, his alter ego, by night (Johnson, 2016; Maki Matsumoto (Earth-616), n.d.). She assisted Murdoch's in-laws, whose daughter was mentally ill, to gain custody of Murdoch's child (Maki Matsumoto (Earth-616), n.d.). Dual opposition with Murdoch/Daredevil and parity with Bullseye calls attention to Del Toro's last name Del Toro, which translates to "of a bull." Although Lady Bullseye fled to Spain, a relationship between Del Toro's Spanish diaspora heritage and bullfighting is not apparent, as bulls refer to rhinoceroses and other animals. Bullseye targets have been frequently depicted in cartoons; for example, Disney's animated masterpiece, *Robin Hood* (Devine, 1973). Allusions to bullfighting would be unlikely because creators of successful comics tend to favor human-animal relationships, and bullfighting angers humans and bulls. Bullfighting, during which a bull dies, is illegal in the United States and Puerto Rico (Cal. Penal Code § 597m, 2017; Eureka Springs, Ark., Code § 6.04.05(B), 2009; Fla. Stat. § 828.121, 2017; Little Rock, Ark., Code § 6–5(5), 2008; Maumelle, Ark., Code § 10–95(f), 2007; Tex. Penal Code § 42.09(1), 2016; W.S.A. 951.08, 2017). "Del Toro" hearkens to bull/cow (White Tiger (Angela Del Toro), n.d.). Cows are sacred in India, the birthplace of the first Bengal White Tiger. The bull is also sacred. Because Del Toro is her father's last name, the message is that bulls are not deities; and that the white tiger is a sacred deity, who prevails in America. Lady Bullseye's name suggests firing a weapon. White tigers are safe inside comfortable intermediate-size zoos in the United States except for the small possibility that a guest could fire a weapon. Lady Bullseye's essence intimidated Del Toro because she saw herself as a target. The relationship between Bullseye and Del Toro suggests liminality, which is reawakened for readers when Lady Bullseye resurrects Del Toro. Lady Bullseye's presence in the United States contrasts sharply with how cows are treated in India.

Lady Bullseye, Maki Matsumoto, was a sex slave owned by the Japanese mafia. She was trafficked with other victims until Bullseye killed the Yakuza mob. Matsumoto was inspired and became Lady Bullseye, a killer. Killing was likely a last resort for her because she had been a slave. A slave is someone, who is released from bondage when working, and then is subordinated in all other aspects. Unlike a prisoner, whose work and life are equally subordinated, Matsumoto's only chance to be free was during the time that she was raped (Copeland, 2016; Lochridge, 2017). Therefore, an alternate opportunity for liberation of her mind and body formulated into a killing spree. Like dairy factory farms that inflict torture on cows and deny them socialization, pleasure, and experiential enjoyment, sex traffickers rob sex, females, and bargained-for-exchange of purpose and meaningfulness (Cusack, 2014c). Many superheroes are inspired when their families are killed by evildoers. Lady Bullseye's desire to kill is released when she is freed from people, who conspired for her to be raped. Further showing different angles of revenge for those, who harm the helpless, Daredevil gained control of the order of ninjas that had affiliated with her, and then he banished her (Angela del Toro (Earth-616), n.d.).

Del Toro has been surrounded by superheroes her entire life; for example, she calls Iron Fist "Uncle Danny" (Angela del Toro (Earth-616), n.d.). Her exposure to Murdoch was endemic. After she ended her career with the

FBI, she joined the New York Police Department. Murdoch was at Riker's Island, while she worked as a vigilante wearing all black. She disobeyed the Superhuman Registration Act (S.R.A.), a law "enforcing the mandatory registration of super-powered individuals with the government. Supporters and critics debated between the rights of the individual" (e.g., "freedom of action and expression") "on one side versus the rights of society at large" (e.g., "safety from danger or harm") "on the other" (Superhuman Registration Act, n.d.). Murdoch recruited Black Widow to assist Angela to make her costume. Black Widow was fostered by a Russian soldier, who caught her after her mother saved her life by defenestrating her from a house that was intentionally incinerated (Natalia Romanova (Earth-616), n.d.). Angela has encountered King Cobra, The Lizard, Deadpool, and others (Angela del Toro (Earth-616), n.d.). Murdoch assumed Uncle Danny's identity and was confronted by Del Toro.

Angela was at home when she was stabbed in the heart by Lady Bullseye (Angela del Toro (Earth-616), n.d.). She was resurrected as a killer serving Lady Bullseye's team leader. Unlike white tiger spirits, which live on, humans are not eternal. Del Toro's resurrection caused destruction. She was cured from her conditioning to harm Murdoch by Black Tarantula, Carlos LaMuerto. "Muerto" means "dead" in Spanish. "Carlos" refers to wheels. He thwarted Lady Bullseye, and removed her from the team. Murdock assumed the power and ranked Angela and Carlos as lieutenants. Bullseye killed numerous civilians and was murdered by Murdock. He was possessed by a demon of the Snakeroot Clan, The Beast. Del Toro's conditioning resurfaced and she began to spy for Snakeroot. She obstructed the chain of command and ordered Foggy Nelson and Dakota North to be killed. She stabbed LaMuerto in the back and threw his body from a rooftop. Angela's control was regained by Master Izo during a battle against The Beast over Murdoch's soul. LaMuerto survived, but blamed himself.

Del Toro was turned against Ava Ayala, her niece, the fifth White Tiger. Del Toro was incarcerated in the Cellar, a super-penitentiary in New York (Angela del Toro (Earth-616), n.d.). Women in incarceration suffer depravity (Copeland, 2016). They are deprived of basic human rights and necessities (e.g., toilet paper and products for menses) (Cusack, 2017f). In prison she had no amulets, was without protection, and had to endure her own humanity without the enhanced spirit of the white tiger to guide, protect, and empower her. Ava has the amulets, which no doubt guided her to prepare for an encounter with Del Toro that saved them together. After Ava gained possession of the mystical amulets, Maker, leader of W.H.I.S.P.E.R. (World Headquarters for International Scientific/Philosophical Experimentation and Research), offered to help Del Toro take revenge against Ava. This offer is consistent with prison economies that torture inmates, who reluctantly participate in black markets for survival (Cusack, 2016). Maker gave to Del Toro mystical amulets from an alternate reality that gave her White Tiger powers from an alternate universe. Del Toro tracked Ava to Rome, Italy. The White Tiger spirit empowering Ava blended with Del Toro's White Tiger spirit causing Ava to become disempowered and Del Toro to be further strengthened. Del Toro joined Maker's New Revengers. The group attacked Ava's group, Avengers Idea Mechanics. Ava took possession of Del Toro's amulets. Del Toro was released from bondage when the amulets were destroyed. Ava and Del Toro became teammates and retired together.

Ava Ayala, the fifth White Tiger, had the most difficulty learning to submit to the white tiger's spirit (Ava Ayala (Earth-616), n.d.; Johnson, 2016). The name "Ava" resonates with "Ave Maria," indicating a departure from African syncretism and deeper connection to Catholicism in the American-born progression of the Ayala family. She is Ayala's sister and Del Toro's aunt. She graduated from Avengers Academy. Her mentor, Tigra, interned for Luke Cage, founder of the Avengers (Ava Ayala (Earth-616), n.d.; Coker, 2016; Johnson, 2016).

> The previous holders of the amulet being her brother and niece, and their time spent as heroes make for a fantastic development down the line. They can serve as one hell of a motivating factor, or it can create some sense of reluctance, and/or hindering her ability to truly control the power. Plus there is the added bonus of her connection with Luke Cage who also happened to be a father figure to her niece Angela. (Johnson, 2016)

Submitting and controlling the power is essential because it can lead to destruction (White Tiger (Hector Ayala), n.d.). Ayala increasingly grew weary and his uncomfortable state replaced the elation that he originally felt. After several near-death experiences, he asked Blackbyrd, a police detective, to return his White Tiger amulets to Sons of the Tiger. He married the love of his life, Holly Gillis. The amulets reentered his life. An upsetting confrontation with his wife stirred him from semi-retirement. The White Tiger attempted to fight crime once again, but before he arrived at a robbery, a police officer was shot. Two thieves robbing a pawn shop framed him. When police arrived, Ayala was holding a television and standing over the body. He was arrested and represented by Murdock and Franklin Nelson, known as Foggy (Hilyerd, 2009).

The attorneys, who White Tiger hires, represent mutations of Americans' perceptions of the justice system and legal professionals (Hilyerd, 2009). These two attorneys are part of a meta-commentary by comic book illustrators. The longest running publication depicting a fictional attorney is a comic book, which set precedent followed by dozens of fictional heroes and villains (e.g., Two-Face/Harvey Dent), who practice law, work in law offices, or are related to lawyers by blood or marriage. During the early 1900s, comic books supplied many children with their first glimpse of the legal profession. "[J]ust like the other superheroes" "adored" by American children, "these attorneys had an impact on them—long before they were introduced to Perry Mason, Atticus Finch or Ally McBeal, and long before they first watched L. A. Law or Boston Legal" (Hilyerd, 2009, p. 160; Lanphear, 2015). Comic books first called attention to "rough and tumble detectives," then to police officers, district attorneys (D.A.s), federal prosecutors (e.g., Kate Spencer, Manhunter), and the United States Attorney General (e.g., Captain Marvel's nemesis, Dr. Sivana) (Hilyerd, 2009, p. 163). The first superhero to wear a mask was created in 1936. He was The Clock, who formerly worked as a D.A. named Brian O'Brien. His vigilante activity resulted from his frustration with the system. Successive D.A. superheroes fit this mold. Well-intended and passionate police officers, attorneys, and judges cannot always create just outcomes for victims and violators. This vigilante fantasy assures readers that revenge and deterrence will occur; and that the justice system is occupied by employees, who actually care. It also fuels fantasies that frustrated justice members can be satisfied by vigilantism. Masked heroes are vigilantes, who have the same agenda as the government. Although they may break the law, they avenge and rescue. The fantasy is that illegal means can create legal ends (Cusack, 2013c; Hoffman, 1991; Zhang, 2015).

Other early district attorney crimefighters expanded, but followed the theme (Hilyerd, 2009). For example, Miss X was a D.A.'s daughter and Iron Skull was an android, who telepathically received requests for help from the New York City D.A. The father of Hawk and Dove, brothers Hank and Don Hall, respectively, was a judge named Irwin Hall. He has been described as the first comic book character to disapprove of vigilantes. Deviating from, and yet adhering to, the theme were villainous gang-affiliated attorneys, such as Caesar Cicero, whose only client was a crime family. Many attorneys with single identities were brought to life in the minds of children, who learned about corruption, crime, and unethical behavior. For example, Assistant District Attorney, Bill Hao, was the first Asian American character, in a 1976 issue of *Iron Fist* (Hilyerd, 2009; Thomas & Kane, 1974). Hao, who was not a superhero, appeared after the Vietnam War ended. Lawyers involved in politics helped illustrators to play-out topical political narratives (Hilyerd, 2009). Jeffrey Haines, first appearing in 1940, was an attorney and Mayor of Pittsburg, Pennsylvania. The incumbent mayor framed Haines after losing the election. Framing is a constant theme in comic books. Major characters, such as White Tiger, have been framed; and minor characters as well, for example, John Doyle, The Zebra.

Privately practicing attorneys, such as Sheldon Drake, demonstrate how attorney's relatives may become involved in the profession to a greater extent than those directly involved in the government's work (Hilyerd, 2009). Jane, Drake's daughter, sleuthed through cases handled by his office. Mixing private practice with private life was a gateway for more female characters (e.g., attorney Darcy Conroy). Between 1940 and 1961, Betty Bates, Lady at Law, was the sole practicing female attorney. She was depicted for 10 years. Another example is Darkhawk, whose mother was attorney Grace Powell.

Female attorneys have been central to the story of Bruce Wayne, Batman. In the movie *Batman Begins*, Katie Holmes plays attorney Rachel Dawes, Bruce Wayne's childhood friend (Hilyerd, 2009). Rachel appeared in the comic book adapted from the screenplay. Selina Kyle, Catwoman, divorced her life of crime and married Wayne (Hilyerd, 2009). Their daughter, Helena, became The Huntress. She and her stepbrother formed a law firm, making her the first female attorney superhero. Several other attorneys were introduced as members of Cranston, Grayson, and Wayne. Their associates included Roger Demarest, Tyler Van Dyne, Frances DeVito, and Charles Bullock. African-American attorney Bullock, Blackwing, was inspired by her. "After being beaten and captured during his first outing as a superhero, Bullock decided that being a junior associate provided enough abuse to satisfy him and was not seen in costume again" (Hilyerd, 2009, pp. 179–180).

Sadomasochistic character traits, such as those exhibited by Bullock, are prevalent in superheroes, for example Judge Alan Welles, Vigilante (Hilyerd, 2009; Kozlovic, 2016). Vigilante "preferred executing anyone he felt was engaged in or aided criminal activities, or preventing his idea of justice from being implemented. He even went so far as to execute a criminal defense attorney who he believed won too often on the basis of what he considered to be technicalities" (Hilyerd, 2009, p. 183). The identity Vigilante humanizes mutants. Murder contrasts with superheroes. It demonstrates "inherent conflict between being a judge on the side of law and order and a vigilante dedicated to wiping out criminals without a trial" (Hilyerd, 2009, p. 183). A third incarnation of Vigilante "became mentally unstable and eventually committed suicide" (Hilyerd, 2009, p. 183). Gregory Wolfe, depicted in *The Flash*, was a former prosecutor and sadistic prison warden, who tortured inmates (Hilyerd, 2009). Wolfe inflicted pain by mentally causing muscle spasms.

"The archetypal character of the retributive antihero—one who makes his own rules and follows his own conscience—is a familiar figure in mass culture, appearing in film, television, video games, and comics. This character represents the frustrations of millions of people who feel powerless and who fantasize about striking back at their enemies, be they real or imagined" (Worcester, 2012, p. 329). Sadomasochistic characters infuse identity into "time-honored debates over justice, morality, and the law" (Worcester, 2012, p. 329). Punishment "represents an inherently political worldview, one that values emotion over reason and unchecked anger over due process" (Worcester, 2012, p. 329). A superheroic Eighth Amendment or due process violation "makes the case for the notion that white-hot rage, channeled into the right kind of self-generated military campaign, has redemptive social value" (Worcester, 2012, pp. 329–330). For punishing sadistic superheroes, "anger is not a feral emotion that should be expelled from the political or legal realm. Instead, it is a dissolvent that allows" audiences to comprehend "things as they really are" (Worcester, 2012, p. 330).

Sadistic, masochistic, misandrist, and misogynistic storylines and attitudes are woven between heroic narratives to capture light and dark aspects of audiences' attention. The primary side may be interested in justice, revenge, superpowers, and other overarching themes. The latent side may be interested in discerning or perceiving what others may experience, withhold, or weaponize. Punisher is an enraged superhero. Surprised by Punisher's emotional drive, Spider-Man asks Punisher "[W]hat's this whole *kick* you're on" (Worcester, 2012, p. 332)? The question reflects Americans' consistent fascination with rage and antagonistic sources of power and psychic fuel. Spider-Man continues, "You said you were a marine—so how come you're fighting over *here?*" (Worcester, 2012, p. 332). Although Marines are unlike the National Guard, Coast Guard, or Army, which may engage in domestic missions, the comment overlooks domestic terrorism; war against intelligentsia (e.g., killings at schools); War on Drugs; and other domestic battlegrounds. Punisher offers a snarky reply, "That's my business, super-hero, not *yours*" (Worcester, 2012, p. 332). His comment refers to earning a living as a Marine, but not as a superhero, though both jobs may be caustic. "Maybe when I'm dead it'll *mean* something" (Worcester, 2012, p. 332). His comment synopsizes the namelessness of being a hero. It also shows his bitterness because his family members were accidently killed during a mafia hit. Spider-Man glibly reflects on Punisher's suffering while arriving at a profound conclusion about the tides of time. Spider-Man says, "[T]hat man's got problems that make *mine* look like a birthday party" (Worcester, 2012, p. 332). Frank Castle, Punisher's dual identity, was in Central Park when shooting began. He said to his wife, "Get *out* of here, honey! *Run*" (Worcester, 2012, p. 332)! He says, "I think I've been—*shot*—Honey. Don't worry—nothing—serious? Honey? Answer m—*no*. Dear lord, *no*. *Noooooo*" (Worcester, 2012, p. 333). Punisher's thoughts move from his shadow. "After a thing like that, I suppose a man *does* go—mad" (Worcester, 2012, p. 333). He disavows his proclivities for anger, dominance-seeking behavior, and sadomasochism that permitted him to be a Marine. Punisher "was always a moralist with an itchy trigger finger, but he needed a catalyst to transform himself into a domestic warrior" (Worcester, 2012, p. 333). "Once his campaign of vengeance began, he jettisoned his civilian identity and assumed the role of the Punisher on a full-time basis. He does not require a mask or a secret identity, because he has no family to protect" (Worcester, 2012, p. 333). Punisher lives through "his inner demons," but occasionally has flashbacks, which he confuses for love (Worcester, 2012, p. 333). "[H]e mostly thinks about his job, which is killing people" (Worcester, 2012, p. 333). He pretends that his sadistic life is a "eulogy" that "threatens to morph into the pursuit of the apocalypse" (Worcester, 2012, p. 343).

Punishing viewpoints and actions may relate to self-rejection. For example, Punisher's family is from Sicily, Italy (Worcester, 2012). After serving three tours of duty in Vietnam, he wanted to reenlist, so he changed his sur name from Castiglione to Castle. At one point, he almost became a priest, but instead became an enraged soldier. He was merited with "the Medal of Honor, the Navy Cross, multiple Silver Stars, Bronze Stars, and Purple Hearts, and the Presidential Medal of Freedom" (Worcester, 2012, p. 333).

> One of its recurrent motifs is the status and legitimacy of the law, both as text and as embodied in specific occupations and individuals, such as judges, lawyers, and police officers. The genre fixates on our obligations to the law, our relationship to the law, and whether, when, and under what conditions acting outside of the law might be considered acceptable. Admittedly, the genre's tough-guy exterior famously conceals an underlying romanticism, and a tendency toward nostalgia, and can thus lapse into melodrama. (Worcester, 2012, p. 334)

Military members struggle to legitimize their surroundings with themselves, and thereby militarize their environments (Cusack, 2015b). Punisher effuses with self-rejection because he is no longer enlisted and cannot legitimize himself apart from revenge. He fuels revenge by having flashbacks about his family. They momentarily alleviate his conflicted, albeit expressed not repressed, militarism.

Sadistic, masochistic, misandrist, and misogynistic storylines and attitudes are disguised as vengeance. These characteristics are "rejectionist" (Worcester, 2012, p. 341). Unlike White Tiger, Punisher "rejects compromise, negotiating, logrolling, deal making, easy living, and empty rhetoric" (Worcester, 2012, p. 341). He focuses on "misgivings," is "unrelenting," and "the campaign is his only solace" (Worcester, 2012, p. 342).

In *Punisher Kills the Marvel Universe*, Punisher ends superheroism by killing every living superhero (Ennis, 1995; Worcester, 2012). He kills Daredevil, even though he was lifelong friends with Murdock.

> The graphic depictions of the Punisher's violent acts are almost saying 'this is what a human body would look like if you did *x* to it.' The cautionary imperative and the pornographic impulse [are] … outré. If his outlook is rejectionist, retributionist, and implicitly (and sometimes explicitly) apocalyptic, it is also filled with deep emotions of dread, guilt, and grief. The anger that drives the character is rooted in moral values and moralistic outrage. He is a hyper-tense, hyper-angry, guilt-wracked killing machine who kills because he cares. In fact, he cares too much, and takes things to excess, which is why his stories are usually cautionary rather than celebratory. (Worcester, 2012, p. 346)

Gang members' inevitable course to join with other gang members (e.g., skinheads) in the U.S. military (e.g., Westside Story's Jets) is examined from an alternate angle in Marvel Edge (Chase, 1995). Punisher becomes insane; kills Nick Fury and S.H.I.E.L.D. after mistakenly blaming them for killing his family; and becomes a mob boss (Worcester, 2012). The mafia undertakes a Machiavellian execution of Frank Castle to sever his connection to society. Punisher defies culture; and, so does Ayala, but Punisher is consistently "inflexible" and obstinate (Worcester, 2012, p. 349). Ayala is emboldened by threats to his privacy and family. White Tiger is neither "cynical" nor "neurotic," but like Punisher he is a "didactic character, which is one reason why he doesn't expend a lot of energy trying to explain or justify his actions" (Worcester, 2012, pp. 348–349).

Problematic emotions may be finite or continuous. Characters' tolerance may be restored after antagonists and villains are defeated. Other emotions and trends toward hatefulness reestablish "injustice" that feeds self-condemnation (Worcester, 2012, p. 335). Cycles of rejection force a "hero, or, more accurately, the antihero, to embark on an unending spree of violence. In these kinds of stories there is no happy ending, at least not for the main character" (Worcester, 2012, pp. 334–335). The "Italian-American antihero" has destroyed "Hispanic, Asian, Native American, and African-American villains, at least one of whom sported gold teeth (a sadistic mercenary named Barracuda, who eventually gets his face blown off)" (Worcester, 2012, p. 335). Some panels are "tasteless and offensive;" but, Punisher is not "a paragon of virtue" (Worcester, 2012, p. 335). He is a psychopath (Cusack, 2015b). Punisher "is an equal-opportunity avenger, and the sheer range of villainy" is how audiences "measure the 'ecstasy' experienced by such a dour mass murderer" (Worcester, 2012, p. 335). Yet, he has been perceived by some readers as preferring to murder minorities. This view is not inconsistent with some liberal views about the U.S. military.

Unlike White Tiger, Punisher's shtick is "that anger is righteous[ness]" that "illuminates, clarifies, and cleanses, and" "belongs in the public realm" (Worcester, 2012, p. 340). Most liberals and conservatives would accept Thomas Hobbes' notion that civil society is where the strong emotions of the state of nature give way to reason and legitimate order.

> Modern political thought is built on the assumption that passions, especially violent passions, are potentially destabilizing, and that the job of the law, social norms, and public institutions is to establish and protect communities where differences can be settled without recourse to blood feuds, internal war, and other forms of unsanctioned, politically illegitimate violence. (Worcester, 2012, p. 340)

Angry characters may be relatable to White Tiger because "anger *is* truth," and White Tiger seeks to shed falsehoods and baggage (Worcester, 2012, p. 340). Both characters could believe that "civil society, the state, and the law itself are tools used by bullies to inflict pain on others;" but, "look[ing] past the veil of the social contract" elucidates that humans are frail (Worcester, 2012, p. 340). White Tigers feel compassion, but sadomasochistic characters are "angry" (Worcester, 2012, p. 340). "His single-mindedness," "morbidity, and" "alienation from everyday life" are similar to what Ayala feels inside, but he lives his pain, whereas Ayala helps others (Worcester, 2012, p. 340). "Perhaps the closest analogue in terms of political theory is provided by the controversial writings of German philosopher Carl Schmitt, who joined the Nazi Party in 1933 but whose theoretical framework nevertheless came under intense fire from leading fascists" (Worcester, 2012, p. 340). Schmitt argued that only parties could evaluate whether their ways of life were threatened by enemies. Swastikas and other artistic elements of Nazism continue to entice outsiders craving to belong.

Minority comic characters have dual identities (U.S. v. Carolene Products, 1938). In the early 1940s, Jeff Dixon, an Apache Indian attorney, donned a skull mask to become the Bronze Terror, also known as Real American #1 (Hilyerd, 2009; Worcester, 2012). The Dakotas' attorney, Michael Blackfeather, had a dormant mutation that awakened in him the ability of flight transforming him into The Werehawk. Sin City's Lucille was the first homosexual attorney. Although she was not a superhero, female homosexuality notifies readers that characters depart from norms. This may flag deviance and pronounce liberation.

Lesbians may intensely experience oppression because their "female role" significantly deviates from normative society requiring "policing work of femininity" and "heterocentricity" (Franklin & Chinn, 1999, p. 309). When comic books first introduced lesbian characters, "lesbians still faced a number of as-yet unpoliticized issues: mothering and child custody, police harassment in and raids on lesbian bars, and subjection to arrest for cross-dressing" (Franklin & Chinn, 1999, p. 310). While male superheroes could wear tights and leotards, sexually masculinized depictions of women were also acceptable to comic book readers. Neither deviation was tolerated in actuality. "Ordinary lesbians dressed up in capes and shiny leotards are not actually superheroes. Nor, exactly, is the lesbian trying to negotiate her way through a hostile legal system" (Franklin & Chinn, 1999, p. 328). A "lesbian hero is magical" (Franklin & Chinn, 1999, p. 328). She may exceed and overpower possibilities available to actual lesbians. "[T]he everyday lesbian" "is not the hero, although she may perform elements of the heroic. Lesbian legal theory is itself the hero" (Franklin & Chinn, 1999, p. 328).

Normative and hyperbolic stylizations "open the question of what 'lesbian' itself means, and who can occupy that position" (Franklin & Chinn, 1999, p. 301). "This is a difficult and challenging balancing act—to talk about and advocate for a sexual identity while insisting that what such an identity means remains fluid" (Franklin & Chinn, 1999, p. 301). This is why "[c]entral to lesbian legal theory is the power of imagination" (Franklin & Chinn, 1999, p. 303). A lesbian comic book character, irrespective of superhero powers, "heroizes the lesbian as locus of the possible, the space in which we can re-imagine and reshape the legal and cultural terrain to make it more livable"

(Franklin & Chinn, 1999, p. 303). Early depictions of lesbian employees were "a bold challenge to legal theory: to grapple with the sometimes gorgeous, sometimes agonizing realities of lesbian life while envisaging a radically alternative reality" (Franklin & Chinn, 1999, p. 303). "In the interplay" "and gaps" "between the terms 'lesbian,' 'legal,' and 'theory,'" "the possible" "limits of the imaginable" are fortified (Franklin & Chinn, 1999, p. 303).

In a comic book, a lesbian's "body is not itself a knowable essence. Instead, the lesbian body is always relational" (Franklin & Chinn, 1999, p. 306). Early characters were not designed to exude "lesbian-centered political activism," but "a richer and more multilayered solution to" the "conundrum" of boredom and oppression (Franklin & Chinn, 1999, p. 320). Lesbian activists, such as the Lesbian Avengers, have committed "direct action[s]" that undoubtedly were empowered, in part, by depictions of lesbian characters and superheroes (Franklin & Chinn, 1999, p. 320). Characters are brought to life, figuratively and practically, by real world politics. During the 1990s, Lesbian Avengers and dozens of similar avenger groups on two continents "operated" using acidic "politics very similar" to patriarchy (Franklin & Chinn, 1999, p. 321). "[A]ny woman was welcome in the group, but the actions the [a]vengers executed were lesbian-focused and devoted to 'lesbian survival and visibility'" (Franklin & Chinn, 1999, p. 321).

While comic books attempted to include diversity, Lesbian Avengers felt overwhelmed by differences.

> [T]he diversity of lesbian communities means that as a direct action, activist group, the Lesbian Avengers is not for everybody, nor should it be. It is for women who want to be involved in activism, work in community, be creative, do shit-work, take responsibility on a regular basis, have their minds blown, change their opinions and share organizing skills. (Franklin & Chinn, 1999, p. 322)

Their first Yippie-like action was on the first day of public school in 1992 (Cusack, 2011; Franklin & Chinn, 1999). Approximately 50 Lesbian Avengers demonstrated with a kilted marching band at an elementary school that opposed queer studies curriculum in New York City. The women were wearing T-shirts that said, "I Was A Lesbian Child;" and they distributed balloons that said, "Ask About Lesbian Lives" (Franklin & Chinn, 1999, p. 322). Like depictions of masked avengers, Lesbian Avengers' actions seemed to be "humorous and confrontational" (Franklin & Chinn, 1999, p. 323). "The atmosphere was almost carnival-like, with the balloons and brass band" (Franklin & Chinn, 1999, p. 324). Unlike superheroes, who fight their enemies, Lesbian

Avengers confronted their enemies' young children when they were likeliest to be unguarded by their parents. They were "hostile," territorial, "open," "and assertive" (Franklin & Chinn, 1999, p. 324). Like anti-hero superheroes, Lesbian Avengers assumed "one of the enduring negative stereotypes about lesbians: that [lesbians] 'recruit' into [their] ranks by taking advantage of the young" (Franklin & Chinn, 1999, p. 324). "In the planning stages of the action, this stereotype was never far from the surface, and caused long and heated debate" (Franklin & Chinn, 1999, p. 324). "[R]ather than running from negative images of lesbians, Lesbian Avengers embraced this myth: Lesbian Avenger t-shirts featured the cartoon bomb on the front, and on the back the slogan 'We Recruit'" (Franklin & Chinn, 1999, p. 324). Their image was weaponized and masculine (Cusack, 2014a, 2015b, 2016). This politicized sexual perspective may have responded to the exclusion of open lesbians from the military (Waranius, 2011). Defying broad cultural associations between heroism and the military, New York City-based Lesbian Avengers marching in the 1993 International Dyke March fabricated "superhero costumes, complete with capes and shields" to pronounce their "philosophy" "that 'we're the superheroes here'" (Cusack, 2015b; Franklin & Chinn, 1999, p. 328). It also says, "some are wives, not heroes" (Stein, 1989).

Lesbian Avengers attempted to radicalize discourse about lesbians by depicting love. By the 1990s, comic books had depicted lesbian romances, but avengers' actions demonstrated new political dimensions. Lesbian Avengers' "multilayered approach to heroizing lesbian love without reifying the monogamous couple is most fully exemplified by the 'Valentine's Day Action,'" "in Bryant Park on February 14, 1993" (Franklin & Chinn, 1999, p. 325). A lesbian sculptor created an effigy of Gertrude Stein's companion, Alice B. Toklas; and Lesbian Avengers placed it next to a sculpture of Stein in Bryant Park. Toklas "was lovingly unveiled" for approximately one hundred attendees, who observed "readings of erotic poetry by lesbian writers and a dramatic recitation of excerpts from Stein's sexually suggestive" poem "Lifting Belly" (Franklin & Chinn, 1999, p. 325; Stein, 1989). They rationalized lewd performances. "While this event could easily have devolved into a sentimental mimesis of the message of St. Valentine's Day—the superiority of coupledom—it was instead an anarchic celebration of lesbian sexualities that culminated in mass waltzing and simulated sex in the falling snow" (Franklin & Chinn, 1999, p. 325). Stein and Toklas "were invoked as foremothers but not 'role models'" (Franklin & Chinn, 1999, p. 325). Through this action, Lesbian Avengers allegedly "both reclaimed the lesbian past and insisted on forging their own lesbian sexual present" (Franklin & Chinn, 1999, p. 325). Public displays of group love, otherness, and freedom from oppression "demonstrate how crucial it is for lesbians to imagine a world that exceeds the bounds of the cultural space" (Franklin & Chinn, 1999, p. 326). For avengers inspired by comic book avengers, "[i]magination is more than just daydreaming: it involves fashioning a set of identities that can move" "through time and space more effectively than the selves to which" society grants "access" (Franklin & Chinn, 1999, p. 326).

Superheroes are neither "flawless nor perfect" (Franklin & Chinn, 1999, p. 327). They "are freaks," "mutants," androgynous, hybrids, and mechanized (Franklin & Chinn, 1999, p. 327). Superheroes relieve traditional desires to believe in "mythic narratives, but those narratives are necessarily connected to the world as we experience it" (Franklin & Chinn, 1999, p. 327). Many individuals, including lesbians, cannot relate to lesbian comic book characters or real-life avengers. "[M]yths are stories" that "might as well be true" because they have the power to transform others (Franklin & Chinn, 1999, p. 327). Mutations are contextualized by myths and liberated by performance of rituals.

Stonewall legal societies (e.g., Stonewall Legal Alliance and Stonewall Bar Association) ritualize a myth (Stonewall Bar Association, n.d.; Stonewall Legal Alliance, n.d.). Stonewall legal societies "raise awareness" and cultivate environments hospitable to open homosexuals and allies (Stonewall Bar Association, n.d.; Stonewall Legal Alliance, n.d.). As part of a legal society, the name suggests that members will reignite protest in the legal arena on behalf of homosexuals and gender-benders; and uses legal rhetoric to supplant mythologization of the first gay rights riot (Westboro Baptist Church, 2008). However, the politicization of the riot is a myth. In 1969, a gay bar was raided for operating without a license (History.com, 2010). Patrons were enjoying invisibility, unmonitored activities, and interactions that did not attempt to live up to society's image of a good person. Drunk patrons offended by the conflagratory confrontation fought police. Rebels and intoxicated patrons dwelling in society's shadow unsurprisingly fought authorities, who demanded that they legitimize and conform. Ultimately, politicization of gayness has resulted in moralized expectations (e.g., marriage and family-life) being levied onto homosexuals. Pressure to be good and participate in conformity with the majority is now at an all-time high. The riot spread from the bar and incinerated order in the surrounding area; however, violence was not the primary reaction (History.com, 2010). The myth holds that a crowd gawked outside the bar until one lesbian and three drag queens were placed into a paddy wagon (History.com, 2010). The crowd responded by lobbing bottles, phallic symbols. The officers retreated into the bar and waited for reinforcement and crowd control, including riot police (Cusack, 2015c; History.com, 2010). Demonstrations sprang around the city and Gay Liberation Front was formed in their wake. "Does it really matter whether it was a diesel dyke who threw the first punch at a police officer outside the Stonewall Bar, way back in the dawn of Lesbian and Gay Liberation, in 1969? The image is symbolic, and has important function as a legend" (Franklin & Chinn, 1999, p. 327). "[T]he lesbian in this legend is a diesel dyke: the most visible, most abjected lesbian identity" (Franklin & Chinn, 1999, p. 328). Lesbian legal theory may be "crucial for lesbians" "playing an essential originary role in the Stonewall Riots" by avenging lesbians inside courthouses (Franklin & Chinn, 1999, p. 327).

"[H]eroic lesbian legal theory is not a comforting, gentle, nurturing 'superwoman'" (Franklin & Chinn, 1999, p. 328). "Like all legendary heroes, lesbian legal theory is a warrior, and warriors must use violence to win justice" (Franklin & Chinn, 1999, p. 328). "Violence is a crucial element in the fantasy life of the oppressed" (Franklin & Chinn, 1999, p. 328). Lesbians may not "expect the powerful to give up power;" they may believe that by using violence and disrespect, lesbians are forced to claim power (Franklin & Chinn, 1999, p. 328).

> Valerie Solanas's SCUM Manifesto (originally published in 1968), a radical (although slightly unhinged) tract for women's liberation, creates a new kind of culture hero, the Society for Cutting Up Men ('SCUM'), a band of 'dominant, secure, self-confident, nasty, violent, selfish, independent, proud, thrill-seeking, freewheeling, arrogant females, who consider themselves fit to rule the universe … by systematically fucking up the system, selectively destroying property, and murder'. (Franklin & Chinn, 1999, p. 328)

Solanas' overt aggression and hostility toward non-lesbian identity "is evident in a recent imaginary lesbian hero, Diane DiMassa's Hothead Paisan, a neo-punk, Uzi-wielding dyke who castrates rapists, pulps homophobes, and engages in wild, raucous sex with sexually indeterminate lovers" (DiMassa, 1999; Franklin & Chinn, 1999, p. 328). Like male superheroes, she attacks evildoers to fill vacancies left by interpersonal and familial displacement. Avengers symbolically emasculate boundaries imposed by evildoers, who parade as justice members and authority figures. Solanas "does not shy away from the lesbian hero's relationship with violence" (Franklin & Chinn, 1999,

p. 328). However, "violence is necessarily more nuanced than" "metaphorically and literally" "cartoonish violence" (Franklin & Chinn, 1999, p. 329).

"[V]iolence is a force that can be used in a variety of ways, just as cartoon superheroes choose to use their powers for good, not evil" (Franklin & Chinn, 1999, p. 329). Violent fantasies, rhetoric, and ideation should end when violence is projected "as an attribute of lesbianism" (Franklin & Chinn, 1999, p. 329). Lesbianism is not "a violent denial of the law's system of heterosexual and male hegemony" (Franklin & Chinn, 1999, p. 329). Violence is like "fire," which is either "good" or "bad" (Franklin & Chinn, 1999, p. 329). "[F] ire has long been a trope lesbians have deployed to represent" lesbianism, but it does not resonate with all lesbians (Franklin & Chinn, 1999, p. 329). Interpersonal violence and harassment in "spiky relationship[s]" does not empower lesbians to cope with men and women in public spaces or past relationships (Franklin & Chinn, 1999, p. 329). It is antithetical to political dominance and legitimate visibility. "[L]inks between women, fire," "and violence exist in a variety of cultures," but do not force lesbians to adopt violent postures toward one another (Franklin & Chinn, 1999, p. 329).

"Fire, and the transformation of fire from destructive to empowering, was also a fundamental imaginary for the Lesbian Avengers" (Franklin & Chinn, 1999, p. 329). Avengers bravely responded to hate crimes (Cusack, 2015c). The residence of a homosexual male and female was firebombed in Oregon. Avengers in Greenwich Village, New York marched. Their neighborhood was populated by homosexuals and targeted by hate crime. Lesbian Avengers ritualistically ate fire at a shrine publicly memorializing the victims. "This action dramatized the membrane between destruction and survival that lesbianism embodies: as Avengers ate fire, other lesbians chanted 'we take the fire within us; we take it and make it our own'" (Franklin & Chinn, 1999, p. 329). The metaphor is morbid. They consume past violence, a symbol of the deceased, and deny their future (i.e., fertility). Although some plants, such as Saw Palmetto, rapidly regenerate after fire, many specimens of nature are permanently altered by it (NPS, n.d.; Texas Parks & Wildlife, n.d.). Acquiring fire rather than water suggests infertility and slaughter. Perhaps they purified the subject of their ceremony. The victim was a lesbian, who lived with a homosexual man. "Just as violence shatters a whole into many pieces, or fire transforms the raw into the cooked, lesbian legal theory unlocks the meanings" of future battles either waged on the pages of comic books, in courthouses, in bedrooms, or on the street (Franklin & Chinn, 1999, p. 330). "Fire burns," but perhaps these spaces ought not to "hold" "it" (Franklin & Chinn, 1999, p. 330). "The hero shows" followers how their "lives can be," yet "leaves" them "standing" (Franklin & Chinn, 1999, p. 330).

Josiah Power was the first gay male attorney (Hilyerd, 2009). Evangeline Whedon and Power's superpowers emerged after they began practicing law. They were ostracized by people prejudiced against superpowers. Power stopped practicing law and founded Superheroes for Hire; and Whedon became the X-men's attorney. During the 1990s, three African-American lawyers were also heroes. Suspiciously bigoted grouping may be evident insofar as one African American character, Shadowhawk, known as Paul Johnstone, was the first HIV-positive comic book character. Reflecting and perpetuating pandemonium in the 1990s, his character was injected with HIV by a mobster, who he prosecuted. Despite the suggested correlation between African Americans and positive HIV status, a correlation between homosexuality and HIV-positive status was not evident. *In toto*, introduction of diseases into comic books softens prejudiced attitudes. It may relate to other tragic subject matter, such as the redeemed love interest of X-Men leader, Charles Xavier, and his nemesis, Magneto, also known as Gabrielle Haller. She was a concentration camp survivor.

Non-lawyers have correlated with minorities (Hilyerd, 2009). A superhero paralegal was the first Hispanic justice member. Marcos Zapata, Relampago (i.e., "Lightning" in Spanish), was illustrated by Azteca Production (Hilyerd, 2009, p. 178). A female former law student, Becky Blake, worked as an intern for Ayala's lawyers, Nelson and Murdock. Blake used a wheelchair. Yet, some non-lawyers were portrayed as being homogenously majoritarian. For example, law student Bill Waring transformed into The Challenger after his father was murdered by a crime syndicate. Reilly Tyne, the son of Spider-Man's clone (i.e., Scarlet Spider) was hired by Nelson. He had a dual identity. Daredevil's spirit and Zarathos, a demon, transform Tyne into the hero Darkdevil.

Homogeneity mainly encompassed "White" male characters (Hilyerd, 2009). Their ethnicities may not have been specified, like some characters with ethnic (e.g., Italian) names. It was also portrayed through their affection for women and close uninhibited relationships with other males veering on homoerotic, which supported dark fantasies that successful White males were secret homosexuals. Comic books in this regard are vengeful because they attack cultural, ethnic, and sexual subordination of majoritarian groups. Characters, such as Gomez Addams, were ambiguously ethnicized (e.g., "*cara mia*," "*ma chere*," and "*bubbeleh*"), but their oddity was justified by kookiness (Hilyerd, 2009). Their homogeneity allowed them to dwell among regular folks, who they ridiculed as being pathetic. *The Addams Family* represents a mutated form of comic books because they appeared in cartoons, on television, and in film. They were not the only characters to transcend zines (e.g., Harvey Birdman) (Hilyerd, 2009).

Majoritarianism and homogeneity are confronted by *Superman* (Siegel & Shudter, 1938). For example, Superman fights Lex Luthor. Superman is not from Earth. He is an extraterrestrial. To accomplish his dual-role as reporter and superhero, and for readers to believe in his existence and ability to fight crime, they must deviate from normative thoughts about law and religion, "Lex" and "Luthor" (e.g., Martin Luther), respectively (Cusack, 2016, 2017a). "Luthor's name even points" to "renunciation of the True Church" (Kozlovic, 2002, p. 14). Luthor is an egocentric "mini-king" (Kozlovic, 2002, p. 14). Superman is neither a criminal nor a heathen. Clark Kent is a Methodist (Cusack, 2016). Ostensibly, Superman's role is not to abolish law or religion, but to complement it in a nonconventional way; however, he challenges and cuts into God narratives that undergird society, law, Christianity, and America. One religious analysis of Superman argued that Superman is a sexy Christic symbol. Superman's given name, Kal-El, means "Star Child" in Kryptonite (Kozlovic, 2002). However, Lucifer, which may be suggested by "Luthor," was an angel of light before his fall (Isaiah 14:12; Revelation 12:1–17). He was said to be the most popular angel. He was a celebrity and a star among the celestial hosts. "Like all good myths (sacred and secular), it had a serious inner core" (Kozlovic, 2016, p. 27). A comparison between Jesus and Superman was published in April 2002 (LazerCannon7, 2014). At that time, Americans were searching for answers and grace in response to the terrorist attacks on September 11, 2001 (Kelly, 2005). An answer to why bad things happen may be "Clex," a balance of Clark and Lex.

White Tiger's attorneys are homogenous and deviant. Like all superheroes, they have flaws and special attributes. Nelson's mother is Rosalind "Razor" Sharpe, an attorney (Daredevil (Matthew Murdock), n.d.; Nelson, Foggy, n.d.). She has a reputation for mercilessness. She abandoned her family shortly after Nelson's birth. Recognizing the reality of American and global familial disintegration, comic books have repeatedly included stories about abandonment, custody, parentage, orphaning, foster parents, and divorce (Franklin & Chinn, 1999; Kozloff, 1981; Maki Matsumoto (Earth-616), n.d.; Natalia Romanova (Earth-616), n.d.). For example, architect Eric Masterson, Thor, consulted family law attorney Samantha Joyce to resolve a custody dispute. Another example is Olivia Lewis, Slingshot, who was Captain Dynamo's biological daughter. His paternity was unknown; and it was believed that she was fathered by the man who raised her, a well-paid attorney in Washington, D.C. A third example is "Professor X of the X-Men," who "consulted attorney Jack White when faced with the possibility of having a court order him to surrender all young mutants to the authorities" (Hilyerd, 2009, p. 192; IPPL v. Institute for Behavioral Research, 1986; Scott, 1987). Some zines have covered new territory; for example, "third sex" problems interlocking with "tender years" doctrines (Franklin & Chinn, 1999, p. 316; Troxel v. Granville, 2000). Custody and visitation may be denied to homosexual partners, who cannot convince the court that they are a child's psychological parent (V.C. v. M.J.B., 2000).

Nelson was raised by his stepmother and father (Daredevil (Matthew Murdock), n.d.). He was roommates with Murdock in college and together they matriculated to Harvard Law School. Like Lady Justice, Murdock is blind. Graphic novels have introduced several characters with physical (e.g., visual and orthopedic) impairments, emotional disturbances, and other health impairments (e.g., specific learning disabilities) (Irwin & Moeller, 2010). Some characters are portrayed as evil, "pitiable," or "super crips" (i.e., use disabilities to fight crime) (Irwin & Moeller, 2010, p. 3). Evil may be defined "as a violation of societal rules, brutal domination and an uncaring disposition" (Kozlovic, 2016, p. 8). "Bizarre" states include, "child hating perversity," which may be "even more 'unnatural' in a woman due to" "iconic associations with birth, nurturing and bonded infant love;" "genetic/mental abnormality;" and "intrapsychic megalomania" whereby the "megalomaniac" has "big ideas and extremely destructive impulses" (Kozlovic, 2016, p. 8). Although many are portrayed as fully participating in family and community life, some characters are their "own worst enem[ies]" (Irwin & Moeller, 2010, p. 9). Emotional impairments seem to be ridiculed and demonized. For example, Joker was admitted to Arkham Asylum. Disabled characters are likelier to be female. "Pitiable" characters (e.g., broken leg) are likelier to be female, whereas evil characters are likelier to be male (Irwin & Moeller, 2010, p. 3). Impairments have become more accepted in society after Christopher Reeve, the actor who played Superman, fell from a polo horse and was paralyzed (Cusack, 2016; Kozlovic, 2002). Murdock became blind, gained heightened senses, and assumed the superhero identity, Daredevil, after he encountered radioactive cargo spilled in a vehicular accident. Murdock defended Nelson from campus bullies. Like Nelson, Murdock was raised by his father and abandoned by his mother. His father was a boxer, Battling Jack. His father was murdered for refusing to throw a fight.

Daredevil's costume was made from Battling Jack's boxing robe. He got revenge on the men, who killed his father. He fought crime along with other superheroes, such as Elektra, Spider-Man, and Wolverine.

Nelson and Murdoch are networked with many attorneys. Attorney Kate Vinokur defended Daredevil; and lawyer Alton Lennox became entangled in an assassination attempt on Foggy Nelson (Hilyerd, 2009). After moving to San Francisco in 1973, Murdock became a partner at Broderick, Sloan, and Murdock. Larry Cranston, a junior partner, was classmates with Murdock and Nelson. Cranston, a professor at Columbia University, passionately hated the duo, and became the villain Mr. Fear. A senior partner, Kerwin J. Broderick, intended to run a criminal enterprise. He deployed alien technology to generate super villains (e.g., Dark Messiah and Angar The Screamer).

Comic books mutate time. This device contrasts with penological aims to control and weaponize time to punish criminals. An alternate version of Daredevil is set in 2099 when Nelson's great-great grandson became the original Daredevil (Hilyerd, 2009). Resurrection Man is another example. The former attorney was an experimental subject of nanotechnology. Blood-borne organisms resurrected him from death. "Time had been good to" The Clock; and in 1992, the original masked superhero became the U.S. president (Hilyerd, 2009, p. 187). Time is relative to earthlings' concept of movement. Supernatural beings may experience time differently than humans. For example, attorney Arkady Dread operated in mafia families with The Others, a group of supernatural beings.

Mortality is a norm faced by superheroes, villains, and humans, such as gang members and police. Replacement may be a form of mortality or immortality. "In 2005, Chicago lawyer Luke Gabriel was inspired by an elderly client to take the client's place as the replacement Mr. Smoke. It was also revealed that X-Men associate, Madrox, the Multiple Man, had a duplicate that had become a lawyer" (Hilyerd, 2009, p. 192). Criminal court judge Michael Hart, the Judge, was killed. After he was resurrected, he killed criminals. Loss of superpowers may result in characters' moral death. "Sharon Ginsberg first appeared as the lawyer for agent Soloman O'Sulivan in the series X-Statix. Her first function was to serve a cease and desist order on X-Force to prevent one of Soloman's clients from appearing on television with the superhero group, but after losing her wings (her superpower) she turned against the legal system" (Hilyerd, 2009, p. 193).

Curses kill avengers' inner-persons. Crimson Avenger, an African-American lawyer from Detroit, bought two guns owned by the previous

Crimson Avenger. The guns were cursed, but she was unaware that when she used them to murder two unpunished murders, she would be "forced her to relive and avenge the death of innocents" (Hilyerd, 2009, p. 193). Criminal killing is a nightmare experienced by some vigilantes, such as a D.A.'s sister, Catalina Flores, known as the Tarantula.

The live action fan film, *White Tiger*, dramaturgically demonstrates how superheroes confront norms within society and alter the meaning of justice and fairness (Huertas, 2016). The gang, who attacked Cindy, Savage Skulls (Savage), was featured in a documentary called *80 Blocks from Tiffany's* (Weis, 1979). The documentary highlighted relevant themes, such as social justice; gender equality; poverty, class, and opportunity; family; and vigilantism. Gang members may be viewed by their neighbors as "outlaws" or "bums" depending on whether community members benefit from "guys sitting around" (Weis, 1979). Gang members are cued into activity on public streets. They are exposed to covert and overt crime. They may participate in crime or deter crime. For example, one community member described their neighborhood as violent, scary, and totally devoid of renovation or maintenance. Dilapidated buildings were abundant, and people feared being accosted. "It was not that unusual" to see a shootout; and when they occurred, unfazed witnesses would flee (Weis, 1979). A migration of inhabitants fled the South Bronx leaving the poorest community members to fend for themselves. Gang members, without job prospects, stayed in the neighborhood. In the course of surviving and preserving the community, gang members assumed a protective role. One member explained the meaning of being a Savage. "If you see a person, who has a little problem, go checkout what it is" (Weis, 1979). A community member said, "They stick together and protect the neighborhood" (Weis, 1979). Other members described their antics, lifestyles, and criminal behavior as "psychopathic" (Weis, 1979). One Savage defended by explaining that a "crazy" person "could go off at the drop of a hat" (Weis, 1979). Savages are not "crazy" (Weis, 1979). On the contrary, they are more regulated than average criminals. One described how he was a "take-off artist" before joining "the club," meaning that he could have targeted any pedestrian (Weis, 1979).

Savage members are like superheroes. They wear bandanas on their faces that render their visages featureless and genderless. Each has a secret identity (e.g., nickname) to avoid detection and implication. Gang members may accept "challenge[s]" to overcome their secret identities; whereas superheroes embrace the inevitability of being challenged because of their secret motives and identities (Weis, 1979). Savages may be motivated by their environments;

whereas superheroes may have pasts that haunt them. Savages may not have "regret" or "responsibilities" (Weis, 1979). They may be reported by the media and sensationalized (Cusack, 2017a). Many savages and superheroes live in post-World War II America. One Black Savage decorated his living area with a Nazi flag (Weis, 1979). Both may take-up combat-style training and experience excruciating defeat (e.g., falling out of a window and breaking one's back). They climb tall buildings. Unlike superheroes, Savages burglarize residences; lower stolen items using ropes; and then exit through front doors; and, Savages publicly "congregate," which may "annoy the pedestrians" (Weis, 1979). Police say that they pose no "real problems" (Weis, 1979). They are recognizable not by costumes, but by their club "colors" (Weis, 1979). Like White Tiger and Spider-Man, they are unarmed and "clean" (Weis, 1979). Savages and superheroes may view their actions as being "antisocial" (Weis, 1979). Whereas superheroes prevent rape, murder, and robbery, Savages perpetrate these crimes. Savages and superheroes attend college and get "wiser" with age (Ellis, 2007; Weis, 1979).

Savages replace broken families. Female members said that they view other male and female members as allies, who they described as "brothers and sisters" (Weis, 1979). Although they may be victimized by criminals, gang life assures them of reprisal. A shopkeeper afraid of Savage Skulls said, "We were afraid of the girls more than we were afraid of the gang" (Weis, 1979). Her comment demonstrates inequality being perceived, but perhaps not experienced by the members. A male member of the club described the perfect woman.

> 'See no evil. Hear no evil.' Man, that's the most righteous woman you could ever have 'cause that's the kind of woman that'll stick by you. She don't need the wedding bells, big fancy cakes, and … poems; and all that wild shit. Just a little lovin', you know; and a little rice; and some herb; and a beer, Man; and boogie all night. (Weis, 1979)

A former leader's wife of five years said that he resisted settling down; and was incarcerated during her first pregnancy for 13 months. Although he did "not care" about her or the children at first, he became more "considerate" of them (Weis, 1979). He began to see the benefits of wanting a job. The documentary did not comment on sexual harassment or other adverse employment conditions affecting men in the 1980s. The former gang leader and another member left the club. They had outgrown the familial roles played by the club.

The two members explained why they left and had "Born Loser" tattoos removed (Weis, 1979).

> That's what the club made me think: one percent of society left out; born loser; and that I really didn't give a hell about nobody in the streets, but my people. We consider ourselves a family 'cause you turnaround, and you hang out there in the streets, and everybody just wants to turnaround and screw you. At that time, we was real tight; never fucked over each other; took care of each other real good. (Weis, 1979)

One said that he was going to remove his tattoo "because it ain't right. I wasn't born to lose" (Weis, 1979). Gang members pressured him to quit a construction job, but he kept it. Father Gigante, a local priest, helped the member to get the job. The member said that he recognized him from the street and thought, "This guy looks like he wants to clean up his act. Let me give him a break" (Weis, 1979). Of his new job, he said "the break worked out pretty good, but it's kind of still screwed up out here. Too many changes. It's like a new life" (Weis, 1979).

Father Gigante's experience with gang life centered around the home, unlike the Savages. While holding a lit cigar, Father Gigante told documentarians that he was in a Greenwich Village gang during the 1940s and 1950s. "That was all part of our neighborhood" (Weis, 1979). He described membership as a "simple, positive activity" because gangs did not participate in "fighting" (Weis, 1979). They rummaged through abandoned buildings to retrieve and sell led and bottles. When Father Gigante was eight years-old, there was "one big war" over a "matter of territorial rights" (Weis, 1979). There was a "peace meeting" during which members played cards and shot craps in the street (Weis, 1979).

He attributed the success of gang membership to a solid home life. (Weis, 1979) "These things developed eventually positively because our families were stable. Our mothers and fathers were there. They were out working. This is probably where we found our salvation in the streets; but, after six o'clock when they were home, they kind of controlled us. The wildest kids got controlled" (Weis, 1979). His parents worked, which may have given him an advantage over gang members whose families were absent. The ex-Savage member said that as a child gang member, life was easy because he took what he wanted. After father Gigante helped him get a job, he had to "hustle for it. That's a big change. It's something else" (Weis, 1979).

Savages discussed intimate partner violence. For example, the former leader's wife said that when they first met, he was "dirty," "mean," and possessed other characteristics that one might anticipate from a gang leader (Weis, 1979). During a 300-person block party, one member struck his girlfriend. She used the term "stroke," not to describe affection, but rather to describe being hit by her boyfriend (Weis, 1979). The emcee of the event set a casual mood. "Just grab a partner. I don't care where they come from" (Weis, 1979). However, the high school-age girl became a battleground. She says that the member, who she "unfortunately" cares for, hit her "just because" another member, named Fly, "was dancing with" her (Weis, 1979). "My old man, he wasn't going to stroke me or anything. All he did was make a mistake, and he hit me by mistake. You know? And then I got this cut on my eye" (Weis, 1979). "He's angry because he knows. He knows" that the other member "loves me; and I like" him "a hell of a lot. You know? So, he's scared that me and" the other member "might have something going with each other. So, that's what happened" (Weis, 1979). "I got stroked by mistake" (Weis, 1979). The other member "digs me and I dig" him (Weis, 1979). "You know? He's alright people. Anything else" (Weis, 1979)?

Gang members' intimate partnerships may be differentiable from the way superheroes' romantic passions are depicted in comics. Nelson and Murdock defended Ayala, but he was convicted. During the trial, Ayala became hostile and had an outburst when the state's attorney questioned him about his marriage. This may evidence his character's ethnic and social role as being protective of his wife. When the verdict was returned, he disarmed a security guard and attempted to escape. He was shot by police. Ayala was posthumously exonerated (White Tiger (Angela Del Toro), n.d.; White Tiger (Hector Ayala), n.d.). Prying into his private life and posthumous exoneration demonstrates the importance of lies and truths in superheroism, the justice system, and families. In the documentary, a member named Frankenstein questioned why the documentarian was reluctant to tell gang members where he lived in Los Angeles, California. It showed that the documentarian feared telling them which neighborhood he lived in because it may have made him a target of gang violence. Frankenstein said, "I could tell you the truth, you can't tell me the truth" (Weis, 1979)? The theme echoes throughout the live action film: transgenderism, bigotry, derogatory language, vigilantism, membership, masking, debt, and backstory all allude to discrepancies between reality and truth. Frankenstein told the documentarian that he would be incapable of living his life in Hunts Point, New York. "You'd be going through a lot of changes, Man" (Weis, 1979). Another said, this is "a land of nowhere," a "disaster" (Weis, 1979). Unlike gentrification, gang members have "nowhere to go" (Weis, 1979). "You can't imagine life here" (Weis, 1979). Another allusion to truth in both films is absence of resources in poor neighborhoods, which correlates with crime and incarceration. In incarceration, inmates are given jobs. These jobs may be their only opportunities to acquire skills beyond high school. They may panhandle or use jobs (e.g., mechanic and gas station attendant) to refine their criminal skills. Work may be emblematic of a club's dissipation. Like women going into the workforce, members working in society may symbolize antistructure within their families. A group of gang members, like the Savage Skulls depicted in the live action film, is emblematic of alternative families and values. Society's pressures to disband are equally destructive to them personally and socially as feminism has been to patriarchy in the home.

One member said that a few shop owners in their community appeared on television begging the police to prevent loitering and crime; and then police reacted.

> Cops [were] on the street corner telling us to get out. We didn't even do nothing. We were just out in the neighborhood cruising, you know, walking around, doing our thing; but, we stopped on the corner to get some beer or something. [T]hey tell us to get out of the block. 'Keep moving.' 'Keep moving.' 'Keep moving.' Get out of the neighborhood. Can't even walk around without getting harassed because when they see us in a rat pack or something, probably think, we going out to look for trouble. (Weis, 1979)

He does not view police as a direct threat (e.g., rival gang), but as a nuisance. They are state employees, who do not have their own militia-like directives (e.g., branches of the military). Their presence affects the gang by weakening their position in the community and limiting their association. In the live-action film, police may not be attuned to the Savages' criminal presence because the gang did not intend to become involved in crime that evening. It may also be that, like the actual Savages, they ride "clean" and their "gang colors" and activities do not cause reasonable articulable suspicion (Cusack, 2015c; NY Penal § 240.10, 2017; U.S. Const. am. 1). Local police complement superheroes. Local culture and the needs of the people transfuse into the superhero, who may work with police to function as a well-regulated militia (U.S. Const. am. 2). However, villains may view police as being inferior; and may derogate superheroes by comparing them to police. For example, in the film *Superman*, Lex Luthor described Superman as "the blue boy" and the "big blue Boy Scout" (Kozlovic, 2002, p. 5; Spengler, 1978–1983). His insult alludes to "boys in blue," a term used to describe police officers. It also demeans Superman's maturity and alien heritage.

Police may focus on prostitution or other crimes possibly committed by Cindy, whose presence may further threaten and harm community members.

Savages may feel that it is their duty to confront and deter Cindy from demoralizing individuals; wasting sex-buyers' families' money; and insinuating herself into the private lives of committed men, whose stability is essential for community prosperity and regeneration. They may not acknowledge Cindy as a potential breeder, generator, protector, and stabilizer, even though she has payed bills for another man and recognizes hardships suffered by her brother, who she is unable to shelter. Like Father Gigante, who was saved by the streets, Cindy's work in prostitution may save her from poverty and alleviate symptoms of her disease (i.e., gender dysphoria) (APA, 2013). However, being confronted by the gang may deter her from prostitution, which is dangerous and illegal.

"[S]avior-style superheroes" such as White Tiger and Spider-Man, have been "most admired" "[a]s were the 'wounded warriors' who recovered," for example Daredevil (Packer, 2009, p. 9). "If only these superheroes were available when Freud or Jung wrote," then there may be more synthesis between the superego and aspirations to be heroic. Freud and Jung "were fond of referencing Greek and Roman myth. They named complexes and mental problems after deities or demons or characters in Greek drama" (Packer, 2009, p. 10). In comics, "demise" has typically "marked the start of a superhero" (Packer, 2009, p. 10). "[I]t is unfathomable to think that Freud would have referenced the American superheroes, even if they were available. Freud was not fond of" heroics (Packer, 2009, p. 10). "He preferred to ally himself with more respectable, more venerable, more classical figures from Greek, Roman, and Egyptian mythology;" "[b]ut Freud's esteem in society has shifted" (Packer, 2009, p. 10). "Similarly, comics' creators were once marginalized, but now they" allegedly "are venerated for their artistic abilities and for their political foresight" (Packer, 2009, p. 10).

Diagnostic and Statistical Manual (DSMV) has renovated Freudian concepts with behavioral science terms (APA, 2013). "Ego," "Oedipus complex," and "drive" "were left over from the Freudian legacy" (Packer, 2009, p. 10). Superheroism tempts analyzers to "turn back time and rename psychopathology after American superheroes instead of Greek gods" (Packer, 2009, p. 10). Unlike a typical psychopath, as diagnosed by the American Psychological Association, "[s]uperheroes turn traumatic events into positive experiences" "even if they retain scars" (Packer, 2009, p. 10). Arguably, charisma may be a sort of mutation that transforms trauma into leadership skills. A psychopath is saved and has the capacity to save others by performing great works (e.g., civic duties) (Cusack, 2017a). "Superhero stories begin after the trauma, not during the trauma" (Packer, 2009, p. 10). Like psychopaths, heroes, and gods, they "reenact the trauma in attempt to achieve catharsis" (Packer, 2009, p. 10). They may not rely on the ego or superego to make decisions. "They simply act" (Packer, 2009, p. 10). Humans (e.g., analysands) may "look *inward* to find truth. Superheroes turn *outward* to bring justice" (Packer, 2009, p. 11). Both may have "second thoughts," "private thoughts," and "dreams" (Packer, 2009, p. 11). "Thought bubbles" illustrate "the double consciousness and introspection and reflection" (Packer, 2009, p. 11). "Some superheroes also dream, and they may act in their dreams" (Packer, 2009, p. 11). "Given the way that superheroes are evolving," "[s]uperheroes have proven to be more adaptable over time than anyone ever imagined" (Packer, 2009, p. 11). "Jung claims that superheroes persist and morph and mutate into many different forms because they represent inherited mythical 'archetypes' that recur almost unchanged from culture to culture, and from era to era. Jung influenced mythographer Joseph Campbell, who ... popularized the concept of the 'monomyth.' Campbell appeared on that ... American ... pulpit known as television" (Packer, 2009, p. 12).

The superhero motif has had a "persistent appeal" (Packer, 2009, p. 12). Superheroes' psychological characteristics' "waxing and waning" "suggest that extrinsic forces interact with intrinsic psychological factors and may even override those theoretical internal drives at times. Extrinsic social, political, and economic factors also produce psychological reactions, regardless of childhood upbringing" (Packer, 2009, p. 12). Some "psychological theorists claimed that superheroes represent subversive sexuality," for example "sadomasochism, same-sex sex, female domination, and sexual fetishism" (Kozlovic, 2016; Packer, 2009, p. 13). Theorists "contend that these cryptic sexual connotations produce untoward but immediate influences on children and could cause ill effects in later generations" (e.g., eating disorders); however, they could cause some children to become more "socially conscious" and "racially progressive" (Chin, 2013; Cusack, 2013b; Packer, 2009, p. 13). These claims may seem apt because American children may be accustomed to envisioning superheroes in Biblical terms. Biblical narratives tend to favor men as dominant figures and subordinate, rather than entertain children. "As Matthew tells the story, King Herod" "ordered a mass infanticide when he learned that a baby boy who was born in Bethlehem might assume his throne. It [is] bad enough to claim that comics [are] *seducing* children; it [is] even worse to hint that the alleged harm caused by comics could compare to mass infanticide" (Packer, 2009, p. 14).

Psychological developments may imitate or spur "cultural changes" causing females to "challenge[]" "designated role[s] in society" (LeGuin, 1987; Packer, 2009, p. 14). Theorists may view "sexual innuendos in every crease and crevice of superhero costumes" as being deleterious to society (Packer, 2009, p. 14). Superheroes' psyches, which suggest to audiences that "violence" is never "gratuitous," may "truly inflame[]" them (Packer, 2009, p. 14). "Superhero sexuality" and "aggression" "is always tempered by the superhero's super ego" (Packer, 2009, p. 15). "That overarching sense of right and wrong, the 'superego,' keeps their sexual and aggressive impulses in check. Supervillains are not subject to the scrutiny of the superego" (Packer, 2009, p. 15). "When superheroes get aggressive, as they often do, they do not show signs of 'intermittent explosive disorder'" (Packer, 2009, p. 15). "They do not lose control and forget why they took a swing" (Packer, 2009, p. 15). "Rather they direct aggression toward a specific, and deserving, target" (Packer, 2009, p. 15). "There is no doubt that stories about being orphaned or abandoned;" "children and mothers" "fend[ing] for themselves;" "mastering social skills;" "or about shedding secret identities to gain greater recognition by peers play into pubescent and adolescent fantasies and push the appeal of superhero stories" (Packer, 2009, p. 16).

Superheroes, for example White Tiger and Superman, are immigrants in America (Kozlovic, 2002). "By infusing immigrant" "concepts into the host … culture, a new American myth emerged. This new superhero myth recreates standard heroic monomyth that appears from culture to culture" (Packer, 2009, p. 16). "This new myth can be compared to a syncretic religion" "that combines old and new" (Packer, 2009, p. 16). Duplicity permits them to "speak unspeakable truth" (Packer, 2009, p. 17). Characters "advocated unpopular positions before real people or politicians" and "were willing to articulate these same sentiments" (Packer, 2009, p. 17). Superheroes' psyches may involve audiences to "push[]" "political agenda[s];" "sacrifice" "social standing;" "incit[e] backlash;" "crusade[] against" "pressur[e];" "condemn" "atrocities;" "innovate[]" "status;" "adapt[]" to "counterculture" "before others adapt[];" and "lose" "pride" (Packer, 2009, p. 17). These actions have not only national and cultural implications, but international and global significance as well.

Iconoclasm is definitive of superheroism because "superheroes' most distinguishing psychological feature" is "the *superego*," which is "a sense of right and wrong" versus "good and evil" (Packer, 2009, p. 18). Superheroes have "trumpeted unprecedented changes in social and sexual mores" "openly espous[ing]" post-feminism and post-secularism (Packer, 2009, p. 17). Drug use, like animal experimentation, is undoubtedly at issue within the realm of superheroes. Experimentation is like drug use because animal subjects aggressively resist experimentation, and therefore compromise any attendant results. Drugs damage takers, and therefore alter their realities, which sublimates the true individual, who took the drugs. Comics challenge audiences to question what their parents (e.g., hippie generation) may have insinuated or communicated about drug use (Cusack, 2015b). Special serums and other drugs may mutate average people and animals into superheroes, but not completely alter their emotional capacities or transform their wills. These changes subtly jab at societies' condonation of drug use, including pharmacological takeover by big pharma (Kelo v. City of New London, 2005). Mask-ulinity is one method for dealing with rejection experienced by youth whose parents suggest to them that they should take prescribed or illegal drugs for self-improvement and behavioral modification (Cusack, 2017e). Social implications of drug use are considered deeply within comic books in which themes persistently revolve around apprehension of drug peddlers, buyers, and users (e.g., villains). These ramifications become embedded touchstones in the lives of youth, who dare to resist drug abuse (e.g., social drinking).

"*[P]syches* move society, and society moves the *psyche*" "and psychology" (Packer, 2009, p. 18). Therapists' resistance to penalizing the psyche, but commitment to treating the psyche, demonstrates their lack of understanding for superheroes' superegos, which are "punitive" (Packer, 2009, p. 18). A punisher "counters the basic instincts" for self-satisfaction, which bad people take at the expense of others (Packer, 2009, p. 18). Vigilantes confront and castigate evildoers, who "make choices" based on "urges" rather than virtues and "conscience" (Packer, 2009, pp. 18–19). A legitimately independent "individual could counter corruption and act as an independent agent, undaunted by political pressures or personal gain. That individual existed in pulp rather than in person" (Packer, 2009, p. 19). By terming superheroics "superegoism," villains are implicitly "sociopaths" (Packer, 2009, p. 19). "Sociopaths possess incomplete" or damaged superegos obsessed with "pursuit of power and personal self-interest" (Packer, 2009, p. 19).

References

16 U.S.C. § 1531, *et seq.* (2017).
42 U.S.C.A. § 5196a-d (2006).

725 ILCS 5/113A-1 (2017).

Abimbola, W. (1997). *Ifá: An exposition of Ifá literary corpus*. New York, NY: Athelia Henrietta Press.

Afridi, K. (2017, January 11). White tiger [don't mind the tail] no tail. Retrieved from https://www.youtube.com/watch?v=glEaXZ-Y2rk

American Psychiatric Association (APA). (2013). *Desk reference to the diagnostic criteria from dsm-5*. Washington, DC: American Psychiatric Publishing.

American Veterinary Medical Association (AVMA). (n.d.). PETS Act (FAQ). Retrieved from https://www.avma.org/KB/Resources/Reference/disaster/Pages/PETS-Act-FAQ.aspx

Angela del Toro (Earth-616). (n.d.). Retrieved from http://marvel.wikia.com/wiki/Angela_del_Toro_(Earth-616)

Animal Legal & Historical Center. (n.d.). Map of states with disaster planning laws. Michigan State University. Retrieved from https://www.animallaw.info/content/map-states-disaster-planning-laws

Antle, B. (2013). *The tiger cubs and the chimp: The true story of how Anjana the chimp helped raise two baby tigers*. New York, NY: Henry Holt and Co.

Ashe. (2008–2014). Ashe: Revista sobre los orishas. Retrieved from http://wwap, w.ashe.com.ve/foro/viewtopic.php?f=1&t=19789&sid=2acdcdb43fbe51d84fd0597cd3baffc5

Association of Zoos and Aquariums (AZA). (n.d.). Retrieved from https://www.aza.org/about-us

Audubon Nature Institute. (n.d.a). Retrieved from https://audubonnatureinstitute.org/

Audubon Nature Institute. (n.d.b). Shelter rules. Retrieved from http://audubonnatureinstitute.org/golf-parks/audubon-park/shelter-rentals/1113-shelter-rules

Audubon Nature Institute. (2016, November 7). White tiger celebrates 20th birthday! Retrieved from https://www.youtube.com/watch?v=tkYEJQjoBz4

Audubon Zoo Volunteer. (2016a, July). Volunteer worked with Suri, the white tigress, who lived at Audubon zoo before Rex and Zulu. Demonstration to save the white tiger. Audubon Zoo, New Orleans, LA.

Audubon Zoo Volunteer. (2016b). Conversation with naturist John about peacock and wolf in a tussle at Audubon Zoo. Fairview Riverside State Park, Covington, LA.

Ava Ayala (Earth-616). (n.d.). Retrieved from http://marvel.wikia.com/wiki/Ava_Ayala_(Earth-616)

Babcock, C. R., & LaFraniere, S. (1992, July 21). The Clintons' finances: A reflection of their state's power structure. *Washington Post*. Retrieved from https://www.washingtonpost.com/archive/politics/1992/07/21/the-clintons-finances-a-reflection-of-their-states-power-structure/c4b6fc4d-abbe-46bf-ae23–31512d77601c/?utm_term=.bc8f5df23ed4

Bacon, P. (1999, August 10). Louisville crowds roar approval for rare white tiger. Rare tiger boosts zoo turnout. *The Courier Journal* (Louisville, Kentucky) B1, B6.

Baihumon. (n.d.). White tiger of the west. Retrieved from http://digimon.wikia.com/wiki/Baihumon; http://digimon.neoseeker.com/wiki/Baihumon

Bean, D. (1961). *West side story*. USA: Seven Arts Productions.

Becknell, C. A., Price, T., & Short, D. (n.d.). Krewe of Zulu. Retrieved from http://www.kreweofzulu.com/history

Bizu, I. (2015). White tiger. On *Moment of madness*. New York, NY: Epic Records.

Blake, W. (1794). Tyger. *Songs of innocence and experience*. Mineola, NY: Dover Publications.

Brown, W. (2008). *Regulating aversion: Tolerance in the age of identity and empire*. Princeton, NJ: Princeton University Press.

Buck, S. (2017). *Iron fist*. Burbank, CA: Marvel Television.

Burkes, C. (2017, May 19). No machine guns for Louisiana kids, House committee decides. *The Times Picayune*. NOLA.com. Retrieved from http://www.nola.com/politics/index.ssf/2017/05/no_machine_guns_for_kids.html

Cal. Penal Code § 597m (2017).

Caummisar, R. L. (1999, August 29). Tiger's 'majestic beauty.' *The Courier-Journal* (Louisville, Kentucky), D2.

Chappell, B. (2017, May 17). One more to go: New Orleans takes down Civil War general's statue. National Public Radio (NPR). Retrieved from http://www.npr.org/sections/thetwo-way/2017/05/17/528745474/one-more-to-go-new-orleans-takes-down-civil-war-generals-statue

Chase, B. (1995). *Marvel edge*. New York, NY: Marvel Comics.

Chicago Botanic Garden. (n.d.). Retrieved from https://www.chicagobotanic.org/butterflies

Chin, W. Y. (2013). Law and order and white power: White supremacist infiltration of law enforcement and the need to eliminate racism in the ranks. *Journal of Law & Social Deviance*, 6, 30–98.

City of Salina v. Blaksley, 72 Kan. 230 (1905).

Cohen, R. S. (2015, September 15). Conversation with Ross Spencer Cohen, Senior Director of Programs and Operations, Hiring Our Heroes, Washington, DC.

Coker, C. H. (2016). *Luke cage*. Burbank, CA: ABC Television Studio.

Copeland, S. (2016). Prison life: My world in the hellish Florida state prison system. *Journal of Law & Social Deviance, 12*, 226–243.

Cusack, C. M. (2006). Volunteered with humane society to care for rescued animals (e.g., pit bulls, puppies, and a goose) post-Hurricane Katrina, Mississippi.

Cusack, C. M. (2007). Conversations in Israel, Jerusalem, Israel.

Cusack, C. M. (2008a). Conversation with PETA Attorney David Favre. People for the Ethical Treatment of Animals (PETA) Headquarters, Norfolk, VA.

Cusack, C. M. (2008b). Conversation with PETA President Ingrid Newkirk. Sublime Restaurant, Fort Lauderdale, FL.

Cusack, C. M. (2010–2016). Observations and comparison of white tigers and black bears reveal that a white tiger is larger than a black bear, Juneau, AK; Miami, FL; New Orleans, LA; Pigeon Forge, TN.

Cusack, C. M. (2011). Placentophagy and embryophagy: An analysis of social deviance within gender, family, or the home (*etude* 1). *Journal of Law & Social Deviance, 1*, 112.

Cusack, C. M. (2012). Nonconsensual insemination: Intimate partner violence, patriarchy, police education and policy. *Journal of Law & Social Deviance*, *4*, 171.

Cusack, C. M. (2013a). A feminist inquiry into intimate partner violence law, policy, policing, and possible prejudices in Alaska. *Journal of Law & Conflict Resolution, 24*.

Cusack, C. M. (2013b). Celebrity justice and gossip blogs: Demographic characteristics of victimized and allegedly criminal celebrities featured on top gossip blogs. *Journal of Law & Social Deviance*, 5, 244–295.

Cusack, C. M. (2013c). Irish in the criminal justice system. *Journal of Law & Social Deviance*, 6, 1.

Cusack, C. M. (2014a). No stroking in the pokey: Promulgating penological policies prohibiting masturbation among inmate populations. *Journal of Law & Social Deviance*, *7*, 80–124.

Cusack, C. M. (2014b). *Pornography and the criminal justice system*. Boca Raton, FL: CRC Press.

Cusack, C. M. (2015a). *Animals, deviance, and sex*. Cambridge: Cambridge Scholars Publishing.

Cusack, C. M. (2015b). *Criminal justice handbook on masculinity, male aggression, and sexuality*. Springfield, IL: Charles C. Thomas.

Cusack, C. M. (2015c). *Hair and justice: Sociolegal significance of hair in criminal justice, constitutional law, and public policy*. Springfield, IL: Charles C. Thomas.

Cusack, C. M. (2016). Save the white tiger. *Journal of Law & Social Deviance*, *12*, 1.

Cusack, C. M. (2017a). *Fish in the Bible: Psychosocial analysis of contemporary meanings, values, and effects of Christian symbolism*. Wilmington, DE: Vernon Press.

Cusack, C. M. (2017b). Male circumcision is unnecessary in America. *Journal of Pregnancy & Reproduction*.

Cusack, C. M. (2017c). Saving captive white tigers: An assessment of an animal law treatise. *Journal of Law & Social Deviance*, *14*, 1.

Cusack, C. M. (2017d, December 6). "Call: From the white tiger" performed with underwater camera, yoga, and paint in person-white tiger spirit habitat, Pensacola, FL.

Cusack, C. M. (2017e, December 7). "Straight face" using feces and countenance to decry bearding, Pensacola, FL.

Cusack, C. M. (2017f, December 8). "Shake the shit outta'er" using sexist usaa representatives, defective edgestar washer, misogynist living direct associates, rhinoceroses, biased contractors, bigoted investigators, Chris Rock, et al., Cyberspace and Pensacola, FL.

Cusack, C. M. (in-press). Foot binding. *Journal of Law & Social Deviance*, *15*.

Cusack, C. M., & Waranius, M. E. (2015). Visual detection of sex offenders and consequential biases among Christians. *Journal of Law & Social Deviance*, *10*, 42–67.

Daredevil (Matthew Murdock). (n.d.). Marvel.com. Retrieved from http://marvel.com/universe/Daredevil_(Matthew_Murdock)#ixzz4fCtC7PAj

Delagrange, M. (2006). Conversation with Mikel Delagrange, attorney at the International Tribunal in The Hague, The Netherlands. Florida International University, College of Law, Miami, FL.

Devine, A. (1973). *Robin Hood*. Burbank, CA: Walt Disney Productions.

DiCaprio, L. (2015). *The revenant*. Los Angeles, CA: New Regency Productions.

DiMassa, D. (1999). *Hothead paisan*. Jersey City, NJ: Cleis Press.

District of Columbia v. Heller, 554 U.S. 570 (2008).

Eason, C. (2007). Fabulous creatures: The white tiger. *Fabulous creatures, mythical monsters, and animal power symbols*. Santa Barbara, CA: Greenwood Press.

Eggler, B. (2012, May 3). One of Audubon zoo's white tigers dies of cancer. *The Times-Picayune*. Retrieved from http://www.nola.com/pets/index.ssf/2012/05/one_of_audubon_zoos_white_tige.html

Ellis, E. (2007). Conversation with Edward Ellis. Member of Playboy Gangsters (P.B.G.). Country Village (C.V.), Carol City, FL.

Ellis, R., & Rose, R. (2016, May 29). Cincinnati zoo kills gorilla to save child who slipped into enclosure. CNN. Retrieved from http://www.cnn.com/2016/05/28/us/zoo-kills-gorilla/

Ennis, G. (1995). *Punisher kills the marvel universe*. New York, NY: Marvel Comics.

Estes, J. (2014, May 21). Bitching retard carries a machine gun in public. Retrieved from https://www.youtube.com/watch?v=iAfcFtSQ0Vs

Eureka Springs, Ark., Code § 6.04.05(B) (2009).

Evans, B. (2017, March 5). King Zulu, Audubon zoo's white Bengal tiger, dies at 20. *The Times-Picayune*. NOLA.com. Retrieved from http://www.nola.com/pets/index.ssf/2017/03/king_zulu_audubon_zoos_white_b.html

Ferguson, C. (1997, December 8). Tiger cubs adorable, but still their wild streak shows: Cubs thrive in captivity. *The Tennessean*, 1A, 2A.

Fihlani, P. (2011, June 30). South Africa's lesbians fear 'corrective rape'. BBC. Retrieved from http://www.bbc.co.uk/news/mobile/world-africa-13908662

Fla. Stat. § 828.121 (2017).

Foxy Gamer Anime. (2013a, November 5). Baihumon hatched!!—Digimon masters online. Retrieved from https://www.youtube.com/watch?v=7ts9bXwLnw8

Foxy Gamer Anime. (2013b, November 5). Baihumon!! skills & stats—Digimon masters online. Retrieved from https://www.youtube.com/watch?v=FjpqjhX7YSo

Franklin, C., & Chinn, S. E. (1999). *Book review: Lesbians, legal theory and other super heroes, Sappho goes to law school*. New York University School of Law Review of Law & Social Change, 301–330.

Ginsberg, D., Kribble, M., & Shucha, B. (2009). Inspiring innovation: Planning, implementing, and evaluating the web 2.0 challenge. *Law Library Journal, 101*(3), 355.

Griffin, J. H., & Bonazzi, R. (2010). *Black like me*. New York, NY: Berkley Books.

Griswold v. Connecticut, 381 U.S. 479 (1965).

Heart-Shaped Herb. (n.d.). Retrieved from http://marvel.wikia.com/wiki/Heart-Shaped_Herb

Hee-sung, K. (2010, January 1). White tiger to roar loud and proud in 2010. Korea.net. Retrieved from http://www.korea.net/NewsFocus/Culture/view?articleId=80148

Hensleigh, J. (2004). *The punisher*. Santa Monica, CA: Lions Gate Films.

Herek, S. (1996). *101 dalmatians*. Burbank, CA: Walt Disney Pictures.

Herzig, R. M. (2015). *Plucked: A history of hair removal*. New York, NY: NYU Press.

Hesse, H. (1957). *Siddhartha*. New York, NY: New Directions Publishing.

High Evolutionary. (n.d.). *Marvel*. Retrieved from http://marvel.com/universe/High_Evolutionary

Hilyerd, W. A. (2009). Hi Superman, I'm a lawyer: A guide to attorneys (and other legal professionals) portrayed in American comic books: 1910–2007. *Widener Law Review, 15*, 159–195.

History.com. (2010). 1969 The Stonewall Riot. A & E Network. Retrieved from http://www.history.com/this-day-in-history/the-stonewall-riot

HJ Res. 69 (2017).

Hoff, B. (1983). *Tao of Pooh*. New York, NY: Penguin Publishing Group.

Hoffman, D. (1991). *Hook*. Culver City, CA: TriStar Pictures.

Hopkins, G. M. (2015). Journal for 1868. *The collected works of Gerard Manely Hopkins: Diaries, journals, and notebooks*. Oxford, UK: Oxford University Press.

Huertas, J. (2016). *White tiger*. New York, NY: West Side Stories. Retrieved from http://moviepilot.com/p/marvels-white-tiger-gets-his-own-fan-film-featuring-a-this-is-us-star/4169984

InvestGold. (n.d.). Retrieved from http://www.investgold.co.za/

IPPL v. Institute for Behavioral Research, 799 F.2d 934 (1986).

Irwin, M., & Moeller, R. (2010). Seeing different: Portrayals of disability in young adult graphic novels. *American Association of School Librarians*, *13*, 1–11.

Itare, I. (2016, June 26). Zulu tribe virginity testing South Africa. Retrieved from https://www.youtube.com/watch?v=eihgKV5Ywjs

Jaques, R. K. (n.d.). "The problem with poop." REL-D 380. Indiana University, Bloomington, IN.

Johnson, M. (2016, November 18). Marvel wants a white tiger Netflix series, here's who we want to cast. Movie Pilot. Retrieved from https://moviepilot.com/posts/4030909

Kasper Cole. (n.d.). Marvel. Retrieved from http://marvel.com/universe/Cole,_Kasper

Kelly, B. (2005). The transformative power of "hot gay sex:" Queering Superman, queering the fan on the televisionwithoutpity "Smallville" boards. *Journal of Film & Television*, *25*(1), 71–82.

Kelo v. City of New London, 545 U.S. 469 (2005).

Kevin Cole (Earth 616). (n.d.). Wikia. Retrieved from http://marvel.wikia.com/wiki/Kevin_Cole_(Earth-616).

Kim, J. J. (1991). A cultural psychiatric study on tattoos of young Korean males. *Yonsei Medical Journal*, *32*(3), 255–262.

Kozloff, S. (1981). Superman as saviour. *Journal of Popular Film & Television*, 9(2), 78–82.

Kozlovic, A. K. (2002). The unholy biblical subtexts and other religious elements built into Superman: The movie (1978) and Superman II (1981). *Journal of Religion & Film*, *7*(1), art. 7.

Kozlovic, A. K. (2016). Superman as Christ-figure: The American pop culture movie messiah. *Journal of Religion & Film*, 6(1), article 5.

Kozuskanich, N. (2008). Originalism, history, and the Second Amendment: What did bearing arms really mean to the founders? *Journal of Constitutional Law, 10*, 413–446.

Lanphear, J. B. (2015). Inherent racism biases woven into America's criminal justice institutions: A reexamination of to kill a mockingbird. *Journal of Law & Social Deviance*, *10*, 69–136.

Larose, G. (2017, March 17). New Orleans stops 'air rights' leasing for balconies for 30 days to review legality. *The Times-Picayune*. NOLA.com. Retrieved from http://www.nola.com/politics/index.ssf/2017/03/new_orleans_stops_air_rights_l.html

La. R.S. § 40:1752 (2017).

Lawrence v. Texas, 539 U.S. 558 (2003).

LazerCannon7. (2014). White tiger dream. Retrieved from https://www.youtube.com/watch?v=geVKSyj-jCY

Leach, M. (1975a). Aries. *Funk & Wagnalls standard dictionary of folklore, mythology, and legend*. Los Angeles, CA: New English Library.

Leach, M. (1975b). Orion. *Funk & Wagnalls standard dictionary of folklore, mythology, and legend*. Los Angeles, CA: New English Library.

LeGuin, U. K. (1987). *The left hand of darkness*. New York, NY: Ace Books.

Levy, E. (2017, February 15). White tiger original producer. Retrieved from https://www.youtube.com/watch?v=x7ckYtr3Ros

Lieberman, L. (1993). White tiger and the mosquitos. *The Hudson Review*, 46(3), 471–476.

Little Rock, Ark., Code § 6–5(5) (2008).

Livo, N. J., & Rietz, S. A. (1991). *Storytelling folklore sourcebook: Stars*. Santa Barbara, CA: Greenwood Press.

Lochridge, M. (2017). *Lochridge's prison adventures*. Prisons Foundations. Retrieved from www.PrisonsFoundation.org

Maki Matsumoto (Earth-616). (n.d.). Retrieved from http://marvel.wikia.com/wiki/Maki_Matsumoto_(Earth-616)

Mardi Gras New Orleans. (n.d.). Mardi Gras history. Retrieved from http://www.mardigrasneworleans.com/history.html

Mardi Gras Parade Schedule. (2016, February 9). 2016 Zulu social aid and pleasure club presents "celebrating 100 years of incorporation." Mardi Gras Parade Schedule. Retrieved from www.mardigrasparadeschedule.com/krewes/zulu/2016/

Maumelle, Ark., Code § 10–95(f) (2007).

McDonald v. City of Chicago, 561 U.S. 742 (2010).

Meridian International Center. (n.d.). Louis Armstrong: Satchmo blows up the world. Retrieved from http://www.meridian.org/jazzambassadors/louis_armstrong/louis_armstrong.php

Meyer, M. D. E. (2013). Slashing Smallville: The interplay of text, audience and production on viewer interpretations of homoeroticism. *Sexuality & Culture*, *17*(3), 476–493.

Miller, W. I. (1996). Surveying law and borders: Sanctuary, redlight districts, and Washington, DC: Some observations on Neuman's anomalous zones. *Stanford Law Review*, *48*, 1235–1246.

Natalia Romanova (Earth-616). (n.d). Wikia. Retrieved from http://marvel.wikia.com/wiki/Natalia_Romanova_(Earth-616)

National Park Service (NPS). (n.d.). Fire management. Retrieved from https://www.nps.gov/cana/learn/nature/upload/fire%20regime.pdf

Nelson, Foggy. (n.d.). Marvel.com. Retrieved from http://marvel.com/universe/Nelson,_Foggy#ixzz4fCssrRME

Nobles, W. P. (2016, February 9). Zulu's Mardi Gras parade set to roll in New Orleans. *The Times-Picayune*. NOLA.com. Retrieved from http://www.mardigras.com/news/2016/02/zulus_mardi_gras_parade_rolls.html

Normand, R. (2017, May 2). Victory on air rights! Vieux Carré property owners, residents & associates. Retrieved from http://vcpora.org/victory-on-air-rights/

Northup, L. (2009). Conversation with Dr. Leslie Northup about "smells and bells." Florida International University, Miami, FL.

NY Penal § 240.10 (2017).

Obergefell v. Hodges, 576 U.S. ___ (2015).

Odusanya, M. (2009). Conversation about Yoruba with Mayowa Odusanya, J.D. Florida International University, College of Law, Miami, FL.

Packer, S. (2009). *Superheroes and superegos: Analyzing the minds behind the masks*. New York, NY: ABC- CLIO.

Packer, S., & Pennington, J. (2014). *A history of evil in popular culture: What Hannibal Lecter, Stephen King, and vampires reveal about America.* Santa Barbara, CA: ABC-CLIO.

Park, E. (1979). Around the mall and beyond + national-zoo white tiger. *Smithsonian, 10*(6), 26.

Peterson, A. T., & Dunworth, D. J. (2004). Appendix C: Mythology in the solar system. In *Mythology in our midst: A guide to cultural references*. Santa Barbara, CA: Greenwood.

Pope, J. (2017, January 6). There never was and never will be a king like Zulu. *The Times-Picayune*. NOLA.com. Retrieved from http://www.nola.com/300/2017/01/first_zulu_parade_1909.html

Prahlad, A. (2005a). Witches. *The greenwood encyclopedia of African American Folklore: Volume 3*. Santa Barbara, CA: Greenwood Press.

Prahlad, A. (2005b). Yoruba. *The Greenwood Encyclopedia of African American Folklore: Volume 3*. Santa Barbara, CA: Greenwood Press.

PrancingPony5656. (n.d.). Horror story: The night of the white tiger part 1, part 2, part 3. Retrieved from https://www.youtube.com/watch?v=RCfjBdsmrAY

Presser v. Illinois, 116 U.S. 252 (1886).

Reeves, G. (2013, March 20). Best semi-automatic pistols. American heroes channel. Retrieved from https://www.youtube.com/watch?v=E-es5xZVnFs

Reno-Gazette Journal. (1998, March 7). p. 19.

Rex. (n.d.). Rex organization. Retrieved from https://www.rexorganization.com/

Rex. (2012, January 27). 2012 Parade explores the ancient Americas. Rex organization. Retrieved from http://www.rexorganization.com/News/2012/2012-parade-explores-the-ancient-americas

Ribar, R. J., Oakes, L. M., & Spalding, T. L. (2004). Infants can rapidly form new categorical representations. *Psychonomic Bulletin & Review, 11*(3), 536–541.

Richter, J. (2016). These days it's hard to tell what's part of the act. *No acute distress*. Carbondale, IL: Southern Illinois University Press.

RS 9:2796 (2017).

Santeria Church of the Orishas. (n.d.). Retrieved from http://santeriachurch.org/

Scott, J. (1987, November 15). Life begins anew for 5 'Silver Spring' monkeys: Trapped in animal rights case, macaques are focus of fresh research at zoo. *Los Angeles Times*. Retrieved from http://articles.latimes.com/1987-11-15/local/me-20966_1_animal-rights

Scott, M. (2017, February 22). How the Zulu coconut was saved from extinction. *The Times-Picayune*. NOLA.com. Retrieved from http://www.nola.com/300/2017/02/zulu_coconut_history_10084552017.html

Sharkey, J. M. (2009). *Minor detail*. Greg Weeks, Stephen Blundell and the online distributed proofreading team. Retrieved from https://www.gutenberg.org/files/28156/28156-h/28156-h.htm

Shen, T. (2010). *A study of Chinese traditional black and white* (Order No. 10367975). Retrieved from ProQuest Dissertations & Theses Global (1868631671).

Siegel, J., & Shudter, J. (1938). *Superman*. Burbank, CA: DC Comics.

South African History Online (SAHO). (2011, April 3). Zulu. Retrieved from http://www.sahistory.org.za/article/zulu

South Florida Sun Sentinel. (1997, February 2). Tiger Photo Reflect Poorly on Zoo, 6G.

Spengler, P. (1978–1983). *Superman*. Burbank, CA: Warner Bros.

Stein, G. (1989). *Lifting belly*. Tallahassee, FL: Naiada Press.

Stewart, A. (2017, May 20). Conversation with Alena ("Ms. Lena") Stewart. Zulu Social Aid & Pleasure Club, New Orleans, LA.

Stonewall Bar Association. (n.d.). Retrieved from www.barassociationdirectory.com

Stonewall Legal Alliance. (n.d.). Florida International University, College of Law, Miami, FL. Retrieved from https://law.fiu.edu/students/organizations/stonewall-legal-alliance/

St. Tammany Sheriff's Office. (2017). Conversation with officers taking the Police Motorcycle Certification Course. Fontainebleau State Park, Mandeville, LA.

Texas Parks & Wildlife. (n.d.). Palmetto State Park. Retrieved from http://tpwd.texas.gov/state-parks/palmetto

Tex. Penal Code § 42.09(1) (2016).

The Institute of Greatly Endangered and Rare Species (T.I.G.E.R.S.). (n.d.). Retrieved from http://www.tigerfriends.com

The Louisville Zoo. (1999, September 3). See the new white tiger. *The Courier-Journal* (Louisville, Kentucky), 15.

The Philadelphia Inquirer. (2008, July 13). A taste of the big easy: Audubon Zoo, N4.

The Times (Shreveport, Louisiana). (1999, January 16). Audubon's white tiger dies, 5B.

The Town Talk (Alexandria, LA). (1999, May 16). Tigers crowned king, D-8.

Thomas, R., & Kane, G. (1974). *Iron fist*. New York, NY: Marvel Comics.

Thomas, R. S. (2003). The white tiger. *Sewanee Theological Review*, 46(2), 291.

Tolson, M. (1999). Delta. *Harlem gallery and other poems of Melvin B. Tolson*. Charlottesville, VA: The University Press of Virginia.

Too, L. (1998). *Essential Feng Shui a step-by-step guide to enhancing your relationships, health, and prosperity* (Ch. 1). New York, NY: Ballantine/Wellspring. Retrieved from http://www.worldcat.org/wcpa/servlet/DCARead?standardNo=0345429044&standardNoType=1&excerpt=true

Troxel v. Granville, 530 U.S. 57 (2000).

Tundra & Loki. (n.d.). The sanctuary's white tigers. Tiger Homes. Retrieved from http://www.tigerhomes.org/animal/wsiberian.cfm

Ugaz, A. Floyd, J., & Wahlen, H. (2011). Freeze a jolly good fellow: Cryonauts and the law. *Journal of Law & Social Deviance*, *11*, 54–200.

U.S. v. Carolene Products, 304 U.S. 144, 153 (1938).

U.S. v. Cruikshank, 92 U.S. 542 (1875).

U.S. v. Lewis, 445 U.S. 55 (1980).

U.S. v. Miller, 307 U.S. 174 (1939).

V.C. v. M.J.B., 748 A.2d 539 (2000).

von Kapff, U. (n.d.). Zulu culture. Retrieved from http://www.zulu-culture.co.za/index.php#.WSOVeWgrLIU

Wakanda. (n.d.). Marvel wikia. Retrieved from http://marvel.wikia.com/wiki/Wakanda

Waranius, M. E. (2008). Conversation with LT Matthew E. Waranius, who rescued two dogs and two humans while flying HH-65 Dolphin helicopters at Air Station Miami, Miami, FL.

Waranius, M. E. (2011). What up with DADT: Addressing confusion from inside the military. *Journal of Law & Social Deviance*, *1*, 56–84.

Weis, G. (1979). *80 Blocks from Tiffany's*. New York, NY: Broadway Video Entertainment.

Westboro Baptist Church. (2008). Debate between Westboro Baptist Church attorneys/members and Professor Jose Gabilondo, with opening comments by democratic candidate for the 18th congressional district, Annette Taddeo. Florida International University College of Law, Miami, FL.

White Tiger. (n.d.). Lego marvel D.C. wiki. Retrieved from http://legomarveldc.wikia.com/wiki/White_Tiger

White Tiger (Angela Del Toro). (n.d.). Marvel wikia. Retrieved from http://marvel.com/universe/White_Tiger_(Angela_Del_Toro)

White Tiger (Evolved Tiger) (Earth-616). (n.d.). Marvel wikia. Retrieved from http://marvel.wikia.com/wiki/White_Tiger_(Evolved_Tiger)_(Earth-616)

White Tiger (Hector Ayala). (n.d.). Marvel wikia. Retrieved from http://marvel.com/universe/White_Tiger_(Hector_Ayala)

White Tiger (New Men). (n.d.). Marvel wikia. Retrieved from http://marvel.com/universe/White_Tiger_(New_Men)

White Tigerzord. (n.d.). Power rangers. Retrieved from http://powerrangers.wikia.com/wiki/White_Tigerzord

Williamson v. Lee Optical Co., 348 U.S. 483 (1955).

Wisch, R. F. (2017). 2016 Statutory amendments table. Animal Legal & Historical Center. Retrieved from https://www.animallaw.info/topic/2016-statutory-amendments-table

Wood, S. (2008, March 4). Two teens shoot bear, tiger at N.J. zoo. Big Cat Rescue. Retrieved from https://bigcatrescue.wordpress.com/2008/03/07/two-teens-shoot-bear-tiger-at-nj-zoo/

Worcester, K. (2012). Comics as legal ideologies: The punisher and the politics of retributive justice. *Law Text Culture*, *16*, 329–350.

World Animal Foundation. (n.d.). Mules. Retrieved from http://www.worldanimalfoundation.org/articles/article/8957973/184611.htm

W.S.A. 951.08 (2017).

Zachariasse, C. (2014, September 16). "Reed dance" a Zulu tradition. Retrieved from https://www.youtube.com/watch?v=DQjJkhnqdFQ

Zhang, H. (2015). Strengthening juvenile rights or doing the opposite: The legal mysteries of the Chinese juvenile justice system behind the "Li gang-rape case." *Journal of Law & Social Deviance*, *10*, 1–41.

Zimmerman, A. (2017, April 28). The saga of Elián Gonzalez: A lost boy who was finally found. *The Daily Beast*. Retrieved from http://www.thedailybeast.com/articles/2017/04/28/the-saga-of-elian-gonzalez-a-lost-boy-who-was-finally-found

Zulu Social Aid & Pleasure Club. (n.d.). Retrieved from http://www.kreweofzulu.com/history